Medieval Conduct

SERIES EDITORS

RITA COPELAND
BARBARA A. HANAWALT
DAVID WALLACE

Sponsored by the Center for Medieval Studies at the University of Minnesota

Volumes in this series study the diversity of medieval cultural histories and practices, including such interrelated issues as gender, class, and social hierarchies; race and ethnicity; geographical relations; definitions of political space; discourses of authority and dissent; educational institutions; canonical and noncanonical literatures; and technologies of textual and visual literacies.

Volume 29
Edited by Kathleen Ashley and Robert L. A. Clark
Medieval Conduct

Volume 28
D. Vance Smith
The Book of the Incipit: Beginnings in the Fourteenth Century

Volume 27
Edited by Glenn Burger and Steven F. Kruger
Queering the Middle Ages

For more books in the series, see pages 229–31.

Medieval Conduct

Kathleen Ashley and
Robert L. A. Clark, Editors

Medieval Cultures, Volume 29
University of Minnesota Press
Minneapolis
London

Published by the University of Minnesota Press
111 Third Avenue South, Suite 290
Minneapolis, MN 55401-2520
http://www.upress.umn.edu

Library of Congress Cataloging-in-Publication Data

Medieval conduct / [edited by] Kathleen Ashley, Robert L. A. Clark.
p. cm. — (Medieval cultures ; v. 29)
Includes bibliographical references and index.
ISBN 0-8166-3575-7 — ISBN 0-8166-3576-5 (pbk.)
1. Literature, Medieval—History and criticism. 2. Conduct of life in literature. I. Ashley, Kathleen M., 1944– II. Clark, Robert L. A. III. Series.
PN681 .M399 2001
809'.02—dc21 00-012314

Printed in the United States of America on acid-free paper

11 10 09 08 07 06 05 04 03 02 01 10 9 8 7 6 5 4 3 2 1

Contents

Acknowledgments

This volume grew out of an initial recognition that there was much of interest to say about conduct literature, a recognition that generated sessions on medieval conduct at the International Congress on Medieval Studies at Western Michigan University for four successive years (1992–1995). We would like to thank the presenters and discussants at those stimulating sessions, as well as the Medieval Institute at Western Michigan for supporting our project in its early stages.

Roberta Krueger read a draft of our introduction and made many helpful suggestions for revision. The two anonymous readers for the University of Minnesota Press provided excellent critiques that have resulted in a better integrated collection.

Finally, we appreciate the encouragement we received from Rita Copeland, coeditor of the Medieval Cultures series, as well as the two editors for the University of Minnesota Press, William Murphy and especially Pieter Martin, who saw the project through its final stages.

INTRODUCTION

Medieval Conduct

Texts, Theories, Practices

Kathleen Ashley and Robert L. A. Clark

The Subject of Medieval Conduct

One of the most problematic sites in contemporary cultural theorizing is the link between text and history. The question of how we theorize the connection between documents or texts and lived practice or performance remains open, as we see from debates within a number of fields—anthropology, history, theater, and mass media studies, to name but a few. Fixed epistemological assumptions about the stability of sign and knowability of referent basic to many disciplines have also been called into question by the insights of poststructuralism. Medieval conduct provides an exemplary location for exploring these theoretical issues. We place equal emphasis on three aspects of medieval conduct—texts, theories, and practices—with the goal of articulating the relationships among them.

Traditionally, when medieval scholarship has entertained the notion of conduct, it has privileged texts, called "conduct" or "courtesy" books. The term "courtesy book" usually refers to prose treatises or poems inculcating the etiquette of court.[1] Within English scholarship, editions of texts addressed to males, like the *Book of Courtesy* or *The Babees Book,* published by the Early English Text Society in the nineteenth century,[2] have provided materials for the writing of the social history of the upper classes. French scholarship took a different approach to such texts, assimilating them to a broad category of moral or didactic literature including sermons, fables, proverbs, mirrors, allegories, and exempla collections.[3] In this categorization, didactic materials were to be distinguished from more "literary" forms such as the lyric or romance.

Early critics noted, however, that there was an easy circulation among kinds of writing *within* the didactic category. To take a specific example, although initially part of preaching materials, exempla were available for incorporation into other didactic texts such as the *Miroir des bonnes femmes,* which in turn was the source for a large proportion of the exempla in the *Livre du Chevalier de la Tour Landry.* Similarly, Philippe de Mézières's rendering into French of the Griselda story was detached from his *Livre de la vertu du sacrement de mariage et réconfort des dames mariées* and incorporated into both the *Ménagier de Paris* and the *Chevalier de la Tour Landry.*

The broader term of "conduct," which we have chosen for our discussion, has been applied to written texts systematizing a society's codes of behavior. Conduct books proliferated in the later Middle Ages,[4] and indeed most of the essays in this volume focus on texts produced during the fourteenth and fifteenth centuries. This proliferation is a pan-European phenomenon that we represent with texts and practices from England, France, Germany, and Italy. During the late Middle Ages and early modern period, a combination of sociohistorical forces was changing religious practices, class structures, patterns of consumption, and political identities. In this period of flux, conduct books provided a guide for literate readers to negotiate new sets of social possibilities. The conventional interpretation of conduct books is that they function in a straightforward, prescriptive mode, subjecting their readers to a hegemonic regime of behavior.[5] But this view leaves untheorized the link between prescription and historical practice—a lack of theorization that has tended to obscure the interest and utility of conduct literature for our understanding of medieval culture.

The evaluation of conduct books has also suffered from their uneasy fit with traditional categories of literary and historical analysis, which have typically privileged subject matter marked as sophisticated, male, and aristocratic. The perceived nonliterariness of conduct literature—its didacticism, its supposedly simple rhetoric—has resulted in its marked absence until recently from literary histories. This exclusion of conduct books from the literary canon is especially true of conduct books addressed to women, which have been construed as belonging to the domain of popular rather than high culture.[6] The identification of many of these works with the bourgeoisie is a further problem since "bourgeois literature" is an unstable category before the early modern period. It is revealing of these exclusionary categories that the only type of conduct book acknowledged in most literary histories has been the male, aristocratic "Mirror for Princes."[7]

Ann Marie Rasmussen's essay provides a penetrating study of this process of literary construction in nineteenth-century German scholarship. She shows how the male literary establishment of the century treated medieval manuscripts in which both male and female conduct texts survived so as to separate discussion of the male- from the female-addressed work. Not only was the male text privileged for scholarly scrutiny, but it was "read" as offering an autobiographical insight into the world of the aristocratic knight, a reading that depended upon suppression of sections advocating ascetic abandonment of the world. The expectation that conduct literature should present a male, aristocratic point of view obviously governed the writing of literary history, as Rasmussen shows.

Until recently, the ideal literary object worthy of study was the "masterpiece" or "classic," defined as a work that transcended the contingencies of its production to offer universal truth to successive generations of readers. By contrast, conduct books were almost always seen as hopelessly contaminated by "history"; this was especially true of those works of conduct considered to be nonelite, nonmale, and unsophisticated. The poststructural revolution in literary studies in the last twenty years has, however, radically undermined the concept that any work can stand outside of history,[8] and literary studies has acquired a panoply of methodologies for analyzing how a text's meaning is conditioned by its material production, circulation, and consumption. These changes in the practice of literary studies, which require that a text be historicized, have breached what used to be the high barrier between Literature and History. As texts that presumably offered access to historical processes, conduct books benefited from the redefinition of the literary task. New editions, translations, and critical studies have returned such texts as the *Ménagier de Paris*, the *Livre du Chevalier de la Tour Landry*, and, above all, Christine de Pizan's works to visibility.[9] The text is now a cultural artifact and, as such, is open to various interpretative strategies, among them the new discourses of history.[10]

Like literary studies, the study of history has undergone recent paradigm shifts that have helped make conduct literature an object of serious scrutiny. As opposed to the traditional historical preference for male, aristocratic, and political or military events, recent trends in socioeconomic history (exemplified by the Annales school) have foregrounded the material conditions, practices, and artifacts of nonelite, everyday life.[11] It was the development of women's history over the last generation, however—with its search for texts and documents about ordinary women's lives—that intensified interest in conduct books. Women's conduct books, which articulated normative female behavior, were often assumed to reflect the real lives of medieval women and to provide information about their social roles and status. More recently, cultural studies has provided sophisticated new theoretical constructs concerning popular culture, ideology, and subjectivity. Since conduct books had always been assigned to popular culture, they were now seen as readily available sites for the cultural analysis of material and bodily practices, especially as these intersected with structures of power.[12]

Expanding the Definition of Conduct Literature

Works conventionally identified as conduct books are an important part of the project of this volume. They include such texts as Christine de Pizan's *Livre des Trois Vertus*, the *Livre du Chevalier de la Tour Landry*, the *Ménagier de Paris*, and Caxton's *Book of Courtesy*. The paradigm shifts in the study of literature and history outlined above make it clear, however, that any discussion of medieval conduct must include more than the analysis of texts; it must also consider the intersection of texts and practices. We will return to this point shortly. Furthermore, our volume makes the argument that the study of medieval conduct must be enlarged to include texts that have not normally been construed as conduct literature. Although not represented by specific discussion here, other genres—for example, drama or romance—have been studied for the ways in which they may have functioned discursively as conduct literature,[13] and we would extend that discussion to nonliterary genres.

The traditional distinction between "didactic" and "literary" texts has been increasingly challenged. Medieval manuscript culture itself asks that we view didactic treatises in the light of other literary products, since manuscripts compiled, often in one volume, romances, religious poems, fabliaux, and moral treatises. A similar dynamic of construction may be observed within specific "literary" works. Robert de Blois's *Beaudous,* for example, is a "romance" that encloses a "miroir" and "enseignment aux dames" and a transvestite narrative—all of which has the effect of destabilizing both genre and gender identity (despite the moralists' pronouncements about "separate" spheres), as Roberta Krueger has shown.[14]

The last three essays in our volume, which take up various devotional practices, contribute to the volume's stated goal of expanding the standard definition of what may qualify as "conduct literature" by teasing out behavioral ideologies in such places as confraternity *laude* and Lollard trial records. Robert Clark's essay, which would be equally at home in a volume on religious devotion, is important for our volume because it shows how devotional programs invade the subject's conduct of her everyday life, specifically in her relationship to home and family. Her pursuit of the devotional program cannot be separated from the way she negotiates the demands of daily living. In a somewhat similar way, Ruth Nissé shows that the Lollards' effort to alter patterns in devotional practice impinged on cultural practices more generally. The kinds of changes the Lollards sought to bring about ultimately required a radical alteration in the way social subjects conducted themselves. In her essay on Italian confraternities, Jennifer Rondeau argues that the statutes through which these groups sought to prescribe and regulate behavior—including, paradoxically, the very commercial activities that had allowed urban laymen to achieve social prominence—betray deep-seated social anxieties even as they promoted their members' spiritual endeavors. These essays work to break down assumed barriers between social life and religious devotion, between the public and private spheres. All three broaden the study of conduct to include texts and practices that more narrowly defined notions of "conduct literature" would exclude. This broadening of the field of inquiry by essays in the volume is complemented by more fluid conceptions of gender, of class identity, and of the ways texts operate in culture through variable appropriation.

Gender

We have noted the crucial role played by scholarship on medieval women in the renewed interest in conduct books. Several essays in this volume draw on this earlier feminist work, which had constructed models of gendered experience. Anna Dronzek's comparison of conduct books addressed to males and females hypothesizes a gendered pedagogical rhetoric, with female learning focused on embodied honor and male learning on abstract honor. Girls were educated using an "experiential model of learning," according to Dronzek, one that presented information through concrete example and even threat of violence. Some contributors move beyond the idea that prescriptive texts are unvarying constructions of the social order through control of the gendered body to a more labile sense of the role of gender in producing cultural arrangements. Thus, in his analysis of medieval devotional guides written for women, Robert Clark argues that the consumers of these texts were enacting complex subjectivities and that their responses to the texts cannot be adequately explained by the model of patriarchal dominance of female conduct. He posits instead the possibility of a ludic space within which the women actively fashioned their devotional conduct.

Other essays, too, contest the notion that there is one coherent model of gender to be imitated through practice, and posit alternative and shifting gender codings (gendering of acts) that can be appropriated, resisted, or parodied, destabilizing any monolithic construction of gendered positions. In particular, the interplay of prescription and performance may produce a multiplicity in gendered subjectivities. Jennifer Rondeau argues that the binaries used by many postmodern theorists of desire—who is the desiring subject, who the object of desire?—are inadequate for understanding the functioning of desire in medieval religious practices. She shows how the male participants in confraternity rituals experience a fluidity of gender positionings relative to the feminine.

Class

Our broadened sense of where we might find ideologies of conduct and the fluidity of gender identities in such texts may also help us problematize fixed notions of class identity. A number of essays in this volume examine the proliferation of conduct manuals in the late medieval period when conduct literature became positively fashionable, as Claire Sponsler and Roberta Krueger suggest. The contributors show that the actual consumers of these texts are not necessarily the inscribed or intended readers. This circulation of conduct books across class lines is directly connected to the social mobility of the emergent bourgeoisie, for whom possessing conduct books became a marker of its ascendancy. Anna Dronzek points out that while texts for boys are usually set in an aristocratic context, they may have been read by wealthy members of the urban middle class. Mark Amos makes the argument that courtesy literature represented a site of struggle between the nobility and nonnoble urban elites, as these two proximate classes attempted to control definitions of "gentle" behavior. According to Amos, the courtesy literature of the late Middle Ages ultimately defines a new division of society into gentlemen and churls (rather than noble and nonnoble), thus producing a single class that includes both the aristocracy and the professional elites. Likewise, in her reception study of the *Miroir des bonnes femmes*, Kathleen Ashley shows that—although women were its inscribed audience—both male and female family members owned (and presumably read) the work and that the owner families belonged to the urban bourgeois elites of Burgundy. As a consequence, Ashley argues, the gendered conduct in the text is encoded into emerging bourgeois family ideologies. At this historical juncture in the fifteenth and sixteenth centuries, the semiotics of gender becomes subsumed within the semiotics of class.

Producing Practices

One of contemporary theory's most profound challenges to traditional social interpretation is to disrupt the assumed link between text and practice. In her essay, Jennifer Rondeau problematizes the discourse-practice binary formulated by Michel de Certeau in *The Writing of History*[15] by showing that both terms are characterized by an instability that renders the binary itself problematic as a critical tool. Rondeau's argument also works to break down the usually undertheorized distinction between prescriptive and descriptive, thus opening up new areas for the study of conduct. The theoretical insight that the content of a text does not necessarily predict its meaning as it is actually put to use is generative of a number of different critical perspectives.

Despite the fact that conduct books offer a set of didactic prescriptions, they can be seen as products to be consumed in a variety of ways, and so they may perform different functions socially. Among the multiple responses possible in relation to dominant ideologies of conduct, there is always the possibility of resistance to or subversion of behavioral scripts. Thus, as James Scott has suggested, the effect of any given ritual or performance cannot be assumed from the written script but must take into account how it is enacted and, hence, potentially variably appropriated.[16] Writing on Lydgate's poem "Dietary," Claire Sponsler analyzes the process by which Lydgate and his publisher produced conduct literature as a commodity for a booming market in which food consumption became a locus for the articulation of new ideologies. The poem, she argues, is addressed to the prosperous householder of unspecified class with advice about how to manage consumption through moderation and restraint. Sponsler argues that the ethos of the poem replaces the traditional lavish and visible consumption of aristocratic elites with a new and attractive bourgeois model of private consumption. In effect, noble codes of conduct have not just been appropriated but transformed.

Beyond the appropriation and transformation of noble codes of conduct already discussed, we might call attention to the presence of subversive modes of response to dominant conduct codes. Ruth Nissé explores the complex interplay between authority and resistance in a body of texts that are not typically considered as dealing with conduct: Lollard heresy trial records. Nissé argues that Lollard parodic practices delegitimized and demystified the orthodox system of devotional ritual—for example, through their skillful manipulation of images, Lollards subverted the orthodox representation of sacred images by the guild-centered, dominant culture—and in the process provided alternative, subversive models of devotional conduct.

Thus, individuals and even groups may become sites of resistance to the "scripts" that the dominant ideology seeks to impose upon them. In Michel de Certeau's terminology, in the face of dominant "strategies" (whose aim is compliance or subjection), individuals deploy "tactics" (whose aim is to undercut or avoid dominant strategies).[17] Indeed, we can take de Certeau's model one step further by identifying whole groups (such as the Lollards) involved in strategies of resistance. This doubleness of the script emerges only at the moment of performance or enactment, at the point when the script itself disappears and becomes practice. Such a realization allows for a more fluid notion of conduct beyond simply such options as resistance, compliance, or subversion. In practice, one could perform some combination of these options, creating new subject positions and new forms of conduct in the process.

Reading texts in the light of reception also changes our understanding of textual production, in that the texts themselves may turn out to be more ambiguous or contradictory than had been previously assumed. We have already noted that the rhetoric of conduct books has been considered rudimentary in its straightforward didacticism. Literary analysis shows, however, that these apparently simple texts may be complex, nuanced, and, ultimately, historically revealing. In her analysis of Christine de Pizan's *Livre des Trois Vertus,* Krueger notes not only Christine's careful matching of fashion advice to the social status of her addressees, but the way in which both fashion and books of conduct made manifest the "volatility of social identity." While condemning the urban merchant woman for her ostentatious fashion display (a display that would be appropriate to the princess), Christine documents the historical change in the European mercantile economy through which the successful trader can purchase a noble lifestyle. This ostensible condemnation of new fashions ironically puts the vivid portrait of a wealthy merchant class "into discursive circulation" and promotes its "undeniable appeal."

Other texts may exploit ambiguities in a deliberate way and thus avoid the monologic. Rasmussen analyzes the juxtaposition of German mother-daughter and father-son advice poems—a technique encouraged by the texts' manuscript tradition—in order to foreground the contrastive play of voices and strategies contained in them. Her reading suggests that conduct literature—long assumed to be univocal and paternalistic—might be marked by a subtle dialogism through which authority could be questioned. Conduct texts may also obfuscate the distinction between moral improvement and socioeconomic mobility, as Anna Dronzek, Mark Amos, and Kathleen Ashley suggest. Caxton's prefaces reveal his awareness of the contentions and contingencies surrounding the terms "noble" and "gentle," and he is able to exploit these ambiguities so as to attract several intended readerships.

The opening up of interpretive possibilities—both for the texts' original and present-day readers—is in fact what all of the essays in the book seek to do through their various emphases on reception, practice, and performance. The theorizing of conduct represented in texts from a broad spectrum of languages and genres allows us to comprehend the extent to which the encoding of social practice is a crucial but intriguingly variable function of medieval—and indeed of any—culture.

NOTES

1. For a detailed discussion of the term "courtesy," with a survey of the extant medieval texts, see J. W. Nicholls, *The Matter of Courtesy: A Study of Medieval Courtesy Books and the Gawain-Poet* (Woodbridge: D. S. Brewer, 1985), especially chapter 1, "Terms, Definitions, and Genres" (7–21). See also H. Rosamund Parsons, "Anglo-Norman Books of Courtesy and Nurture," *PMLA* 44 (1929): 383–455; Fred Benjamin Millett, *English Courtesy Literature before 1557*, Bulletin of the Departments of History and Political and Economic Science in Queen's University, Kingston, Ontario, Canada, no. 30 (Kingston: Jackson Press, 1919). For discussion of a slightly later period, see John Edward Mason, *Gentlefolk in the Making: Studies in the History of English Courtesy Literature and Related Topics from 1531 to 1774* (Philadelphia: University of Pennsylvania Press, 1935).

2. See *Caxton's Book of Curtesye*, ed. Frederick J. Furnivall, EETS e.s. 3 (1868); *Early English Meals and Manners*, ed. F. J. Furnivall, EETS o.s. 32 (1868); *A Fifteenth-Century Courtesy Book*, ed. R. W. Chambers, EETS o.s. 148 (1914).

3. See, for example, the volume of the *Grundriss der romanischen Literaturen des Mittelalters* devoted to *La littérature didactique, allégorique, et satirique* in which a section is devoted to "la didactique mondaine," broken down into further subcategories including "contenance de table" and "proverbes," among others (*La littérature didactique, allégorique, et satirique*, vol. 6 of *Grundriss der romanischen Literaturen des Mittelalters* [Heidelberg: Carl Winter, 1970]).

4. Reasons for this proliferation are analyzed by Claire Sponsler in "Conduct Books and Good Governance," chapter 3 in *Drama and Resistance: Bodies, Goods, and Theatricality in Late Medieval England* (Minneapolis: University of Minnesota Press, 1997), 50–74. See also Suzanne W. Hull, *Chaste, Silent, and Obedient: English Books for Women 1475–1640* (San Marino, Calif.: Huntington Library, 1982), 1–30.

5. See Alice A. Hentsch, *De la littérature didactique du moyen âge s'adressant spécialement aux femmes* (Halle, Germany: Cahors, 1903).

6. Diane Bornstein's pioneering work, *The Lady in the Tower: Medieval Courtesy Literature for Women* (Hamden, Conn.: Archon Books, 1983), however, marked the beginning of serious study of female conduct literature.

7. Denis Hollier's *A New History of French Literature* (Cambridge: Harvard University Press, 1989) was advertised as "a panorama of literature in its cultural context" and announces in its introduction that it will set the classical canon next to its rivals and opponents, asking not "What is literature?" but "What is not?" Yet this massive tome contains not one reference to female conduct books, including those of Geoffroy de la Tour Landry or the Ménagier de Paris; there is, however, a section on a male conduct book, Guillaume Budé's 1517 *Le livre de l'institution du prince*, a humanist mirror for princes (136–39). The most comprehensive survey of the male mirrors is Wilhelm Berges's *Die Fürstenspiegel des hohen und späten Mittelalters* (Verlag Karl W. Hiersemann, 1938). For discussions of medieval English examples, see Judith Ferster, *Fictions of Advice: The Literature and Politics of Counsel in Late Medieval England* (Philadelphia: University of Pennsylvania Press, 1996), and R. F. Green, *Poets and Princepleasers: Literature and the English Court in the Late Middle*

Ages (Toronto: University of Toronto Press, 1980). Other general discussions of the genre include Lester K. Born's introduction to his edition of *The Education of a Christian Prince* by Desiderius Erasmus (1936; New York: Octagon, 1987) and Allan H. Gilbert, *Machiavelli's Prince and Its Forerunners* (Durham, N.C.: Duke University Press, 1938).

8. See "The Forms of Power and the Power of Forms in the Renaissance," in *Genre* 15 (1982), for early articulation of the "New Historicism." For an exploration of the fraught relationship between literature and history, see *Post-Structuralism and the Question of History*, ed. Derek Attridge, Geoff Bennington, and Robert Young (Cambridge: Cambridge University Press, 1987).

9. The recent critical work of Roberta Krueger has explored the connections between conduct literature and the self-fashioning of the aristocratic women; see "*Chascune selon son estat:* Women's Education and Social Class in the Conduct Books of Christine de Pizan and Anne de France," *Papers on French Seventeenth Century Literature* 24 (1997): 19–34.

10. For examples of such interpretive strategies as well as a reflexive look at the "historicist enterprise," see *New Historical Literary Study: Essays on Reproducing Texts, Representing History*, ed. Jeffrey N. Cox and Larry J. Reynolds (Princeton, N.J.: Princeton University Press, 1993).

11. Closely associated with the journal *Annales: Economies, sociétés, civilisations*, founded by Lucien Fèbvre and Marc Bloch in 1929, the Annales school broke with the dominant positivist approach to history, seeking the broadest possible rapprochement with the human sciences. An informed discussion of these developments in French historiography may be found in Roger Chartier's *Cultural History: Between Practices and Representations*, trans. Lydia Cochrane (Ithaca, N.Y.: Cornell University Press, 1988); and Aaron J. Gurevich, "Medieval Culture and Mentality according to the New French Historiography," *Archives européennes de sociologie* 24 (1983): 167–95.

12. For an example of such a discussion, see Claire Sponsler's chapter cited above in note 4.

13. For example, Kathleen Ashley, "Medieval Courtesy Literature and Dramatic Mirrors of Female Conduct," in *The Ideology of Conduct*, ed. Nancy Armstrong and Leonard Tennenhouse (New York: Methuen, 1987), 25–38. Without making the argument explicitly, a number of studies seem to be implying that lay readers were using romance narratives to explore appropriate conduct, especially that of males with power. See Karen Jambeck's article, "The *Fables* of Marie de France: A Mirror of Princes," in Chantal Maréchal's *In Quest of Marie de France: A Twelfth-Century Poet* (Lewiston, N.Y.: Edward Mellen, 1992), 59–106; Harriet Spiegel, "The Male Animal in the Fables of Marie de France," in *Medieval Masculinities: Regarding Men in the Middle Ages*, ed. Clare A. Lees (Minneapolis: University of Minnesota Press, 1994), 111–26. See also Chaucer's *Tale of Melibee*, which Carolyn Colette has recently argued should be read in the context of conduct literature, "Heeding the Counsel of Prudence: A Context for the *Melibee*," *Chaucer Review* 29 (1995): 416–33.

14. See Krueger's "Constructing Sexual Identities in Robert de Blois' Didactic Poetry," chapter 6 in her *Women Readers and the Ideology of Gender in Old French Verse Romance* (Cambridge: Cambridge University Press, 1993), 156–82; also her "Intergeneric Combination and the Anxiety of Gender in *Le livre du Chevalier de la Tour Landry pour l'enseignement de ses filles*," *Esprit créateur* 33 (1993): 61–72.

15. Michel de Certeau, *The Writing of History,* trans. Tom Conley (New York: Columbia University Press, 1988).

16. See James C. Scott, *Domination and the Arts of Resistance: Hidden Transcripts* (New Haven: Yale University Press, 1990).

17. This distinction is made by de Certeau in *The Practice of Everyday Life,* trans. Steven Rendall (Berkeley: University of California Press, 1984), 34–39.

1

Eating Lessons

Lydgate's "Dietary" and Consumer Conduct

Claire Sponsler

In Book IV of his *Chroniques,* Jean Froissart describes a meeting with an English squire named Henry Chrystede, who tells Froissart the following story.[1] Chrystede, who had been brought up in Ireland and was fluent in the language, was put in charge of four Irish kings who had come to Dublin to declare their submission to the English crown during Richard II's expedition to Ireland in 1394–95. Chrystede's task, during the month he spent with the Irish kings, was to educate them in the customs of the English, refashioning their behavior, bearing, and dress, for they were, Chrystede claims, uncouth and boorish men. During the first days he spent in their company, Chrystede observed their behavior while dining, noting with disapproval that they allowed their minstrels and servants to sit at the same table with them, to eat from their plates, and to drink from their goblets. Chrystede tolerated these practices for three days, but on the fourth day he had the tables in the hall rearranged and laid in the "correct" manner, seating the four kings at the high table, the minstrels at a separate table, and the servants at yet another table. This reconfiguration angered the Irish kings, who refused to eat, on the grounds that such arrangements were contrary to the customs with which they had been brought up. Chrystede replied that their previous eating arrangement was not a reasonable one and that they would have to abandon it and adopt the English style, since that was what King Richard wished.

Perceiving that a change in table manners was a necessary accessory to political submission, the Irish kings complied.[2]

These eating lessons make visible the sometimes hidden connections between politeness and politics—connections not lost on the participants. Chrystede takes proper table manners as a sign not only of civility, but also of political allegiance, a point the Irish kings themselves quickly come to see. To be fully incorporated within the English national community, to become obedient subjects of Richard II, the Irish kings are required to cast aside their native customs—customs whose barbarity is signaled, for Chrystede and presumably other Englishmen of his class, by the promiscuous fraternization of elites with commoners. The refusal of the Irish kings to eat, followed by their ultimate acquiescence to English norms, replicates within the dining hall the larger battles being fought outside as the Irish are forced under English rule.

The link between table manners and subjection figured in Froissart's account underscores the importance of eating as a cultural practice in the societies of premodern Europe. From the ritual eating of Christ's body during communion to carnival displays involving excess consumption to fasting by religious women, the seemingly simple act of eating was freighted with complex cultural meanings.[3] Given this centrality of food as a symbol and of eating as a ritual and cultural practice, it is perhaps not surprising that many early conduct poems focus on various aspects of eating, including such things as proper seating order, correct techniques for serving, and decorous ways of ingesting food. Noting the frequency with which such concerns manifest themselves in early conduct literature, Norbert Elias, in his pioneering study of early modern civility, calls attention to the way that the early modern civilizing machine used table manners to inculcate and disseminate new norms of gentility and decorum.[4] As the nation-state was formed along new lines of inclusion and exclusion, Elias argues, new forms of behavior were fashioned to ratify social divisions through the notion of *civilité*. The adoption of innovations such as individual plates and forks, along with prohibitions against uncivil behavior at table, were in Elias's view methods for separating elites from commoners through the use of table manners as a way of signaling status and apportioning power. Although Elias identifies these impulses as new to the sixteenth century, they were already at work much earlier, as Froissart's anecdote makes clear.

John Lydgate's "Dietary," a conduct poem written in the first half of the fifteenth century, enters into the processes of differentiating subjects, displaying status, and allotting power identified by Elias. What is particularly interesting is that the poem does so by linking conduct with what Roland Barthes has called "the empire of things," foregrounding consumer behavior as a central feature of the project of social and economic sorting.[5] In the "Dietary," eating is understood to be a specific form of consumption, one laden with symbolic and material value for the individual consumer. But eating is an especially complicated form of consumption, both because of the nature of the product consumed and because of the nature of the act of consumption. Although food consumption overlaps with other forms of consumerism, it differs sharply from them in that it involves the most embodied and elemental form of consumption: the food taken in by the body. Unlike other kinds of consumer goods that remain external to the body, food penetrates the self and then disappears (though traces of food can be charted on the body, as it appears either fat or thin, healthy or sick). Eating thus raises the specter of boundary violation and loss of bodily integrity; in other words, the stakes may be higher for food consumption than for the use of other consumer products. This perhaps explains why the production of food—procedures for growing, marketing, preparing, and serving it—were within late medieval culture such important concerns, as victualing regulations and sumptuary laws make clear.

While eating can be a highly social act, as Froissart's account reminds us, the "Dietary" strikingly foregrounds private eating, offering advice about the dietary practices of the individual food consumer dining alone. The poem thus provides a glimpse of the role of private eating in the everyday life of fifteenth-century England. In so doing, it lets us see how ideas about consumption that emphasized public largesse—ideas that strongly influenced aristocratic consumerism—were being reshaped to stress privacy, inwardness, and the care of the self, all of which addressed the new cultural needs of a new group of consumers somewhat lower on the socioeconomic ladder.[6]

What complicates things even further is that the "Dietary" provides this glimpse of private consumption through a representational medium—the conduct poem—that was itself a commodity, a consumer object available for purchase. As recent scholarship has emphasized, changes in commercial publishing were important stimuli for the proliferation of conduct literature in the fifteenth century.[7] As paper replaced parchment, manuscript books became cheaper and more widely available.[8] A flourishing trade in second-hand books also made expensive and relatively scarce manuscripts accessible to a wider range of readers.[9] At the same time, many of those who had learned to read for business purposes now sought other kinds of reading material, especially works offering entertainment and education. As a consequence, the production of books of all kinds came to be a profit-making activity, and books began to be marketed in ways that appealed to a readership with a vested interest in commercial activity and self-enhancement.[10] The London copyist John Shirley, whose connection to Lydgate was so close that he has been described as Lydgate's publisher and agent, was responsible for disseminating a great deal of Lydgate's writings, perhaps in order to turn a profit.[11] The large number of copies of the "Dietary" suggests that fifteenth-century copyists were attuned to the potential marketability of Lydgate's advice about food consumption.

Following the lead of Fernand Braudel, historians have argued that the defining transformation of the West was not just the industrial revolution and its early capitalist precursors, but a consumer revolution representing a shift in the tastes and buying habits of consumers as well as a cultural reorientation that changed a whole set of attitudes and social formations. Although this revolution is usually located in the eighteenth century, a case can be made for its earliest stages occurring in the fifteenth and sixteenth centuries.[12] Chandra Mukerji, for instance, charts the rise of a "consumerist culture" in fifteenth- and sixteenth-century Europe; focusing on commercial rather than industrial capitalism, Mukerji argues that consumerism predates capitalism and, in fact, sets the stage for it. As evidence, Mukerji points to the proliferation of early consumer goods, including printed texts, and then draws on the work of cultural anthropologists to scrutinize how consumer goods acquired symbolic and communicative force.[13]

Late medieval conduct books were part of this proliferation of items of consumption, bearing considerable symbolic value both as cultural objects—that is, as status symbols attesting to the social and economic arrival of those able to purchase and read them—and in terms of their contents. Conduct books sold themselves not only by appealing to their purchasers' taste for didactic and educational reading material but also by commodifying manners, packaging behavior as a way of ensuring socioeconomic mobility and personal happiness. *The Babees Book* of around 1475 stresses, for instance, that "governaunce" will lead to "lastynge blysse" and "self auaunce,"[14] promising that self-discipline will pay off handsomely and that the reader should therefore eagerly embrace the advice the book proffers. As this and other similar examples suggest, part of the success of conduct books as commodities seems in fact attributable precisely to their ability to market conduct and hence themselves.

Probably as a result of some combination of Lydgate's stature as a writer and the poem's specific contents, the "Dietary" was to all appearances a strong commercial success. Some fifty manuscripts of the poem survive, making it by far the most widely disseminated of Lydgate's poems and the most popular didactic verse in Middle English. The longest version of the poem, British Museum MS Lansdowne 699, consists of twenty-one eight-line stanzas, beginning with the three-stanza "Doctrine for Pestilence," which typically appears separately.[15] This version is unique in its insertion of eight extra stanzas between stanzas one and two. What Lansdowne 699 presents, then, is an unusually full picture of advice about the care of the self, particularly dietary practices. It will be this version that my subsequent discussion of the poem focuses on.

From the broadest perspective, care of the self and dietary practices can be viewed as playing an important role in the inscription of the body into culture at any historical juncture—a process which Pierre Bourdieu calls "embodiment." This inscription into culture occurs through the oblique form of a "structural apprenticeship," or forgotten education process, which teaches the subject like "conductorless orchestration."[16] Bourdieu borrows from Marcel Mauss the term "habitus" to describe this structural apprenticeship whereby individuals absorb a culture's norms and standards. By habitus Mauss means all the learned behaviors of the body—its motions, gestures, and postures. These bodily behaviors, Mauss argues, vary not just between individuals but between societies, and so in them we can see the whole content of the culture as it is expressed on and through individual bodies.[17]

Although a full understanding of medieval conduct poems focusing on eating is possible only through theories of consumption, to which I shall turn shortly, the notion of habitus nonetheless usefully foregrounds the way that dietary practices and rules intersect with both the body and culture, operating where the two overlap. Claude Lévi-Strauss has famously shown that it is only when food enters into culture—when it is cooked—that it becomes subject to cultural meanings and social uses.[18] Once it has been enculturated, food—like other social activities—becomes embedded in systems of signification where it attracts various kinds of regulations that work to limit and categorize its potential meanings and uses at any particular historical juncture. Because food so intimately concerns the body—which it invades, sustains, and then abandons as it is eaten, digested, and excreted—it almost inevitably becomes linked with attitudes toward the body, particularly, as Mary Douglas has demonstrated, with anxieties about bodily borders, anxieties that are themselves tied to broader social and cosmological tensions.[19]

Certainly such anxieties figure in Lansdowne 699, which understands the consequences of missteps in diet and other bodily behaviors to be sickness, discomfort, and even death. The poem explicitly pitches itself as an aid to be used to ward off illness, styling itself a "receiht" (l. 168), that is, an apothecary's prescription beneficial for anyone seeking to "resiste the strok of pestilence" (l. 2). The poem's goal is to preserve health by protecting the body and, to a lesser extent, the soul. And its focus is on the individual body, understood as an engine of consumption—not just of food, but also of emotions, thoughts, other personal activities, and even social relations.

As this suggests, the poem explicitly links eating practices to other behaviors, with the result that diet is positioned not as an isolated aspect of life but as one among many other interdependent consumer activities. In what might seem a natural reflex, Lydgate interweaves advice about what, when, and how much to eat with other recommendations that directly bear on the health of the body, such as getting enough sleep, breathing clean air, rising early, and avoiding overwork. Drink good wine and eat wholesome meats, he advises; do not overeat or dine too late in the evening; avoid fruit, use spices, he admonishes. Eschew black mists, don't frequent stews or baths, walk in gardens, don't sleep at noon, he adds. All of this advice, whether directly subsumed under the rubric "diet" or not, converges on the theme of safeguarding the body against the dangers of excess consumption. "Voide awey al surfete & excesse" (l. 50), Lydgate urges, and instead embrace "temperat diet, temperat travaile" (l. 99) as the best medicine for physical ills.

But Lydgate also, and perhaps unexpectedly, expands his scope beyond the body's well-being into broader social and moral concerns, cautioning his readers to shun the company of known troublemakers such as dice players, to dress and maintain a household that reflects one's status and income, to be content with one's lot, and to be charitable. Be courteous in your speech, do no violence toward poor people, avoid those who sow trouble, and live in peace with your neighbors, Lydgate advises. With "thi bettir be war for to stryve, / Ageyn thi felaw no quarell do contryve, / With thi soget to fihten it were shame" (ll. 124–26), Lydgate warns, mapping out a social hierarchy of superiors, fellows, and subjects with whom the reader must peacefully coexist in order to remain healthy. Be meek during times of troubles and glad in poverty, never complaining whatever your lot might be. "Yiff phisik lak," Lydgate adds, "make this thi gouernance" (104).

What connects these disparate recommendations about bodily and social behaviors is an emphasis on the body as a site of consumption. A conceptual map of the "Dietary" would sketch a human body at the center of the picture and encircle it with randomly arranged objects—food, air, sleep, clothing, income, other humans—all intersecting the central body. The individual's dilemma is to figure out which and how much of these objects to absorb in order to maintain a state of physical, social, and spiritual well-being. Perhaps not surprisingly, penetrable bodily boundaries call for special vigilance, and the reader is warned to exercise caution about what comes into contact with not only the mouth, but also the nose ("Smelle swote thynges," "eschewe mystis blake" [ll. 7, 8]), ears ("To euery tale soone yif not credence" [l. 105]), skin ("keep fro cold thyn hed" [l. 25]), and sexual organs ("With women aged flesshly have na a do" [l. 29]).[20] Only the eyes require no special policing. At heart, what Lydgate's "Dietary" offers is advice for regulating the intake of various materials into the body, whatever those materials happen to be. In other words, the poem teaches the reader how to be a good consumer who can safely negotiate the dangers associated with a world of plenitude.

In an article entitled "The Body in Consumer Culture," Mike Featherstone analyzes the way the consumer culture of late capitalist societies encourages individuals to manage their bodies by adopting instrumental means of controlling bodily deterioration and decay, a strategy Featherstone argues is endorsed by national bureaucracies eager to defray health costs by shifting the burden and expense of bodily maintenance onto the individual.[21] Consumer images of beautiful, fit bodies bombard the twentieth-century viewer, selling the idea that the body is "a vehicle of pleasure and self-expression" (18) while also emphasizing the importance of appearance and the right look. Featherstone argues that the reward for what he calls "ascetic body work" is no longer health or spiritual salvation, as once was the case, but rather enhanced appearance and therefore a more marketable self, better able to compete for its share of wealth, success, and happiness (18).

Lydgate's "Dietary" rather obviously challenges Featherstone's teleological construction of the history of dietary regulation, at least in terms of his assertion that desires for a marketable self are exclusive to late capitalist culture, since Lydgate's poem makes abundantly clear the market advantages accruing to the person who is adept at dietary self-regulation. These market advantages are presented by Lydgate chiefly as avoidance of loss of present privilege. The thrust of the poem's advice is that if you want to hold on to what you now possess—in terms of both health and socioeconomic standing—you had best follow the poem's advice for controlling consumption. Although it is true that Lydgate is concerned with spiritual as well as material results, concluding his poem by stating that moderation and charity are the keys to "al the welthe / Of sowle & bodi" (ll. 161–62), it would be a mistake not to see Lydgate's representation of both soul and body, spiritual and material aspects of human existence, as contributing to an economy of self-maintenance, including maintenance of social and economic standing—based on well-regulated consumption.

To whom is Lydgate's consumer advice directed? The poem opens by constructing a universal reader, addressing all who wish to be healthy and escape sickness: "Who will been holle & kepe hym from sekenesse" (l. 1). This seemingly universal reader is, however, delimited in a number of ways. First of all, the reader is assumed to be male, as is made clear in the poem's advice about avoiding brothels (l. 14) and having nothing to do with "women aged flesshly" (l. 29), not to mention the frequent use of masculine pronouns and repeated references to men (e.g., "Ther be thre lechees consarue a mannys myht" [l. 61]). Second, although at least one version of the poem, MS Rawlinson C. 86, addresses a "sonn," and although Rossell Hope Robbins claims that most copies of the poem appear in instructional manuscripts aimed at educating young boys, there is little evidence in the poem to suggest that a juvenile readership was what Lydgate had in mind.[22] The reader of the poem is in fact imagined to be an adult, neither very young nor very old, though of sufficient years to be concerned about health, to have a household, and to have an established income and a network of social relations—in short, the reader is assumed to be in a position to need the advice about consumer behavior the poem offers.[23] The tone of the poem is also relevant here, since although it makes its suggestions in the form of imperatives—"With thi neihbore live in rest & pes" (l. 120), "eschew excesse of labour" (l. 36), "Be nat to pensiff" (l. 147)—those imperatives are hardly onerous, as these examples suggest. Who would not want to live peaceably with neighbors, avoid working too hard, and be cheerful? Such advice seems less a series of commands of the sort found, for example, in conduct poems aimed at servants and apprentices, than a gentle model of not just desirable but actually profitable behavior.

In status, the implied reader of Lydgate's poem would seem to belong to the property-owning, fairly prosperous classes—that is, urban or provincial householders of some substance. In the first place, the poem assumes a reader who has to watch out for the dangers of overconsumption of food, drink, and sexual and social pleasures. There is no sense of lack of material comforts conveyed in the poem; certainly it does not address subsistence-level readers, but those who have already attained prosperity. The specific food items mentioned in the poem—especially "gret flessh" (l. 17), fruits, chickens, sauces, "holsom spices" (l. 22), "holsom meetis" (l. 6), and good wine—all suggest a fairly high income. And while such food items would once have been exclusive to aristocratic diets, by Lydgate's time they were within reach of bourgeois consumers, given the increasing prosperity and greater availability of foodstuffs in the late fourteenth and fifteenth centuries in England.[24]

Although the poem makes reference to court in the lines "Withynne thi coort suffre no divisioun, / Which in thyn housold shal cause gret encrece" (ll. 117–18), it in fact offers little evidence of targeting a specifically aristocratic audience. Instead it seems directed at prosperous householders of the gentry or bourgeoisie who have both superiors, "thi bettir," as well as inferiors, "thi soget" (ll. 124, 126), and who might be susceptible to arguments urging charitable giving as a way of winning material rewards (ll. 133–36) as well as to advice about being "gentil in table manners" as a means for social advance (l. 110). The poem is aware of poverty and the limits of income, not only in this admonition to be charitable, but also in its awareness that some people are unable to afford medicines (ll. 69–70) or the aid of apothecaries (ll. 166–68) and in its warning not to do "violence" to poor people (l. 107). But the poor are clearly outside the scope of the target audience, mentioned in the poem chiefly because their poverty increases opportunities for the kinds of "healthy" spiritual and material behaviors that will profit the poem's readers. As this treatment of the poor suggests, there is a clear sense of social hierarchy in the poem, and the reader is advised to stay in his place within it (be "mery lik thi degre" [l. 103]), be "clenly claad aftir thyn estat" [l. 121]). Although the reader is admonished to avoid overwork, there is little evidence of labor in the poem, a telling omission I shall return to later. Instead, the implied reader lives a leisured life, one in which advice to sleep late (ll. 23–24) would be possible.

The poem's location of its consumer advice within the setting of a well-to-do household is of particular interest. In a discussion of another late medieval conduct poem, "What the Good Wife Taught Her Daughter," Felicity Riddy has argued that the household had a crucial function within what she calls the "bourgeois ethos," that loose yet distinctive set of values shared by the citizens or freemen of late medieval towns who "enjoyed privileges in relation to trade, the law, and the tenure of property."[25] As a center of production and trade, the preindustrial urban household, which consisted of apprentices and servants as well as the kin group, embraced a cluster of values, including piety, stability, hierarchy, ambition, diligence, and respectability, all of which helped ensure the success of the household's economic enterprises.

It is worth noting, however, that the household was also a unit of *consumption* as well as production. The various members of the household—whether family, servants, apprentices, or guests—had to be maintained, which involved an often considerable outlay to purchase food and clothing, in particular. Christopher Dyer notes in his study of living standards that late medieval statistics tend to privilege the household as a unit of consumption to such an extent that it is possible to sketch out household expenditures, but rarely individual consumerism.[26] This suggests that late medieval consumption was typically thought of, or at least recorded as, a corporate activity of the whole household, not as an individual activity.

Lydgate's poem is unusual in the glimpse it offers of the householder as privileged consumer within the household unit. The poem positions its reader as head of the household, charging him with its maintenance—"Aftir thi rent mayntene thyn houshold" (l. 148)—and demonstrating an awareness of his responsibilities. We even see the householder dining communally, being cautioned not to allow discord at his table (ll. 113–14). But the poem's chief focus is on his personal consumption practices rather than those of the household group. In its foregrounding of the individual, the poem seems related to a specific historical phenomenon—the increasing privatization of eating in the late Middle Ages. Already, in Froissart's account of the dining practices of the Irish kings, we can see the encroachment of standards of privacy beginning to separate social groups and eventually even individuals who no longer dine communally in the hall or at the same tables sharing the same utensils.[27] In effect, a politics of individualism and differentiation comes to replace commonalty. The individual consumer in Lydgate's poem shares in this politics, as he is asked to think first and foremost of his own private eating habits, disregarding the wider patterns of consumption taking place around him in his household.

The implied reader of the "Dietary"—prosperous, leisured householder—meshes reasonably well with what we know of Lydgate's actual readers, that is, those who commissioned many of his works. Although best known as the favored propagandist of the Lancastrian rulers of early fifteenth-century England, Lydgate was patronized by a wider circle of men and women, most of them residing on the high end of the socioeconomic scale and including London merchants as well as the provincial nobility and gentry of East Anglia. In addition, Lydgate's writings reached an even wider audience through Shirley's efforts. In thinking about potential readership, it is suggestive that although some copies of the "Dietary" are in commonplace books compiled for an individual owner, many other copies appear in what Derek Pearsall calls "speculative anthologies," not commissioned by one reader but geared for the widest possible audience in the hopes that the manuscript could be sold once assembled.[28] Walter Schirmer, in fact, argues that Lydgate wrote his conduct poems for a bourgeois public, eager for instruction, and that his literary forays into the popular advice genre could only have enhanced his reputation among a wider audience.[29] This might well be the case, but it is worth remembering that the "Dietary" presupposes a fair amount of affluence and would seem to target arrivistes rather than aspirants to socioeconomic success.

MS Lansdowne 699—which shares the tastes of Harley 2251, a manuscript Pearsall describes as "virtually a Lydgate anthology" catering to all comers[30]—is a collection of Lydgate poems written partly on vellum and partly on paper in a quarto volume of the fifteenth century.[31] Its contents include the fable of two merchants; *Guy of Warwick;* "The Churl and the Bird"; "Horse, Goose, and Sheep"; *The Livis and Passions of Seynt Albon and Seynt Amphival;* and Lydgate's begging poem "The Letter to Gloucester," among others. The "Dietary," at folio 85v–88, is sandwiched between the conduct poem "Stans puer ad mensam" and "Descriptio garcionis" (more commonly known as "The Ballad of Jack Hare"), the latter a poem about a "ffroward knave . . . And a sloggard" (l. 1–2), who drinks, plays dice, gossips, and generally represents the flip side of the restrained adolescent male behavior modeled by "Stans puer." Nothing is known about the owner of this manuscript, although it is obviously designed to cater to a wide range of tastes—religious, historical-romantic, didactic, and practical. It is possible Lansdowne 699 was a speculative anthology of the sort described by Pearsall, put together in the hopes that it would find a buyer and thus aiming to be as all-inclusive of bourgeois tastes as it could be.[32]

Many of the other copies of the "Dietary" appear in such speculative anthologies, although at least one manuscript containing the poem, Egerton 1995, was a commonplace book compiled by an individual owner, and another manuscript, Sloan 3554, contains a Latin version, hinting at a different sort of reader than those at whom the vernacular anthologies were aimed. More representative of the latter is Shirley's Add.16165, which is packed with all kinds of material, is manageable in size, was clearly designed to be consulted regularly, and is indeed well-worn and scribbled over. Add.16165 includes the "Dietary" along with romance, history, treatises on etiquette and hunting, miscellaneous information, and gnomic verses.[33] Both Harley 2251 and Add.34360, which also contain copies of the "Dietary," derive from a lost Shirley codex, Eleanor Hammond has argued, and so were probably aimed at a broad readership. Among the other items in Harley 2251 are Lydgate's "Ballad of Jack Hare," his "Gentlewoman's Lament," and the *Court of Sapience,* all texts that would be consistent with "gentle" tastes.[34]

We should not discount the possibility that the readers of such manuscripts would have been interested in advice about diet for strictly health-oriented reasons—as a way to avoid the sickness and even death envisioned as the result of bad eating habits. But they might also have been attracted to Lydgate's poem for reasons related to new needs and opportunities developing within their particular segment of late medieval consumer society. Recent work in the theory and history of consumption has emphasized the role of consumer goods in making and communicating cultural meaning.[35] Goods, these theories argue, come into play in the definition and redefinition of gender, to preserve traditions and ideals, to sustain and transform lifestyles, and even to spur social change. For these theories, consumer goods—or what Mary Douglas and Baron Isherwood call the "visible part" of culture—are thus seen as mediums and even creators of cultural meaning, making meaning discernible and available for social continuity and change.[36] In what to my knowledge is the single best study of consumption, Grant McCracken demonstrates how material objects contribute "to the construction of the culturally constituted world precisely because they are a vital, visible record of cultural meaning that is otherwise intangible." In this sense they are "performative," McCracken argues, because they "give cultural meaning a concreteness for the individual that it would not otherwise have."[37]

Within the incipient consumer society of fifteenth-century England, advice about how to regulate food consumption and integrate eating into a larger pattern of social behaviors might have been welcome, especially among prosperous—perhaps especially *newly* prosperous—householders. Historians of food have demonstrated that in medieval Europe, diet was socially stratified, with meat, fish, wines, and spices consumed by the wealthy, grains and ale by poorer people. In other words, food consumption was coded for status. During the late fourteenth and fifteenth centuries, however, food, and especially meat, was relatively plentiful.[38] What this meant was that as food became more widely available its utility as a consumer good able to create and disseminate cultural meanings expanded. As Stephen Mennell notes, the civilizing of appetite that began in late medieval conduct books was at least partly related to an increasing security, regularity, reliability, and variety of food supplies.[39] Certainly it is difficult to imagine Lydgate's "Dietary" being written in a context of food dearth; the poem presumes an abundance of food, an abundance whose very existence poses new problems and calls for new behaviors.[40]

Despite its growing availability, food remained the single largest item in household expenditures across all social strata, though the proportion of expenditure on food diminished as total income increased. According to Dyer, for example, a small clerical household in the 1450s, that of two chantry priests in Dorset, spent more than half its £20 per annum on food, while earls required no more than a quarter of their spending to cover food expenses.[41] Although food cost more in towns, by the later Middle Ages townsmen appear to have enjoyed better diets than their rural counterparts, and the numerous regulations applying to the victualing trades show the particular concern of urban authorities with maintaining a steady food supply.[42] The picture we get, then, is of food as a central item of consumption by late medieval consumers, but an item increasingly available to more and more consumers, especially those living in towns and cities.

Given this context of increased abundance of food, it is perhaps not surprising that the "Dietary" privileges consumption over production. Lydgate's poem is clearly about consuming the end products of someone else's act of labor and its emphasis is on managing consumption, not on producing more comestibles. The poem shows no concern about how food is grown, harvested, shipped, or traded; it is in fact oblivious to the processes whereby food reaches the consumer's table. Instead, in the poem, labor and work are removed from the realms of material production and transported into the terrain of consumption, with the result that consumption becomes a form of work. The poem does not present us with a producer but with a consumer, and that consumer is seen as a laborer in that he must expend considerable effort in order to manage his consumption. And clearly the poem sees the work of managing consumption as fraught with peril and open to failure at every turn. A laborer tilling his fields could hardly face more anxieties about his work than the consumer constructed by Lydgate's poem.

Michel de Certeau's understanding of consumer behavior helps us see some of the repercussions of the poem's treatment of consumption as work.[43] In *The Practice of Everyday Life,* de Certeau seeks to develop a model of consumption as the realm of the use of an object by those who are not its makers, that is, to find the production in the act of consumption. Traditionally understood, consumption is the domain of passivity and inertia, a site not of practice or action but of absence and waste. Using the categories of "strategies" and "tactics" to describe the signifying practices of consumption, de Certeau attempts to trace the various practices by which consumers seize their chances and turn alien forces to their own ends, transforming seemingly passive consumption into acts of resistance. For de Certeau, power can never fully dominate the social space, and the tactics of consumption show the local processes whereby power is eluded. In de Certeau's view, then, consumption is work and it is also resistance.

It is fairly easy to see how in the "Dietary" consumption is constructed as active, not passive; that, after all, is the cornerstone of the poem's point that the individual consumer needs to take charge of his own consumer practices. But where, if anywhere, in Lydgate's poem is the resistance de Certeau posits as part of consumer behavior? From the point of view of someone like Bryan Turner, who from a post-Foucauldian perspective has described the role of dietary management in producing docile and disciplined bodies in late capitalist societies, the "Dietary" would clearly evince hegemonic forces at work and allow no opportunities for resistance.[44] Just as modern regimes of dieting, jogging, and cosmetics seek to control disaffected and alienated citizens of the late twentieth century, so the dietary advice proffered by Lydgate disciplines bourgeois appetites, Turner would be likely to say, encouraging prosperous groups in the middle social strata to limit their consumption and hence their status. Precisely because food consumption was socially stratified, eating lent itself to the negotiation of status in the sense that differentiation of material lifestyles played a role in status differentiation. The recipes of the urban-bourgeois Ménagier de Paris, for instance, resemble those of courtly cookbooks, suggesting an emulation of courtly eating by those in lower social strata, and some of the surviving English cooking books from the fifteenth century show a strikingly similar pattern.[45] Elias's discussion of table manners, in fact, focuses on just such competition and conflict between social groups; for Elias, standards of politeness became a way for one group to differentiate itself from another and to gain power, since cultural tastes, social organization, economic power, intellectual fashions, and forms of behavior all are inseparable. Certainly it is not hard to imagine how Lydgate's stressing of restrained consumption would mesh with a top-down apportioning of both material (the food itself) and symbolic resources (what food signifies, especially in terms of the cultural capital it represents), encouraging those of the well-off but still middling social groups willingly and under the guise of what is best for personal health to restrict their own access to food and all it stood for. From this perspective, the "Dietary" seems at one with the attempt of sumptuary laws to limit conspicuous food consumption to elites, and hence to preserve their status-enhancing hold on largesse.

But to see the "Dietary" in this light alone would, I believe, be a misreading of the cultural work of Lydgate's poem. What sets the poem off from sumptuary legislation and returns us to de Certeau's insistence on the resistance offered by consumer tactics, is the substitution it offers: in place of the considerable social and gustatory advantages of lavish food consumption and highly visible largesse, the poem holds out another form of cultural capital, one based less on the public display of goods than on the private transformation of them. In this way, the "Dietary" makes a gesture predicted by de Certeau, in which the passive consumer becomes an active user and resister. The prosperous householder of Lydgate's poem is not encouraged to follow food consumption patterns associated with elites, but instead is offered a new way of eating, one which allows him to escape direct competition with aristocratic privilege by retreating into the enclosed space of private consumption whose value rests less on public approbation than on individual health and happiness.

One way to make sense of this bypassing of elite patterns of consumption as a marker of status for the prosperous bourgeoisie is through Bourdieu's theorizing of symbolic capital, which he deliberately opposes to an (inadequate) economism or materialism that would deny the existence of symbolic or ritualistic means of establishing social relations and reproducing the economic order, including structures of domination.[46] For Bourdieu, all agents participating in cultural practices interact with symbolic goods that through their diffusion produce and reproduce agents within a specific social and economic sphere. Although Bourdieu refuses any reduction to the purely economic, he nonetheless insists that symbolic capital be seen as material in the sense that it is created by material forces—such as social institutions, labor practices, and power structures—and has material impacts—raising or lowering status and maintaining patterns of social relations. Symbolic capital can always be put to the service of other kinds of capital, Bourdieu claims, and provides a way of charting the symbolic struggles waged on the cultural field. It also serves as a way of ordering and controlling the pursuit of specific economic ends, for example valuing "a given type of goods as worthy of being pursued and conserved." At the same time, symbolic capital masks the arbitrariness of the valuing of goods, reinforcing "the well-grounded illusion that the value of the goods it designates as desirable is in the nature of things, just as interest in these goods is in the nature of men."[47]

Part of the value of symbolic goods, Bourdieu argues in his essay, "The Market of Symbolic Goods," is to maintain cultural distinctions, to mark their producers and consumers with the signs of legitimacy and distinction that enhance their cultural status. The production of competent consumers is also required in order to ensure the desired valuation of the symbolic good being produced and such consumers are often produced through institutions like the educational system. There is always, according to Bourdieu, competition at work for the power "to grant cultural consecration," competition that takes place among various agents of cultural authority.[48] Symbolic goods, Bourdieu reminds us, are produced within systems of social relations that give them their worth; they have no autonomous meaning or value apart from those social relations.

From Bourdieu's perspective, Lydgate's "Dietary" would function as a privatized educational system designed to produce competent consumers able properly to value symbolic goods—in this case, food—and hence to maintain cultural distinctions at a time when food items once confined to the aristocracy are becoming more widely available and thus weakening earlier distinctions. At the same time, the "Dietary" also provides a way of assigning meaning to the act of eating. McCracken argues that an important way in which meaning is transferred from the culturally constituted world to goods is through advertising: advertising is "a kind of conduit" pouring meaning from the culturally constituted world to goods; advertising replaces the old meanings of goods with new ones and keeps us up-to-date on "the present state and stock of cultural meaning" in goods. For the fifteenth century, the "Dietary" served some of the same functions now performed by the ad agency. It not only marketed conduct but also acted as a conduit for transferring meaning from what McCracken calls the culturally constituted world, or social reality, to goods.

But the fact that Lydgate's poem does not educate the reader into elite patterns of food consumption, does not teach conspicuous consumption and largesse, suggests a new valuation of food as a symbolic good. The central tenet of this new valuation is moderation, a term directly opposed to conspicuous consumption and largesse. Again and again,

Lydgate's poem stresses "measure," cautioning against "Greedi souper" (l. 73) while endorsing "fedyng mesurable" (l. 108) and "Temperat diet" (l. 63). "Voide awey al surfete & excesse" (l. 50), Lydgate urges, since "Off mykil or litel cometh al infirmyte" (l. 77). "Moderat foode," he concludes, "yeueth to man his helthe" (l. 163).

It is not difficult to see how this emphasis on moderation would mesh well with the ethos of the bourgeois household described by Riddy, with its elevating of piety, stability, diligence, ambition, and respectability. But the emphasis on moderation moves those bourgeois values into the world of consumption, offering a model for a new, specifically bourgeois way of being a consumer. Lydgate's poem holds out the promise of mastery over the self and social reality as a consequence of mastery of consumption. By moderating food intake, the "Dietary" suggests, one can attain not only health but wealth, success, and happiness. Thus consumerism becomes productive in that it, like other forms of labor, is understood to lead to material satisfaction. By moving this work of consumption into the privacy of the household and, even further, onto the body of the individual who eats the food, the "Dietary" opens a new, albeit highly confined, space for bourgeois consumption and self-construction: not the great hall of aristocratic feasts, but the private table of the solitary eater.

The social sciences ask us to think of the self and culture as a process, created and maintained as a result of specific individual and collective efforts. In a similar vein, McCracken suggests that we see the consumer as someone who is at work on the cultural project of making a self.[49] Consumer goods offer individuals the raw materials to shape a self by concretizing cultural notions of what it means to be a certain kind of person—man, woman, parent, citizen, youth, professional, and so on. In the "Dietary," prosperous late medieval consumers are offered the most commonplace of consumer goods—food—as just such raw material. And through the conduit of Lydgate's advice, they are offered a way of shaping their own distinctive patterns of food consumption based on an ethos of privacy and moderation. By emphasizing consumerism as an activity, as something requiring effort, the poem creates the consumer as a producer—of self, of social standing, and of cultural value. If Chrystede's experience with the Irish kings reveals how eating can be the locus of class and political allegiance, then Lydgate's poem shows how the individual can actively participate in changing those allegiances. In its confident assertion that the self can be not just safeguarded but also reshaped through conscious control of eating practices, the "Dietary," with its shift from an ethos of aristocratic conspicuous public consumption to one of private moderation, testifies to the awakening powers of the self-fashioning bourgeois consumer, a consumer whose heirs are very much still in existence.

Notes

1. Jean Froissart, *Oeuvres,* ed. Kervyn Lettenhove, 15 vols. (Brussels: Victor DeVaux, 1867), 15: 167–78.

2. Margaret Visser, in *The Rituals of Dinner: The Origins, Evolution, Eccentricities, and Meaning of Table Manners* (New York: Grover Weidenfeld, 1991), 318, notes that sharing not just tables but also plates and cutlery at meals suggested that people shared intimacy, an intimacy deemed inappropriate when it involved social unequals.

3. The best-known study of the cultural significance of food in medieval Europe is Caroline Walker Bynum, *Holy Feast and Holy Fast: The Religious Significance of Food to Medieval Women* (Berkeley: University of California Press, 1987). More generally, anthropologists have emphasized the link between dietary regulations and cultural categories: Mary Douglas, for example, in a discussion of Hebrew dietary rules, observes that "It would seem that whenever a people are aware of encroachment and danger, dietary rules controlling what goes into the body would serve as a vivid analogy of the corpus of their cultural categories at risk"; see Mary Douglas, "Deciphering a Meal," *Daedalus* 101 (1972): 79.

4. Norbert Elias, *The History of Manners,* vol. 1 of *The Civilizing Process,* 2 vols., trans. Edmund Jephcott (New York: Pantheon, 1982); originally published in 1939 as *Über den Prozess der Zivilisation.*

5. Roland Barthes, "Le monde-objet," in *Essais critiques* (Paris: Editions du Seuil, 1964), 19–28. Available in English translation by Richard Howard in *Calligram: Essays in New Art History from France,* ed. Norman Bryson (Cambridge: Cambridge University Press, 1988), 107–15.

6. For largesse as a guiding principle of aristocratic consumerism, see Christopher Dyer, *Standards of Living in the Later Middle Ages: Social Change in England, c. 1200–1520* (Cambridge: Cambridge University Press, 1989), especially 91.

7. For the contours of these developments see Carol Meale, "Patrons, Buyers, and Owners," in *Book Production and Publishing in Britain, 1375–1475,* ed. Jeremy Griffiths and Derek Pearsall (Cambridge: Cambridge University Press, 1989), 201–38.

8. On prices of books, see H. E. Bell, "The Price of Books in Medieval England," *The Library,* 4th series, 17 (1936): 312–32. For a discussion of late medieval English book buyers see Meale, "Patrons, Buyers, and Owners." On the impact of paper, see R. J. Lyall, "Materials: The Paper Revolution," in *Book Production and Publishing,* 11–29.

9. Curt F. Bühler, in *The Fifteenth-Century Book: The Scribes, the Printers, the Decorators* (Philadelphia: University of Pennsylvania Press, 1960), notes that "The trade in books

throughout the Middle Ages was largely a second-hand business; only with the invention of printing did a new-book market become commonplace" (33).

10. For a useful survey of early English conduct literature, see Jonathan Nicholls, *The Matter of Courtesy: Medieval Courtesy Books and the Gawain-Poet* (Woodbridge, Suffolk, England: D. S. Brewer, 1985); Nicholls notes the resemblance between rules for monastic refectories and courtesy-book advice on table manners (22–27). Anglo-Norman conduct poems are discussed by H. Rosamund Parsons in "Anglo-Norman Books of Courtesy and Nurture," *PMLA* 44 (1929): 383–455. For the relationship of English conduct poems to the Latin *facetus* tradition, see Sister Mary Theresa Brentano, *Relationship of the Latin Facetus Literature to the Medieval English Courtesy Poems* (Lawrence: University of Kansas Press, 1935), especially 37–65. For conduct poems treating table manners, see also Stefan Glixelli, "Les contenances de table," *Romania* 47 (1918): 1–40. Finally, for texts of the extant English conduct poems, see *Manners and Meals in Olden Time,* ed. Frederick J. Furnivall, EETS os 32 (London, 1868).

11. Lydgate's networks of patrons and readers as well as his relations with Shirley are described by Derek Pearsall in *John Lydgate* (Charlottesville: University of Virginia Press, 1970), 71–79. For East Anglian literary patronage, see S. Moore, "Patrons of Letters in Norfolk and Suffolk, c. 1450," *PMLA* 27 (1912): 188–207 and 28 (1913): 79–106. For Shirley's role as a disseminator of Lydgate's writings, see Margaret Connolly, *John Shirley: Book Production and the Noble Household in Fifteenth-Century England* (Aldershot, England: Ashgate, 1998); Connolly challenges the notion that Shirley was a commercial bookseller, but agrees that he was responsible for copying and putting into circulation much of Lydgate's work.

12. Chandra Mukerji, *From Graven Images: Patterns of Modern Materialism* (New York: Columbia University Press, 1983). For an argument favoring the eighteenth-century origins of consumerism, see *The Birth of a Consumer Society: The Commercialization of Eighteenth-Century England,* ed. Neil McKendrick, John Brewer, and J. H. Plumb (Bloomington: Indiana University Press, 1982).

13. Mukerji, *From Graven Images,* 12.

14. *The Babees Book* (MS. Harl. 5086), in *Manners and Meals in Olden Time,* 9, ll. 216–17.

15. MS Lansdowne 699, fols. 85v–88; printed in *The Minor Poems of John Lydgate,* ed. Henry N. MacCracken, 2 vols., EETS es 107 and os 192 (Oxford: Oxford University Press, 1934), 2: 702–7. For a list of manscripts of Lydgate's "Dietary" and the "Doctrine for Pestilence," see Carleton Brown and Rossell Hope Robbins, *The Index of Middle English Verse* (New York: Columbia University Press, 1943), entries 824, 1418, and 4112; as well as *A Manual of the Writings in Middle English, 1050–1500,* ed. Albert E. Hartung (New Haven: Connecticut Academy of Arts and Sciences, 1967–1993), 6: 2092–94.

16. Pierre Bourdieu, *Outline of a Theory of Practice,* trans. Richard Nice (Cambridge: Cambridge University Press, 1977), 89, 95.

17. Marcel Mauss, "Techniques of the Body," *Economy and Society* 2 (1973): 73.

18. Claude Lévi-Strauss, *The Raw and the Cooked,* Introduction to a Science of Mythology, 1 (London: Jonathan Cape, 1970).

19. For this view, see Mary Douglas, *Purity and Danger: An Analysis of Concepts of Pollution and Taboo* (New York: Praeger, 1966).

20. Michel Jeanneret has recently explored the relationship between food and talk in the Renaissance, reminding us that the tongue has a social as well as an alimentary role and that the mouth is an organ of speaking as well as eating; see his *A Feast of Words: Banquets and Table Talk in the Renaissance,* trans. Jeremy Whiteley and Emma Hughes (Chicago: University of Chicago Press, 1991). Originally published in 1987 as *Des mets et des mots: Banquets et propos de table à la Renaissance.*

21. Mike Featherstone, "The Body in Consumer Culture," *Theory, Culture, and Society* 1, no. 2 (1982): 18–33.

22. Rossell Hope Robbins, *Secular Lyrics of the Fourteenth and Fifteenth Centuries* (Oxford: Clarendon, 1952), 251, believes the poem was used by schoolchildren since it is found in collections of instructional poems and is linked to the "Stans puer ad mensam" tradition; but as Pearsall, in *John Lydgate,* 220, observes, it is difficult to know what children made of much of its advice, such as avoiding sexual contact with older women.

23. MS Rawlinson C. 86, printed in Robbins, *Secular Lyrics,* 73–81. This version lacks the three stanzas of the "Doctrine for Pestilence" and also, much more drastically, omits stanzas five through twelve, which is to say that it omits all of the dietary advice.

24. See Dyer, *Standards of Living,* 190–202.

25. Felicity Riddy, "Mother Knows Best: Reading Social Change in a Courtesy Text," *Speculum* 71 (1996): 67.

26. Dyer, *Standards of Living,* 49 and passim.

27. Patricia Fumerton, in *Cultural Aesthetics: Renaissance Literature and the Practice of Social Ornament* (Chicago: University of Chicago Press, 1991), 111–67, describes the process by which aristocratic subjects in the Jacobean period removed themselves from communal to solitary dining and as a result created "a subjectivity that separated itself from publicly centered forms of living" (128). Mark Girouard, in *Life in the English Country House,* 104–8, charts the architectural changes that ran parallel to the increasing desire for mealtime privacy.

28. Pearsall, *John Lydgate,* 76.

29. Walter F. Schirmer, *John Lydgate: A Study in the Culture of the Fifteenth Century,* trans. Ann E. Keep (London: Methuen, 1962), 109–10. Schirmer's study originally appeared as *John Lydgate: Ein Kulturbild aus dem 15 Jahrhundert* in 1952. Lydgate's other conduct poems include "Stans puer ad mensam"; "The Treatise for Lavenders," which advises the servants of Lady Sibille Boys on how to wash her clothes; "Duodecim abusiones"; "Four Things Make a Man a Fool"; and an uncompleted adaptation of the *Secreta secretorum.* He also wrote a tract on the "Nine Properties of Wine," which resembles the "Dietary" in its cataloging of the salubrious effects of wine, though it lacks prescriptive advice.

30. Pearsall, *John Lydgate,* 76.

31. For a description of the manuscript, including a complete list of its contents, see *A Catalogue of the Lansdowne Manuscripts in the British Museum* ([London], 1819).

32. Pearsall, *John Lydgate,* 76.

33. H. S. Bennett, *Chaucer and the Fifteenth Century* (Oxford: Clarendon, 1948), 164.

34. See Eleanor P. Hammond, "Two British Museum Manuscripts," *Anglia* 28 (1905): 1–28; "Ashmole 59 and other Shirley Manuscripts," *Anglia* 30 (1907): 320–48.

35. In Marshall Sahlins's structural analysis of consumption, goods are an "object-code," a nonlinguistic way for a community to communicate cultural meaning; see his *Culture and Practical Reason* (Chicago: University of Chicago Press, 1976), 178.

36. Mary Douglas and Baron Isherwood, *The World of Goods: Towards an Anthropology of Consumption* (New York: Norton, 1978), 66.

37. Grant McCracken, *Culture and Consumption: New Approaches to the Symbolic Character of Consumer Goods and Activities* (Bloomington: Indiana University Press, 1988), especially 74. McCracken also presents a useful overview of recent studies of consumerism.

38. See Dyer, *Standards of Living*, 55–71, for aristocratic diets; see 152–57 for peasant diets.

39. Stephen Mennell, *All Manners of Food: Eating and Taste in England and France from the Middle Ages to the Present*, 2d ed. (Urbana: University of Illinois Press, 1996), 32.

40. For overviews of food in premodern England, see Gerard Brett, *Dinner Is Served: A History of Dining in England, 1400–1900* (Hamden, Conn.: Archon Books, 1969); Bridget Ann Henisch, *Fast and Feast: Food in Medieval Society* (University Park: Pennsylvania State University Press, 1976); and C. Anne Wilson, *Food and Drink in Britain from the Stone Age to Recent Times* (London: Constable, 1973).

41. Dyer, *Standards of Living*, 55.

42. Ibid., 197–98, 210. By the early fifteenth century, Dyer claims, noncereal foods accounted for 37 percent of the cost of urban building workers' diets (202).

43. Michel de Certeau, *The Practice of Everyday Life*, trans. Steven F. Randall (Berkeley: University of California Press, 1984). For a useful discussion of de Certeau's book, see Mark Poster, "The Question of Agency: Michel de Certeau and the History of Consumerism," *Diacritics* 22, no. 2 (1992): 94–107. As Poster points out, one oversight of de Certeau's theory of consumption is that as a theory it is not historical: it does not consider historical differences in tactics of consumption, and it does not consider the relation between tactics of consumption and the strategies of marginalized groups at different historical junctures (107).

44. Bryan Turner, "The Discourse of Diet," *Theory, Culture, and Society* 1, no. 1 (1982): 1–14.

45. See Mennell, *All Manners of Food*, 60–61.

46. Pierre Bourdieu, *The Logic of Practice*, trans. Richard Nice (Stanford, Calif.: Stanford University Press, 1990), especially 112–14.

47. Ibid., 121.

48. Bourdieu, "The Market of Symbolic Goods," *Poetics* 14 (1985): 24.

49. McCracken, *Culture and Consumption*, 88.

2

"For Manners Make Man"

Bourdieu, de Certeau, and the Common Appropriation of Noble Manners in the *Book of Courtesy*

Mark Addison Amos

England in the fifteenth century saw a number of economic and social shifts that further challenged the already blurring line dividing her nobility from her most powerful commoners. As the ruling bureaucracy became increasingly secularized and the importance of the Commons grew, many urban professionals attained positions of great power and influence. At the same time, the development of England's international, capitalistic cloth trade concentrated unprecedented wealth and financial power in the hands of London's merchant and entrepreneurial guilds; and as London Companies replaced England's barons as the Crown's major source of finances, formal political power soon followed. A number of titles and terms of address link the members of the urban elite and the nobility, averring a growing recognition that those commoners ennobled by education or profession were coming to join those noble by birth, occupying similarly dominant positions in relation to the rest of the society. By the late fifteenth century, each of the groups composing the secular elite was accorded high status because of its wealth and power, and each possessed a great autonomy: legal powers of oversight and regulation, traditionally in the hands of local lords, were in urban centers given to the ruling members of a guild or profession. Elevated de facto by their increasing economic and political power, members of

London's urban elite were formally ennobled through the custom of entitling mayors and aldermen, a practice that institutionalized the widening separation between the urban elite and lesser commoners.

With the shifting of power and prestige that accompanied the elevation of merchants, financiers, and professionals came a commensurate threat to the symbolic distinction of the aristocracy, undermining the stability of a traditional aristocratic identity already weakened by the internecine strife of the Wars of the Roses and diluted by the rapid spread of literacy down the social ladder. Issues of class image and individual status were foregrounded as each of the groups inhabiting the interlocking social sphere of London's urban patriciate was engaged in a struggle to define and reify its elite class identity. Labrousse delineates the stages of this process of identity production: "the social changes more slowly than the economic, and the mental more slowly than the social."[1] An investigation of the negotiations and confections involved in the emergence of such new social configurations—a process Foucault terms *Entstehung*[2]—necessarily involves identifying and tracing the physical and literary trappings of wealth and power, those artifacts and practices that communicate a social value far beyond their use-value. Critics and theorists of contemporary culture, Pierre Bourdieu and Michel de Certeau offer analyses and heuristics for examining and analyzing the symbolic values negotiated by the use and dissemination of these cultural markers, and, as we will see, provide valuable insights for reading historical and literary shifts in perception and consumption in terms of economies of symbolic capital. Their work offers paradigms for reading the relationship between these two classes and for interpreting the way that cultural practices (objects, texts, and behaviors) and textual representations function in the struggle between them, allowing us to examine the ways these symbols and behaviors are appropriated and deployed by the urban elite, and the ways they resonate on both sides of the porous border dividing these two proximate classes.

One of the most value-laden and contested sites for this symbolic struggle, one that underwrites and validates many other status objects and behaviors, is courtesy literature, for the behaviors it defines and delineates are at once the most group-dependent and individually enacted form of display. Unsurprisingly, as each of these two constituencies sought methods of producing and displaying a recognizable culture amid these shifts of power, England saw an explosion in the production and consumption of conduct literature—a popularity furthered by the advent of printing technology.[3] Examining the *Liber niger,* a household ordinance commissioned by Edward IV, A. R. Myers neatly summarizes the complex relationship between the cultural elite and its conduct literature:

> Fifteenth-century society was competitive and fluid, yet wished to maintain respect for order and degree. It is no accident that this century, when the number of "bourgeois gentilhommes" was quickly increasing, saw the appearance of more books on etiquette than ever before, telling one how to behave in courtly circles and devoting special attention to subtle differences and equivalences of rank.[4]

Eagerly consumed by those on both sides of the shifting status border, many of these didactic texts reveal an ideological lability as they reflect and affect the new social relationships being negotiated, and so allow us to map out the shared and conflicting interests and reading practices of those at the border of gentility, the nobility and the urban elite. My discussion will break into two parts, both shaped and informed by Bourdieu's and de Certeau's social/textual theories of modern behavior and consumption: an examination of the historical objects and practices at stake in this struggle for image and identity, and a reading of the *Book of Courtesy,* a book of manners printed in the late fifteenth century by William Caxton. As a text selected and printed by England's first publisher, the *Book of Courtesy* was influential not only because it was disseminated in (relatively) great numbers, but also because Caxton explicitly directs his texts at those composing London's ruling elite, the "grete lordes gentilmen & marchauntes" at the center of these issues of class identity, and so this text offers us a point of entry both into the issues of identity confronting these colliding classes and into the usefulness of these theories of modern consumption in examining medieval society and texts.

Spectacle and display are important elements in almost every arena of medieval society—ecclesiastical, civic, royal, martial—but the high status and civic functioning of the groups composing the secular elite, especially guilds, demanded repeated and sumptuous public displays of support for the church, city, or nation. Medieval public display of extravagant, outward signs of a group's honor—including feasting, livery (for both noble retainers and guildsmen), candles, barges, and banners, to name only the most obvious—required from a collective both significant financial investment and also a less visible but more important investment in its reputation within the greater community. As we would suspect, the more elevated the social status of a group, the greater is its concern for its corporate image, and the greater the likelihood that it would impose behavioral regulations on its members in order to define and maintain an esteemed corporate identity.[5] As the traditionally dominant class, the nobility had an extraordinary investment in its image as the honor class and in maintaining the exclusivity of that image. Analyzing the conflicts between modern proximate classes, social theorist Pierre Bourdieu has argued that "conducts of honor"—those behaviors whose intent or effect enhances the regard in which a status group is held—should most usefully be "seen no longer as the product of obedience to rules or submission to values (which they also are, since they are experienced as such), but as the product of a more or less conscious pursuit of the accumulation of symbolic capital."[6] On a variety of fronts, as we will see, each of these two powerful groups was engaged in a quest for honor and privilege. Bourdieu sees the accumulation and display of cultural capital in the quest for honor as structured to achieve "distinction." Defining the dominant class by exclusion, "distinction" is that field of socially produced tastes that no other class or group can achieve, a set of cultural codes that invisibly and insistently privilege the nobility. Achieving and maintaining its distinction, the validated group attempts to impose on those they oppress "the cultural dispossession which provides the best apparent justification for economic dispossession" (386).[7] The centrality of reputation and display to the lived and imagined identities of the aristocracy and the urban elite heightens the importance of distinction and the necessity of recourse to symbolic strategies in order to define and maintain that distinction. As noted above, this cultural field includes not only material artifacts but also modes of action and systems of thought.

Both communally and individually, the newly empowered urban elite were seeking a recognition hitherto reserved for the noble class, and in pursuit of this honor were acquiring and displaying objects and behaviors of authority that were traditionally noble. Individually, members of the professional elite were seeking to acquire and display aristocratic status objects including luxurious clothing, heraldic coats of arms, and country estates. Communally, the more elite corporations were investing in large guild halls, armorial bearings, and land in the country. Since powerful commoners were inhabiting political and social spheres that increasingly interlocked with the nobility, the display that had always been a part of guild activities now took on an even greater importance.

As one might expect, such forays into noble symbolism were not greeted with enthusiasm by those benefiting from a sharp class distinction, and the aristocracy sought to seal the increasingly porous border to close the social ranks behind itself. The lavish dress of the wealthy commoners in particular alarmed the gentlefolk, who responded to this threat to their distinctiveness by enacting articles of sumptuary legislation throughout the fifteenth century. These laws sought to restrict the types of cloth and fur that citizens were allowed to wear by demarcating boundaries along lines of class and income. The general trend of such legislation, which proved unenforceable, was to narrow the privileged groups by raising and refining the wealth standards required for admission into those groups. Claire Sponsler offers an intriguing complication to this issue, ascribing the progressively restrictive laws not to the nobility, but to those wealthy merchants in the Commons seeking to advance themselves socially while thwarting the advance of others.[8]

Addressing the malleable value of status objects, Bourdieu observes that the dissemination of such an artifact necessarily decreases its worth, for wider distribution threatens the "rarity and distinctive value" of that cultural asset (*Distinction,* 229). However, it is not simply a devaluation of the object that occurs; the activity of appropriation itself has a value. In his exploration of actions and practices, Michel de Certeau develops the concept of consumption as a secondary production: to each conservative, hegemonic production "corresponds *another* production, called 'consumption.'"[9] De Certeau notes that such consumption-production allows those in the previously excluded group to "take on the power that dominates production" (32). In the later Middle Ages, the dissemination of heraldic crests functioned in this way: frequently sought by members of London's professional elite, these cultural markers became more widespread, and they were adapted by their new users. Indeed, entire guilds were granted coats of arms, thereby elevating and "ennobling" the entire company.[10] Individual commoners also adopted these cultural markers, reproducing them, altering them, and aligning them with their own life experiences and group identity. For example, some merchants modified their heraldic crests to include images representing their occupation: cloves for the grocer or mercer, goblets or buckles for the goldsmith.[11] De Certeau argues that in such re-uses, "assimilating" signifies not only "becoming similar to" but also "*making* something similar" (166). Although not all such heraldic deviations were accepted as armorial, in their merchant incarnation these crests functioned as business logos or trademarks, and guild ordinances protected such marks as a property right. In de Certeau's terms, such "procedures of consumption" have "metaphorized the dominant order: they made it function in another register" (32). Just as the merchants had followed the aristocratic concern with inventing an honored historical past—evidenced by their interest in heraldry in general and family crests in particular—aping and then appropriating modes of noble display, so too did they begin to mimic noble modes of *self*-display.

Situated on the edge of a noble class they could never fully enter, these influential commoners looked to adapt as their own not only noble objects, but also the exclusive and excluding noble modes of conduct, and with them the attendant structures of belief. The fifteenth century saw the leaders of powerful guilds follow the noble class division and institutionalize a class-based hierarchy within the structure of their guilds: the liverymen at the top of the guild structure divided their guilds into two houses and permanently relegated the poorer members to the lesser house. On occasion, these commoners appropriated noble terms for mannered behavior: in the records of the mercers, apprentices are instructed to be "lowly and curteis" in deference to liveried members of their own guild.[12] The mercers, one of the most powerful guilds in the country, even followed the aristocracy's emphasis on lineage, instituting their own birth restrictions for membership.[13]

As they had met the common appropriation of traditionally aristocratic dress with restrictive legislation, so too did the aristocratic class meet these common assimilations of noble symbolism and behavior with reaffirmations of traditional noble images and fictions, especially the concept of "gentilesse." Both the literature and history of the later Middle Ages suggest that the concept of noble courtesy is central to aristocratic self-consciousness and distinction: standing as a supplement to gentle birth, economic superiority, and martial accomplishment, noble courtesy both reflects noble identity and actively constitutes it.[14] Bourdieu summarizes the interplay between the dominant social position and the rarified actions of the elite: "The very life-style of the holders of power contributes to the power that makes it possible, because its true conditions of possibility remain unrecognized, so that it can be perceived not only as the legitimate manifestation of power but as the foundation of its legitimacy" (*Logic,* 139). As other markers and behaviors central to noble identity were being challenged and appropriated in the fifteenth century, the nobility emphasized its traditional discourse of behavior in order to ensure the distinction of its image in the present. Bourdieu defines class identity through his concept of habitus, a concept quite useful for examining the separations and intersections of these two dominant groups in the late Middle Ages. A habitus comprises "systems of durable, transposable dispositions, structured structures predisposed to function as structuring structures" (*Logic,* 53). Composing both unconscious ideology and conscious practice, these systems are "principles which generate and organize practices and representations that can be objectively adapted to their outcomes without presupposing a conscious aiming at ends or an express mastery of the operations necessary in order to attain them" (*Logic,* 53). De Certeau argues that this structural nature of habitus renders it static and limits its use in examining resistant or emergent groups, for it assumes a firm tie among practices, a suitable field for their enactment, and a "collective principle of administration." Additionally, it recognizes neither varied reading practices nor the multiple uses of texts.[15]

In their quest to consolidate their traditional identity, aristocrats naturally turned to romances depicting traditional noble behaviors—an extraordinarily popular genre in the fifteenth century[16]—and books of manners that sought to instill those nostalgic values into contemporary noble children. In many respects these texts constitute an educational program in aristocratic *noriture* that offers the noble classes mechanisms for retrenching their class privileges. Basing his definition on Edward IV's *Liber niger,* Richard Firth Green defines *noriture* as "including, ideally, not only manners in the narrow sense but also a basic literacy, a familiarity with improving stories, and a mastery of certain literary, musical, and linguistic accomplishments."[17] Ostensibly aimed at educating gentle youths and the newly arrived courtier in aristocratic comportment, manuals of noble behavior sought to concretize an abstract class superiority into recognizable and practical actions in an effort to distinguish the noble from the common.

Textual presentations of these behaviors of privilege, however, make that program in noble education available for appropriation by the powerful common lay readership. The appeal of an aristocratic education for those seeking to enhance their class status is clear, for it would convey to the new elite the honor code of a community with which their own was becoming increasingly consonant, so it is unsurprising that historical and literary evidence argues that these encodings of aristocratic *noriture* were eagerly sought after and appropriated by the urban elite.[18]

In medieval courtesy literature, the language of morality everywhere links polite behavior to a moral valuation: as the texts offer advice on personal hygiene, table etiquette, and conversational niceties, they detail the rewards and punishments for these activities in terms of virtue and vice. This ethical level provides a transcendental motivation for a rarefied and self-consciously chosen limit to one's activities, the controlling of affect through an act of the will that noble manners entail. Intended to direct the actions and shape the thoughts of their readers, these texts situate themselves on the border between practice and the theorizing of that practice, and must be read as a mixture of reflection and direction, not as history. Treating early works printed in France, Roger Chartier notes the ephemeral character of didactic literature intended to shape the behavior and thought of its readers: "a great many texts had the precise function of disappearing as discourse and of producing, on the practical level, modes of conduct and behavior that were accepted as legitimate with respect to current social or religious norms" (6). Bourdieu describes the habitus itself in a way that echoes the function of these self-consuming artifacts: the habitus is "embodied history, internalized as a second nature and so forgotten as history—the active presence of the whole past of which it is the product" (*Logic,* 56). Each of the constituencies involved in the struggle over class honor in the late Middle Ages sought the distinction offered by such rarefied and artful behavior, and each sought to naturalize those behaviors into an innate and unquestioned code of superiority.

De Certeau's image of readers is useful here: "readers are travellers; they move across lands belonging to someone else, like nomads poaching their way across fields they did not write, despoiling the wealth of

Egypt to enjoy it themselves" (174). This metaphor has particular value when unpacked in light of the relationship between an aristocracy threatened with the loss of a secure class identity and a class of powerful commoners eager to join the nobility in forming an honor class, for it highlights the fact that these new readers are unwelcome invaders whose presence threatens real damage to those whose noble readings it has appropriated. Equally significant is the fact that the pilfered readings would have had different meanings for each of the two constituencies: the Egyptian farmers and the nomadic poachers, the aristocrat and the commoner. An application of de Certeau's idea of productive consumption to the act of reading proves invaluable in discovering and delineating these divergent meanings. While de Certeau follows other reader-response theorists in acknowledging that each reading questions and modifies the text, he emphasizes the centrality of social fields to the reading act:

> Reading is thus situated at the point where *social* stratification (class relationships) and *poetic* operations (the practitioner's constructions of a text) intersect: a social hierarchization seeks to make the reader conform to the "information" distributed by an elite (or semi-elite); reading operations manipulate the reader by insinuating their inventiveness into the cracks in a cultural orthodoxy. (172; emphasis in original)

De Certeau identifies two broad categories of practices of consumption that are dependent upon the class relationship between the producer and the consumer: strategies and tactics. He terms "strategic" any use or consumption that verifies the values of the commodity and supports the traditional hierarchy. In contrast to these he posits "tactics," uses resulting from the disparity between a dominant producer and a disempowered consumer. Originating from a disadvantaged position, a tactical reading invades a text and imposes a fragmentary reading contrary to its orthodox reading: "a tactic is a calculated action determined by the absence of a proper locus. . . . In short, a tactic is an art of the weak" (36, 37). I view noble readings of aristocratic courtesy literature as conservative and "strategic," and common readings of these same texts as "tactical," seeking to colonize meaning in such a way as to enable the commoners to negotiate between their own experiences and an aristocratic text that seeks to exclude them. The meanings of these poached readings must be located in reference to the sociocultural institutions through which culture, belief, and values are transmitted: the noble culture that designed them and the urban elite culture that appropriates them.

The retrenching of the aristocracy into those traditional stories and behaviors that display and demand privilege, however, was complicated by the waning of the noble household as the educational center of aristocratic youth. The education of noble children alongside the children of merchants and wealthy professionals certainly complicated the process of transmitting traditional aristocratic culture;[19] the fact that these children were increasingly raised outside of the traditional identity-producing institution emphasized the need for alternate avenues through which a collective noble identity might be transmitted, a need that courtesy literature addressed. Green notes that the institution of henchmen in the fifteenth century certainly contributed to the need for such primers of aristocratic behaviors, inviting into the court youths not necessarily bred to nobility.[20] Formalizing the education of these youths, a process embodied in the master of the henchmen, would certainly have contributed to the increasing use of behavioral manuals at court. This formalizing represents a fundamental shift in the relationship of the court to its charges: the need for a textual education in how to live in a given social context suggests that the readers are living in circumstances rather different from those described. Elias summarizes:

> People living in the example-setting circle do not need books in order to know how "one" behaves. This is obvious; it is therefore important to ascertain with what intentions and for which public these precepts are written and printed—precepts which are originally the distinguishing secret of the narrow circles of the court aristocracy. (100)

The difficulty that these texts must negotiate is how to make court life available to an audience not of the court and simultaneously to organize their information so as to restrict access to it. The paradigm of formal and textual examples of court life would have suited both constituencies of the urban elite, for neither the professional elite nor the lesser gentry reader was likely to have lived experience in the court. As a result, both aristocratic and apprentice households were increasingly likely to be engaged in the *noriture* of their respective charges, and each group would require a mediator to translate the aristocratic rhetorical strategies and demonstrative approaches into terms more commensurate with its *mentalité*. Courtesy literature offers itself as just such a mediator.

Given even the narrowest of bridges, the gap between noble paradigms and elite common ones could be traversed, and many works of courtesy literature present their noble fictions and didactic elements in ways consonant with components of the urban honor identity, thereby offering to non-nobles these artifacts of noble tradition as building blocks for constructing a new, socially valid urban identity. Bourdieu credits the habitus with an adaptability that allows for the incorporation of means external to the habitus as long as the desired ends are within: "being the product of a particular class of objective regularities, the habitus tends to generate all the 'reasonable,' 'common-sense,' behaviours (and only these) which are possible within the limits of these regularities, and which are likely to be positively sanctioned because they are objectively adjusted to the logic characteristic of a particular field, whose objective future they anticipate" (*Logic,* 55–56). Even though the royal household ordinance commissioned by Edward IV sought to exclude commoners as it systematized learning and defined and supported the noble power of knowledge, the structures it forwarded—*lettrure* and *noriture*—were presented in a way consonant with the guild habitus, as we will see, and so did not prove resistant to being co-opted by the emerging professional elite. Indeed, William Caxton defines an educational program for the common constituency of London's ruling elite similar to this noble paradigm in the prologue to his *Dialogues in French and English,* his handbook of French phrases for the traveling merchant:

> Yf ye haue children,
> So chastyse them with the rodde,
> And enforme them
> With good maners
> the tyme that they be yong;
> Send them to the schole
> To lerne rede and to write,
> That they resemble not bestis. (9, 11.31–38)[21]

Like noble children, merchant children must learn both *lettrure,* to "rede and to write,"[22] and *noriture,* to exhibit "good maners" in order to be human and "resemble not bestis." Marketing these noble texts for an audience that expressly includes common readers, however powerful, dislocates noble behavior from the noble habitus that engendered and supports it and opens the texts to an alternate reading, offering aristocratic modes of conduct as a field for the self-transformation of the professional elite in what de Certeau would term a "guileful ruse of *different* interests and desires" (35), in this case, the interests and desires of the rising urban elite.

The typical work of didactic courtesy literature was designed to inculcate values and behavior, and focused on serving at table, general table manners, and personal and religious hygiene, offering general recommendations concerning proper measure, generosity, and deference to elders and other superiors. The range of these texts is striking: some resemble more a list of directives than an organized didactic lesson, offering simple cause-and-effect statements that locate the final arbiter of polite behavior in the *mentalité* of the audience of one's social performance; others make concerted efforts to support their admonitions with a moral teleology in hopes that their readers will internalize the proscriptions and will then self-regulate their behavior. In the motivations and rewards associated with the behavior it encourages, *The Babees Book* seeks to restrict its use to those of the noble habitus. Digressing from a discussion of the need to be attentive in one's duties, the poet touts the incalculable value of a noble upbringing: "And yif ye shoulde at god aske yow a bone / Als to the worlde, better in noo degre / Mihte yee desire thanne nurtred forto be" (ll. 115–19).[23]

For his audience of "grete lordes gentilmen & marchauntes" Caxton selected and published a number of works of courtesy literature; in 1477 he published two. The shorter, John Lydgate's "Stans puer ad mensam," was widely circulated and enjoyed a long-lived popularity: the fifty extant copies date from the early fourteenth to the mid-sixteenth centuries. This ninety-nine-line poem addressed to children is little concerned with offering a moral underpinning, and consists in the main of simple cause-and-effect statements: "Be nat to hasty on brede for to byte, / Of gredynesse lest men woulde the endwyte" (27–28).[24] In the same year that he published "Stans puer," Caxton published another behavioral manual, the *Book of Courtesy.* Longer and far more complex, this

524-line poem invites interpretation within a number of different discourses. As with "Stans puer," its popularity attests to its wide appeal: three other editions were printed within twenty-five years of Caxton's. It, too, is addressed to children and treats concerns in which even modern children need instruction, such as the hazards of spitting, the drawbacks of talking with one's mouth full, and the importance of a clean nose. Unlike the shorter texts, it offers scant space to serving at table, a discussion comprising only four of its seventy-six stanzas. The *Book of Courtesy* carries its discussion out of the narrow noble court, treating behavior appropriate to social situations in the church, in the hall, and on the street. Discussing relationships and issues not treated in the other works, this poem also engages with theoretical issues of mannered behavior: the contingency of polite action, suitable models for imitation, genuine courtesy versus insincere foppishness, and the cultural dividends of literature. Many of these issues are inappropriate for children, and it is these issues in particular that reflect concerns addressed in legal statutes and guild regulations, opening the poem up for a non-noble reading that validates an elevated image for the urban elite.

The poem begins by introducing itself as an instructional manual for "Lytyl John," advising its young charge to begin each day by remembering God with prayer, combing his hair, cleaning his eyes, purging his nose, and washing his hands. The poem links the actions of John's daily routine to their appropriate reward or punishment. For devout prayers he will be rewarded by the Virgin Mary: "The blesside lady / wil quyte you your mede" (l. 35).[25] For congenial behavior he will gain the praise of his peers: "Dispose you to be so compenable [companionable] / That men may of you reporte for commendable" (ll. 151–52). This poem follows other courtesy books in frequently returning to moral concerns in an attempt to motivate a noble readership seeking ontological verification of its elevated status.

Throughout this complex text, the ethical/religious and the social are intertwined as God and cleanliness are forwarded as defining the virtuous life. From its opening, the *Book of Courtesy* announces the moral purpose undergirding its discussion of courteous behavior:

> Vyce or vertue to folowe ande enpresse
> In mynde / ande therfore / to styre & remeue
> You from vice / ande to vertue addresse

That one to folowe / and that other teschewe
I haue deuysed you / this lytyl newe
Instruccion / acordynge vnto your age
Playne in sentence / but playner in langage. (8–14)

Such an address to children, promising age-specific instruction "Playne in sentence" and "playner in langage" is common in medieval books of courtesy, and this focus makes these texts particularly effective vehicles for inculcating cultural values and naturalizing the behaviors they advise: "When distinctive dispositions are accepted and acquired as self-evident from early childhood, they have all the appearances of naturally distinguished nature, a difference which contains its own legitimation" (Bourdieu, *Logic,* 139). The linking of social actions to moral consequences in the *Book of Courtesy* is common in books of manners, and likely pedagogically sound—serving as an effective way to indoctrinate children into a certain set of social behaviors by depicting these standards as serving a greater, moral good. Yet, as we will see, what the text advances as "virtue to folwe" is staged as noble behavior and the vices "teschewe," violations of decorum. This conflation of the practical and the moral defines a discourse that naturalizes class superiority.

In concert with its moral foundation, the *Book of Courtesy* motivates its readers by discussing the importance of the impression one makes on others:

Kepe you so cloos / that men haue no conseite
To say of you / ony langage or vilonye
Bicause ye ete your mete / vnmannerly. (243–45)

John is reminded that all of his actions may have social consequences and advised to take care to avoid being seen as "vnmannerly" in a number of social situations. Since the gaze to which he responds is located outside of himself, John must be ever vigilant in controlling how he is viewed.

But loke my child / to folkes that ye mete
Ye speke fayr / with wordes of plesaunce
Demure and curtoys / of your demenaunce
To hym that is your felawe and pere
Gyue ye fair langage / and a frendly chere. (59–63)

Again, we have the conflation of the social and the moral: to be viewed as properly courteous, one must go beyond the rules here outlined, and eschew folly and love honesty. Interestingly, what defines this honesty, or at least what will lead one's peers to define one as honest, is proper measure: "Lete maner & mesure / be your gydes tweyne" (125). Washed and combed at the poem's opening, little John is directed:

And or ye passe / out of your loggynge
Euery garment / that ye shal on were
Awayte wel / that it be so syttynge
As to your degre / semeth accordynge
Thenne wil men saye / forsoth this child is he
That is wel taught / and louyth honeste. (50–56)

Honesty, then, includes representing oneself accurately, and beginning with this early passage John is told that he will be praised for fitting himself to his "degre" in society. In this early iteration of the necessity of maintaining oneself in a manner befitting one's status, the text reveals its anxiety that the cultural markers of noble behavior are open to co-optation and colonization, even by those it expressly seeks to exclude. Its fear is well-founded, for as Bourdieu notes, all cultural markers are open to appropriation. Although this admonition to represent one's station in society would seem to bar a reading sympathetic to the powerful commoners' quest for an image commensurate with their financial capital, it would have suited both halves of the ruling elite: the polyvalent interpretations of the sumptuary laws noted above suggest that noblemen would have read it as proscribing commoners dressing as nobles, while the elevated commoners would have seen it as rewarding their raised status with raised levels of luxury. De Certeau's paradigm would note that this action would allow the urban elite to "maintain their difference in the very space that the occupier was organizing" (33).

Again *The Babees Book* serves to bring the *Book of Courtesy* 's openness to tactical readings into relief. Having proclaimed noble *noriture* as the greatest boon imaginable, *The Babees Book* ends on an even more hyperbolic note:

And mygtefulle god, that suffred peynes smerte,
In curtesye he make yow so experte,

> That thurhe your nurture and youre governaunce
> In lastyng blysse yee mowe your self auaunce! (213–17)

Although the promise of everlasting bliss could be expected to have universal appeal, by locating its rewards beyond the social, the poem speaks directly to a nobility seeking to confirm its superior status through structured behavior, and offers little to those who seek through their behavior to gain respect for themselves and for their status group in this temporal world. Not that the powerful commoners of London's elite were unconcerned with moral issues—their bylaws argue otherwise—but social advancement and validation were more likely to be the immediate goals of commoners adopting noble manners. The *Book of Courtesy*, on the other hand, speaks to both the noble and the urban constituencies, balancing its moral grounding with practical concerns of social advancement, and thereby inviting tactical readings by acknowledging the increasing, and increasingly non-noble, literate population. John is to curry the favor of his "felawe and pere" not for moral reasons, but for practical ones: such behavior is useful not merely for signifying one's status, but also for gaining advantage and rank.

> Loke who doth best / and hym ensiewe ye
> And in especyal / vse ye attendaunce
> Wherein ye shal your self best auaunce. (117–19)

John is told to imitate the behavior of successful men, especially those who may help him "auaunce"; clearly this type of advancement differs from the "auaunce" into "lastyng blysse" promised in texts like *The Babees Book*. This juxtaposition speaks to the individualism encouraged within the shared language of the habitus of the courtly community and the habitus of the guild structure. As Bourdieu argues, for a practice or discourse to aid in the construction of a habitus, it must offer its consumers collective practices and beliefs consonant with their own structures of thought: "The corrections and adjustments the agents themselves consciously carry out presuppose mastery of a common code; and undertakings of collective mobilization cannot succeed without a minimum of concordance between the *habitus* of the mobilizing agents . . . and the dispositions of those who recognize themselves in their practices or words" (*Logic,* 59). Within their institutional structures, both court and guild rewarded individual initiative with recognition and advancement.

Resisting the ontological admonitions that seek to lock up and direct readings toward conservative ends, the *Book of Courtesy*'s "tactical" statement of self-advancement is bracketed in one of the few moments of this poem located wholly within a conservative, nostalgic presentation of the feudal court—the situation that dominates so many other manner books. Although the relevance of the feudal, lord-vassal relationship that underwrites the behaviors and rewards of courtesy books such as *The Babees Book* was already waning in the fifteenth century, the scene recalls an inherited habitus central to aristocratic identity as it provides its noble readers with a nostalgic image of an ordered society in which their distinction was unchallenged. Such a circumscription of manners and behaviors seeks to limit its purview and to welcome only a nostalgic reading unavailable to a common audience. Notably, Caxton did not publish the popular *Babees Book* for his dual-class audience.

In the *Book of Courtesy,* John is instructed that he must not only control himself, but also be canny and subtle in his observation of others, to perceive how others perceive, especially in dealings with his master:

> Regarde also the loke ande contenaunce
> Of your maister / or of your souereyne
> So shal ye best preue. what is in his plesance
> Or els displesaunce / this is soth serteyne
> The chere discouerith / often both tweyne
> And eke þe chere / somtyme may you addresse
> In thingis / þt langage may not them expresse. (127–33)

At first reading this passage seems traditional and conservative, focusing as it does on the desirability of reading the countenance of one's lord; however, its placement immediately after the advice to seek out those who may best advance the student's own situation suggests that attentiveness in serving one's lord is self-serving. The poem's presentation invites us to see that even such apparently conservative and class-affirming precepts may be redirected and deployed from without for one's own personal gain and advancement: one asks what he can do for his lord in order to determine what his lord can do for him.

One of the poem's longest discussions explores loose speech and slander, an issue central both to the noble house—where servants and underlings must be made to keep secrets—and to powerful commoners—whose guilds levied severe punishments for the crime. John is admonished not to spread rumors, to "kepe alway secree [for] Besy reporte of mischief is chief noryse," and to "Passe forth [his] way in scilence & in pees"—yet he is at the same time encouraged to "Here and see" (134–35, 139–40). For what purpose is John to gather information if he is never to speak? As we would suspect, the text does note the proper circumstances for disclosing such information, "yf the caas require," but restricts such disclosure by delineating "seuen condicions" that the speaker must observe (141, 143). Given the moral tone of courtesy literature, we naturally expect the seven conditions to follow those typical of confession manuals and require the speaker to explore the moral ramifications of speaking, or at least to question the necessity of imparting what one knows, to assess the damage that might result, or to evaluate the trustworthiness of his knowledge or his listeners. Yet John is directed:

> Auyse you wel / what ye saye / & in what place
> Of whom / & to whom in your mynde compace
> How ye shal speke / & whan take good hede
> This councelith the wise man withoute drede. (144–47)

Instead of the expected ethical advice concerning the effect or veracity of the student's report, he is given rhetorical advice to make his speech as effective as possible. Here again the text entrusts its charge with a seemingly subversive directive: gather information clandestinely and ascertain how best to divulge it. And again, the text locates the arbiter of that behavior outside of John's conscious control. At the conclusion of this discussion, the poet shifts his focus and recalls St. Augustine's admonition to avoid "the vice / of vyle detraccion" and instructs little John to turn away "Suche a detractour / from the table / As vnworthy / and also reprochable" (163, 167–68). A firm, moral stance to be sure, but one belied by the lengthy, pragmatic, and self-advancing discussion that precedes it. The admonition here speaks to a code shared by the two groups, for both household ordinances and guild regulations give much treatment to the proper use of information, proffering restrictions aimed at keeping such secrets within the institution.

Among the many aspects of life it addresses, the *Book of Courtesy* offers a reading list "of bookes enornede with eloquence" wherein one will "fynde / bothe plesir & lernynge" (310, 311). Clearly, the poem is addressing itself to an elite population seeking a cultural and intellectual superiority commensurate with—and validating of—a political and social superiority. The poem assumes that its audience is both leisured (to some degree) and possessed of a literacy beyond the rudimentary. Both constituencies in the ruling elite were literate,[26] yet increasingly, literacy was not restricted to the dominant classes: extrapolating from the records of the clerk of the consistory court of Edward IV, who registered 40 percent of the witnesses to appear before him as literate in Latin, Sylvia Thrupp estimates that by the 1470s, 50 percent of *all* London lay males would have been able to read English.[27] Bourdieu notes that an ongoing rise in the literate population reduces the cultural value of reading itself, and so in order to protect the exclusivity of the act, reading must be further restricted to a validated and sanctioned canon, creating a "hierarchy of readers" (*Distinction,* 229). The particular authors and titles that the poet recommends are revealing. John is advised to "Redeth gower in his wrytynge moralle . . . Redeth his bookes / callede confessionalle," and to "Beholde Ocklyf in his translacion," especially "His traytye / entitlede of regymente *[De regimine principum]*" (323, 335, 351, 363). The poet laments the death of "chaucer / maister galfryde":

> O fader and founder of ornate eloquence
> That enlumened hast all our bretayne . . .
> Redeth my chylde / redeth his bookes
> Refuseth none . . . (ll. 330–45)

The final author is "dan Iohn lydgate" and John is directed to "Redeth his volumes / that ben large & wyde" (365, 386). The text's modern editor marks this emphasis on insular poets, calling it "a wise man's advice on the books his little Jack should read, the best English poets,—then Gower, Chaucer, Occleve, and Lydgate,—not the Catechism and Latin Grammar."[28] Significantly, the *Book of Courtesy* recommends only insular poets, and only their English-language texts. This selection would have had an immediate appeal to common readers lacking the traditional aristocratic emphasis on French. As the selections of poems is specified, so too is the method of reading these texts. Frequently, a book of courtesy will offer itself as a reading lesson, seeking to make efficient use of the youthful audience it inscribes by suggesting that the reader familiarize himself with unfamiliar terms: "Eke, swete children yf there be eny worde / That yee kenne nouhte, spyrre whils yee yt ken" (*The Babees Book,* 36–39). The reading process recommended in the *Book of Courtesy* is quite different, both rhetorical and literary:

> Seche ye therfore / and in caas ye fynde
> Such gleynors fressh as haue some apparence
> Of fayr langage / yet take hem & unbynde
> And preue ye / what they be in existence
> Colourd in langage / sauerly in sentence
> And doubte not my childe / withoute drede
> It wil prouffite to see such thingis & red[e]. (421–27)

This text extends beyond recommending the "basic literacy" and "familiarity with improving stories" that Green includes in his description of the broad goals of aristocratic *noriture,* prescribing a detailed reading that seeks to "unbynde And preue" the "fayr langage" conveying a profitable sentence. Although the "prouffite" is not defined, clearly this curriculum goes beyond pastime reading to avoid idleness: it offers texts in English to those seeking to increase their cultural capital, both to those seeking to protect their inheritance and to those investing in a symbolic capital not theirs by birth. The prescribed reading method implies what de Certeau calls "the fiction of the 'treasury' hidden in the work, a sort of strong-box full of meaning, [one] obviously not based on the productivity of the reader, but on the *social institution* that over determines his relation with the text" (171). That social institution would in the narrowest sense be the court—more broadly, the court of opinion—and the text is here trying to ensure that its meaning is accessible only to those within the privileged class that has the power to define that meaning.

Accusing himself of having "Degressed somwhat" in his discussion of English authors, the poet of the *Book of Courtesy* then returns to advise his charge on the particulars of mannered behavior:

> Thenne lityl Iohn / I counceyl you that ye
> Take hede to the norture / that men vse
> New founde /or auncyent whether it be

So shal no man / your curtoisye refuse
The guyse & custom / my child shal you excuse
Mennys werkis / haue often enterchaunge
That nowe is norture / somtyme had be strange.

Thingis whilom vsed /ben now leyd a syde
And newe feetis / dayly ben contreuide
Mennys actes / can in no plyte abyde
They be changeable ande ofte meuide
Thingis somtyme alowed / is now repreuid
And after this / shal thinges vp aryse
That men set now / but at lytyl pryse. (435–48)

At the same time the poem stresses the demonstrative apparatuses of aristocratic "norture," it defines that essential component and marker of noble behavior in a way that acknowledges its contingency—"changeable ande ofte meuide"—and even reversibility: "Thingis somtyme alowed / is now repreuid." Similarly, the poem emphasizes noble behavior's dependence on customs of the time—"New founde / or auncyent." Although earlier in the poem John is directed to choose an avatar of good moral character—"Enforce you vnto hym conformed to be / That can moste good / ande hath humanyte" (209–10)—here the emphasis is on ensuring that he is au courant: he is advised to "haunte / The guyse of them / that do most manerly" (449–50). Seemingly simple advice, yet John is cautioned:

But beware of vnthryft Ruskyn galant
Counterfeter of vnconnyng curtoisy
His tacchis ben enfecte with viloyne. (451–53)

The poet then details Ruskyn's futile and embarrassing attempts to mimic gentle courtesy: lousy-headed and unable to bow properly, he serves as a stern warning that those seeking to ape noble manners may themselves appear "apysshe." The poem announces that the unsuccessful affectation of behaviors not one's own, or not of one's class, will be read as insignificant or comical. The fact that the *Book of Courtesy* insists on the ontological restriction of polite behavior to the aristocracy at the same time it acknowledges the contingency of such behavior—arguing that noble habitudes cannot be successfully adopted by those not to the manners born—marks an awareness that those behaviors it forwards in an attempt to guard against appropriation may themselves be appropriated.[29] The class-specific valence of the poet's report on these laughable attempts at gentle courtesy suggests that the charge of "vilonye" would threaten not only villainy, but also villein-y.

Contemporary literature and statutes aver that powerful commoners, especially merchants, were often mocked for their social ambitions and propensity for mannered and self-conscious behavior. Of Chaucer's Merchant, Jill Mann declares, "the professional facade is the basis of our knowledge," for Chaucer "directs our attention to the Merchant's "*manner* of giving a certain impression of his status" (102). Even into the early sixteenth century, powerful commoners, and merchants in particular, still lacked positive images to which they could attach symbolic valences.[30] The *Book of Courtesy* warns us of the possibility that such obviously affected behavior will be seen as foppish: "Fetis new founden by foolis vnprouffitable" (487). To guard against seeming foolish, we must not only "be manerly resonable" in our array, but also both cunning and honest:

> Take hede my chyld to suche as be connyng
> So shal ye best worship conquere & wynne
> Enforce you in al your demenynge
> To folowe vertu / & fro folye declynynge
> And waite wel that ye loue honesty
> Which is acordynge vnto humanyte. (478–86)

Here "honesty," earlier linked to fitting oneself to one's station in life, is linked to "humanyte" in a move that naturalizes the contemporary divisions of society and seeks to resist the sociopolitical shifts the poem elsewhere negotiates.

On the social level the *Book of Courtesy* likewise asks its readers to address the ways others perceive them, yet in its addition of the moral discourse of virtue and vice it interrogates the distinction between sign and essence:

> For that is a token of wantoun inconstance
> Whiche wil appeyre your name & disauance
> The wise man saith who hath these thingis thre

Is not lyke a goode man for to be . . .
These ben þe signes / the wiseman seith sikerly
Of suche a wight / as is vnmanerly nyce
And is ful likely disposid vnto vyce. (110)

At first reading, this admonition seems to echo the warning that behaving in an unmannerly way will cause one to be seen as disposed to vice.

Interpreting the sign-value of certain behaviors on the authority of a "wise man," the poet problematizes the distinction between exterior/interior and sign/essence by telling us that these behaviors signal people who *are* disposed to vice. A strategic and conservative reading argues that one's manners reflect a seemingly essential inner state. However, the emphasis of a tactical reading is constructionist: changing one's exterior behavior *effects* an inner change. Thus the tactical warning—behaving churlishly makes one a churl—and its hopeful converse—behaving nobly can make one noble: one's manners (or any program of behavior) can lead to a fundamental inner transformation. The *Book of Courtesy,* in both its operations and in its forwarding of reputation as the touchstone of behavior, provides many examples of this slippage between observer and observed, between behavior and character, and suggests that manners and moral essence are not distinct categories but necessarily related effects. For those elite only by profession this transformative power of conscious behavior modification is heightened, for they are not merely assuming a collective representation to which they were born, they are assigning themselves a *mentalité* not their own. This transformative potential—a program by which one could not only change one's appearance on the social level, but also seemingly transform oneself on the moral level—speaks to the urban elite's construction of its honor code out of elements of noble identity.

In Caxton's prologue to the *Book of Good Manners,* a text treating the condition of all levels of society from servant to king, he reiterates the view foregrounded in his *Dialogues in French and English* that those who are unmannered are "bestis": "the condycious & maners of the comyn people whiche without enformacion & lernyng ben rude and not manered lyke vnto beestis brute accordyng to an olde prouerbe. he that is not manerd is no man. for maners make man."[31] These formulations divide society into two groups, mannered men and unmannered beasts, a description that rewrites the dichotomy from noble/common to mannered/unmannered or elite/common, thereby inscribing his powerful common readers into the validated, superior group. Such a division is consonant with that forwarded in the *Book of St. Albans,* printed by one of Caxton's competitors for an audience similar to his,[32] which bases its nine degrees of gentle status on four criteria: birth, achievement, wealth, and service. Significantly, all but noble birth are available to the common half of London's ruling elite, and even that can be retroactively acquired through the acquisition of armorial bearings. Open to common appropriation along lines similar to the *Book of Courtesy, St. Albans* was frequently reprinted and adapted for a variety of uses. This fifteenth-century text traces its division of society into two groups, gentlemen and churls, back to the blessings and curses bestowed on Seth and Cain. Presenting this teleology of a societal division that inscribes the readers of courtesy literature—both aristocratic and non-noble—into a single class unified against the masses is an effort to ontologize the professional elite into that class whose manners and superiority had always already been ontologized (in part to prevent this kind of co-optation). Such a move collapses the distinction between a dominant, noble reading and an emergent, resistant common reading, appealing to the practice of competitive self-assertiveness and self-fashioning at work in the cultures of *both* the aristocracy and the professional elite.

NOTES

1. E. Labrousse, preface to *Aspects de l'histoire sociale et politique du Loir-et-Cher 1848–1914,* by G. Dupeux (Paris: Mouton, 1962), xi.

2. My view of the process involved in such an emerging group's quest for a social recognition commensurate with its enhanced financial and political status has been influenced by Michel Foucault's theoretical discussions, most directly by "Nietzsche, Genealogy, History," in *Language, Counter-Memory, Practice,* ed. and intro. Donald F. Bouchard, trans. Bouchard and Sherry Simon, 139–64 (Ithaca, N.Y.: Cornell University Press, 1977); see especially 148–52.

3. Contrary to conventional wisdom, the explosion in books of manners predates the then unimaginable volume of books made possible with the printing press. For a representative selection of fifteenth-century courtesy literature, see the more than twenty examples collected in *Early English Meals and Manners,* ed. Frederick J. Furnivall, EETS o.s. 32 (London: Kegan Paul, Trench, Trübner, 1868; reprinted 1894).

4. A. R. Myers, ed. and intro., *The Household of Edward IV: The "Black Book" and the Ordinance of 1478* (Manchester: Manchester University Press, 1959).

5. Ben McRee's examination of guilds supports this view: he finds that guilds with behavioral restrictions "owned property worth, on the average, more than three times as

much as gilds without such provisions" (116); "Religious Gilds and the Regulation of Behavior in Late Medieval Towns," in *People, Politics, and Community in the Later Middle Ages,* ed. Joel Rosenthal and Colin Richmond, (New York: St. Martin's Press, 1987) 108–22.

6. *The Logic of Practice,* trans. Richard Nice (1980; Stanford, Calif.: Stanford University Press, 1990), 16.

7. Bourdieu develops his definition of "distinction" most fully in *Distinction: A Social Critique of the Judgement of Taste,* trans. Richard Nice (Cambridge: Cambridge University Press, 1984).

8. See Claire Sponsler, "Narrating the Social Order: Medieval Clothing Laws," *Clio* 21 (1992): 265–83.

9. Michel de Certeau, *The Practice of Everyday Life,* trans. Steven Rendall (Berkeley: University of California Press, 1984), xii. De Certeau predicates his theories and schema on the modern world; indeed he does not himself see the medieval period as one for which they would be particularly relevant, declaring, "[i]n the middle ages, the text was framed by the four, or seven, interpretations of which it was held to be susceptible" (xxii).

10. For a full discussion of London guilds and coats of arms, see J. Bromley and H. Child, *The Armorial Bearings of the Guilds of London* (London: F. Warner, 1960).

11. Sylvia Thrupp, "The Gilds," in *Cambridge Economic History,* vol. 3, *Economic Organization and Policies in the Middle Ages,* ed. Eileen Power and M. M. Postan (London: Routledge and Sons, 1933), 276; for her discussion of armorial bearings, see *The Merchant Class of Medieval London: 1300–1500* (1948; reprint, Ann Arbor: University of Michigan Press, 1976), 140, 249–54.

12. *Acts of Court of the Mercers' Company 1453–1527,* ed. Lætitia Lyell and Frank D. Watney (Cambridge: Cambridge University Press, 1936), 60, 85–86; Merchant Tailors' Minutes, 1488–93, fol. 45; Kingdon, vol. 2 [1431], quoted in Thrupp, *Merchant Class,* 165–66.

13. A regulation of the mercers' guild states: "nobody of the said mystery should take an apprentice who had carried packs in the country nor the son of a villein"; *Mercers' Acts,* xi.

14. One need only think of the fourteenth-century alliterative poem *Sir Gawain and the Green Knight,* where Gawain demonstrates his nobility by supplementing his high birth with his peerless mastery of the conventions of polite behavior, as demonstrated by his absolute propriety in word and deed; see Jonathan Nicholls, *The Matter of Courtesy: Medieval Courtesy Books and the "Gawain" Poet* (Suffolk, England: D. S. Brewer, 1984).

15. Bourdieu is aware that his concept of habitus runs the "risk of being both schematic and formal," and warns against it being seen as "designat[ing] a system of acquired, permanent, generative dispositions" (*Logic,* 290). De Certeau offers specific objections to Bourdieu's articulation in "Foucault and Bourdieu," *Everyday,* 45–60.

16. For a discussion of the romances of this period, see H. S. Bennett, *English Books and Readers, 1475–1557* (Cambridge: Cambridge University Press, 1969), 140–48.

17. Richard Firth Green, *Poets and Princepleasers: Literature and the English Court in the Late Middle Ages* (Toronto: University of Toronto Press, 1980), 90.

18. Norbert Elias offers a valuable exploration of the historical development and dissemination of mannered behavior down the social scale. Throughout, he asserts that the downward spread was imposed: "Stricter control of impulses and emotions is first imposed by those of high social rank on their social inferiors, or, at most, their social equals"

(*The History of Manners*, 2 vols., trans. Edmund Jephcott [1939; reprint, New York: Pantheon Books, 1982], vol. 1, *The Civilizing Process*, 137). While this view seems accurate for the Enlightenment, I am arguing for a more voluntary acquisition of elite manners in the Middle Ages.

19. For discussions of the nature of formal education in the later Middle Ages, see Nicholas Orme, *Education and Society in Medieval and Renaissance England* (London: Hambledon Press, 1989), and *From Childhood and Chivalry* (London: Methuen, 1984).

20. *Poets and Princepleasers*, 79–83. For a helpful discussion on the use of courtesy literature in noble education, see Nicholls, *The Matter of Courtesy*, 57–74.

21. William Caxton, trans., *Dialogues in French and English*, ed. H. Bradley, EETS e.s. 79 (London: Kegan Paul, Trench, Trübner, 1900).

22. For a discussion of the importance of literacy and education for merchant children in particular, see Thrupp, *Merchant Class*, 234–87.

23. *The Babees Book, or A "Lytyl Reporte" of How Young People Should Behave*, in *Early English Meals and Manners*, ed. Frederick J. Furnivall, (London: Trübner, 1868), 254.

24. "Stans puer ad mensam," in *Early English Meals and Manners*, ed. Furnivall, 277.

25. *Caxton's "Book of Curtesye,"* ed. Frederick J. Furnivall, EETS e.s. 3, 1–53 (London: Trübner, 1868), 9.

26. Addressing the effectiveness of the noble educational programs, Orme concludes that by the late fourteenth century virtually all of the aristocracy would have "learnt enough Latin to follow a missal or a breviary, but would have been most fluent in the reading and writing of French and English" (*Education and Society*, 154, 228). Examining the literacy rate among guildsmen, measured by the ability to sign one's name, David Cressy finds that the members of the Mercers, Scriveners, Merchants, Vintners, Grocers, Saddlers, and Apothecaries guilds were wholly literate by the end of the fifteenth century; *Literacy and the Social Order: Reading and Writing in Tudor and Stuart England* (New York: Cambridge University Press, 1980), 134, table 6.7.

27. See *Merchant Class*, 156–58.

28. *Caxton's "Book of Curtesye,"* viii–ix.

29. This nervous gesture, and the repeated insistence on an honest fitting of oneself to one's station, suggests that Bourdieu's attention to the apparent "naturalness" of privileged culture could be usefully tempered with attention to the worried nature some of these elite texts bespeak.

30. Jill Mann discusses the presentation of merchants in estates satire in *Chaucer and Medieval Estates Satire: The Literature of Social Classes and the "General Prologue" to the "Canterbury Tales"* (Cambridge: Cambridge University Press, 1973), 99–103. In her survey of fictional literature, Laura Stephenson finds that for the most part, merchants are portrayed as stock vice figures akin to Avarice well into the sixteenth century; see *Praise and Paradox: Merchants and Craftsmen in Elizabethan Popular Literature* (Cambridge: Cambridge University Press, 1984).

31. Jacques Legrand, *The Book of Good Manners*, trans. William Caxton (Ann Arbor, Michigan: University Microforms, Early English Books, 1470–1640, reel 1227), n.p.

32. The Caxton scholar William Blades has edited a facsimile edition, *The Book of St. Albans* (London: Trübner, 1881).

3

"Nouvelles choses"

Social instability and the problem of fashion in the *Livre du Chevalier de la Tour Landry*, the *Ménagier de Paris*, and Christine de Pizan's *Livre des trois vertus*

Roberta L. Krueger

> *From what is taken by most scholars to be the beginnings of an institutionalized fashion cycle in the West, namely, fourteenth-century Burgundian court life, up to the present, fashion has repeatedly, if not exclusively, drawn upon certain recurrent instabilities in the social identities of Western men and women.*
>
> Fred Davis, *Fashion, Culture, and Identity*

The vexed relationship between women's fashion, gender roles, desire, sexuality, social distinction, ethics, community, and textual commentary—which can be witnessed today in the contrast between the profashion hype of *Cosmopolitan* or the Style channel and the somber social analysis of *No Sweat,* a recent manifesto against unethical labor practices in the globalization of textile production[1]—finds its tangled roots in the late medieval period. Then, as now, the domain of women's dress was a highly conflicted area surrounded by ethical ambivalence as it evoked, paradoxically and simultaneously, positive impulses for self-expression; the desire for youth, beauty, and love; apprehension about sexual transgressions and the breakdown of social distinctions; and moral qualms about the social inequalities fashion accentuates between those who display their surplus wealth and those who labor out of necessity to produce objects of luxury. Now, as then, both fashion and commentary about women's apparel reflect the social instabilities and inequities that women attempt to negotiate through dress.[2]

Cultural historians, sociologists, and anthropologists have analyzed the key social, economic, and political roles played by cloth and clothing as objects of exchange, as valued commodities, as symbolic expressions of power, and as a means by which individuals express identity and demarcate social differences.[3] Fashion, which accentuates, flaunts, and toys with those differences, goes one step further by announcing that social identities are unstable and subject to change.[4] It is little wonder, then, that dress and fashion are recurring topics of magazines and how-to books for women today, or that literature instructing women in the formation of social identities in which clothing played a key role was in vogue at the very time that the "fashion system" originated in European culture.

At first glance, medieval didactic literature appears antithetically opposed to fashion (unlike the popular press today), for many texts voiced repeated condemnations of new and seductive styles. Along with sermons and sumptuary laws, fashion bashing in conduct literature has been viewed as part of a widespread and largely ineffective attempt to regulate women's dress.[5] Historians often turn to conduct books for evidence of the moral outrage provoked by sartorial change, as well as for documentation of the existence of the styles themselves.[6] Literary critics have not failed to note that railings against excess, seductive styling, and novelty in women's dress are recurrent topics of the moralists' discourse, as we shall see.

But the links between fashion and books of conduct go deeper than the latter's frequent denouncements of "desguiseures" and "oultrages." The simultaneous proliferation of conduct books and the rise of fashion invite us to read these cultural systems as contingent phenomena that attempted to negotiate, in distinct and seemingly opposing ways, the ambivalence and volatility of social identity in a period of intense historical change. As objects of material and symbolic culture that take their meaning from the complex discursive, economic, social, and political matrices in which they were produced, consumed, and circulated, fashion and manuals of conduct share common features whose analysis can shed light on their deeper significance. If fashion operates like a discourse—in that it establishes a semiotic system of communication and that it functions symbolically to express relations of power[7]—then conduct books also function as objects of fashion, as material possessions that bring distinction to their readers, linking them to groups of others and helping them construct identities of gender, sexuality, and class.[8] Fashion and conduct books are also similar in the ways that they fail. Despite the common attempt of the fashion system and conduct books to impose a distinctive order that would bring social advantage to the moralist, the reader, or the wearer, the sartorial and discursive systems bear witness to the incapacity of individuals to fix behavior, create identity, or shape communities in ways that would assure their superiority. Although stylish attire and didactic literature are entrenched in the symbolic order that they both represent and attempt to manipulate, both fashion and conduct books register the instability of social identities and reveal the ethical conflicts that arise whenever human subjects attempt to construct their social selves.

Three conduct books for women written within thirty-five years of each other in northern France illustrate the dynamic intersection of fashion and conduct books in late medieval culture: *Le livre du Chevalier de la Tour Landry pour l'enseignement de ses filles* (1371–1372), which was written by a provincial aristocratic for his young daughters;[9] *Le Ménagier de Paris* (1394), compiled by a prosperous businessman for his fifteen-year-old bride, an orphan of noble birth;[10] and Christine de Pizan's *Livre des Trois Vertus* of 1405, a companion to her *Cité des dames* of the same year, which was written for the young Princess Margaret of Burgundy, who was only eleven when she married the dauphin, Louis de Guyenne, in the previous year.[11]

Written within different social venues, for diverse readers, and employing distinct narratorial strategies, these three books nonetheless intersect in important ways. Christine's later work incorporates both the clerical attack on luxury of the *Chevalier de la Tour Landry* and the bourgeois appreciation of clothing and linens within the household of the *Ménagier de Paris*. It is quite possible that Christine had read the *Livre du Chevalier de la Tour Landry*, for the arguments advanced by "la Dame de la Tour" in the governess's letter used in *Le livre du duc des vrais amans* and *Le livre des Trois Vertus* repeat many of those used by the wife of the Chevalier de la Tour Landry in his book, as Anne Marie De Gendt has shown.[12] Christine may also have known the *Ménagier de Paris,* for its ideals of domestic management are echoed in Books II and III of *Le livre des Trois Vertus* (as we shall see). The books circulated in common circles throughout the fifteenth century: the library consulted by Anne de France, for example, contains both *Chevalier de la Tour Landry* and *Le livre des Trois Vertus.*[13] In one manuscript, Bibliothèque de l'Arsenal 3356 in Paris, the *Livre du Chevalier de la Tour Landry* and Christine's *Le livre des Trois Vertus,* are compiled together. The Ménagier de Paris includes the story of Griseldis, which he has modified (as we shall see) from Philippe de Mézières's Old French translation of Petrarch's Latin version; a sparser version of Griseldis appears in Christine's companion text to the *Livre des Trois Vertus,* the *Cité des dames.*[14] Attesting to the vogue of this tale in which clothing encodes class and moral virtue so poignantly (as we shall see), in five fifteenth-century manuscripts the *Livre du Chevalier de la Tour Landry* is followed by "Le mireoir des dames mariées: Griselidis, la noble marquise de Saluce."[15]

The encyclopedic *Ménagier de Paris* is extant in only three manuscripts, but both the *Chevalier de la Tour Landry* and the *Livre des Trois Vertus* circulated very widely, in luxury manuscripts, in paper manuscripts, and in early printed editions, and both were translated into other languages.[16] Paper manuscripts of Christine's and the Chevalier's work suggest their appeal to broader bourgeois audiences;[17] vellum manuscripts with an opening illumination attest also to their continued circulation among wealthy households as well. Thus, these books circulated in similar circles, sometimes together, and in the company of similar texts throughout the later European Middle Ages, during which time the connections between dress and the social, economic, and moral order became ever more complex, and "fashion" began to extend its lure in Western culture.

Readers of conduct books could not have been unaware of the vogue for fashion that spread from courts to wealthy households in urban centers throughout late medieval Europe.[18] Until the mid–fourteenth century, distinctive clothing marked the different social classes, but change of styles was subtle and gradual. The tunic, a robe shaped in rectangular form and draped and gathered, was the basic unit of clothing, which might vary in length and fabric according to occupation and rank. Peasants wore short, rough clothes for ease of work; noble men and women in the leisure of court wore longer robes, and they prized a variety of fine fabrics: fine cottons and linens, silk, taffetas, brocades. The dress of noblemen and women was similarly based upon the flowing robe, as can be observed in manuscript illuminations before 1350; one finds the terms *chemise, bliaut,* and *chainse* used to describe both male and female clothing. As Jane Burns has shown, clothing in thirteenth-century courtly texts was a focus for the expression and display of sexual desire and was often a site where male and female gender roles could intermingle.[19]

In the mid–fourteenth century, apparently almost simultaneously throughout elite European societies, style gave way to fashion, which cultural historians have defined as dress that intends to "startle, captivate, offend or otherwise engage the sensibilities of some culturally preponderant public."[20] Sometime between 1330 and 1350, the rectangular tunic fell out of favor, to be replaced by clothing with rounded sleeves that was more closely molded to the body.[21] Noble men's and women's dress became more sharply differentiated. Male styles were probably the first to change, and their new features were the most boldly distinctive: men donned short formfitting pourpoints or doublets that exposed their legs, which were later swathed in multicolored fabric, known as *mi-parti.* Noblewomen's dress was distinguished by a tightening of the bodice, revealing the female shape, and by plunging necklines. Some years later, both men and women adopted the *houppelande,* a showy great cloak with expansive sleeves that could be lined with fur. Men wore the *houppelande* open to reveal their hose; women fastened their cloaks at the waist. Later costumes were sewn together from small pieces and sometimes had decorative slits and slashes. These fashions sacrificed economy for style, since "dagged" construction wasted material and individually sized clothing could not be handed down as easily.[22]

Both sexes wore increasingly elaborate headdresses throughout the later Middle Ages. Women's headdresses, whose former purpose had been to cloak women's heads and hair with modesty and decorum, became objects of display that accentuated the hair and face. Popular female styles included the *chaperon,* or hood; the *bourrelet,* a rounded, reticulated headdress; the horned headdress; and, later in the fifteenth century, the *hennin,* a high, pointed headdress with a gauze covering and train. Late medieval costume for wealthy nobles and bourgeois accentuated sexual differences, flirted with cross-dressing, flaunted the erotic silhouettes of male and female bodies, displayed the wealth and taste of the wearer, blurred social distinctions—and apparently did so with an increasingly rapid pace of changing styles through which men and women vied with one another for novelty and distinction.

Contemporaneously with and in similar venues as the spread of stylish clothing, late medieval French conduct books traveled from courtly settings into lower aristocratic and bourgeois households. Instructional texts achieved special prominence at the court of Charles V, who enhanced the royal library with a program of vernacular translations, including Nicole Oresme's translations into French of Aristotle's *Nicomachean Ethics, Politics,* and the pseudo-Aristotelian *Economics* (a treatise on household management).[23] Charles VI and the dukes of Burgundy, Berry, and Orléans also sponsored numerous didactic works, among them works of Christine, which were often lavishly prepared and illustrated.[24] Advice about women was often included in twelfth- and thirteenth-century tracts,[25] and several separate works for women predate the fourteenth century, notably Robert de Blois's *Chastoiement des dames.*[26] However, the appearance and rapid dissemination of no less than three discrete works on female conduct within a forty-year period for such varied audiences—for provincial aristocrats *(Livre du Chevalier de la Tour Landry),* for a Parisian bourgeoise (the *Ménagier de Paris*), and for a mixed audience ranging from royal court to poorest subject (the *Livre des Trois Vertus*)—marks a new prominence and popularity of books for women. New styles and new books for women circulated contemporaneously, probably often within the same prosperous courts and households.

The simultaneous dissemination of fashion and books for women from court to wealthy household was fostered by important socioeconomic changes, including the continued growth of urban centers, the enrichment and expansion of the merchant class, an expanding market of textiles and luxury goods, technological innovations in weaving and later in printing, and a widening public of consumers and readers. At the same time, the demographic crisis of the fourteenth century— the political and economic instability rising from the vicissitudes of the Hundred Years' War and the Black Death—led to a disintegration of traditional societies that permitted new modes of social expression, intensified the reaction against social upstarts, and called forth the desire to reimpose "order" and articulate boundaries. Even as the majority of French people suffered the ill effects of plague, famine, and war, members of royal and ducal courts—perhaps seeking to secure their precarious power through symbolic means—indulged in greater expense for clothing and luxurious display than ever before.[27] The rage for conspicuous consumption among the highest families of France was most notorious at the court of Charles VI, under his queen, Isabeau de Bavière.[28] The desire to enrich royal coffers during times of war and civil strife contributed to the fiscal and social instability of the later Middle Ages.[29] At the same time, expanded markets for luxury goods and textiles enriched the families of merchants and artisans, who could now afford to vie with the aristocracy in consumption and display.

The new styles and their attendant social transformations provoked censure and opposition in a variety of discursive contexts. Beginning as early as Charlemagne's restrictions on furs in 808, a series of royal sumptuary ordinances in France attempted to regulate not only sartorial display but also ownership and display of precious metals, jewels, and household silver.[30] Philippe le Bel's law was particularly restrictive of bourgeois men and women, who were forbidden to wear gray squirrel, ermine, gold, or precious stones, who could not own more than a pair of dresses a year, and whose gowns could not be made of more than an amount of material commensurate with income.[31] Although no new royal edicts are recorded in France during the period 1372–1405, the motivations that underlay such regulations, which were widespread throughout Europe, remained strong. Whether sumptuary laws were instituted to maintain class distinctions and promote recognition of one's peers, to regulate women's sexual morality, to curb the ill effects of luxury on an impoverished populace, to contain the inflation of dowries, to increase the value of the royal treasury by making precious fabrics, and especially gold and silver, scarce, to protect trade—or a combination of several elements—depends on particular historical contexts, and their aims have been much discussed.[32] As Hunt points out, even if sumptuary laws "failed" to transform behavior and were impossible to enforce uniformly, the regulatory impulse was firmly entrenched in early modern culture.[33] Even more prevalent than official ordinances were the persistent condemnations of fashion from priests, clerics, chroniclers, and lay moralists—further proof that the desire for fashion pervaded courts and households throughout Europe.[34]

Within such volatile social and discursive spaces, our late medieval conduct books for women paradoxically became objects of fashion and promoted self-fashioning even as they decried the lure of new styles. The *Livre du Chevalier de la Tour Landry*, the *Ménagier de Paris*, and the *Livre des Trois Vertus* all demonstrate the emergence of fashion as a contested area of women's agency and transgression, as a means for women's social transformation, and as a site in which conflicted ethical relationships are manifest. Even as the moralist's lament against fashion grows more pointed from the Chevalier de la Tour Landry to Christine de Pizan, dress becomes increasingly valorized as an area over which women exerted ever greater control within the court, the manor, and the household. With growing complexity, the Chevalier, the Ménagier, and Christine reveal how clothing not only expresses women's symbolic capital but also implicates them in a tissue of unequal social relationships. By talking about clothing, the moralists also put matters of dress into discursive circulation and promote the popularity of books like their own.

The earliest book, the *Livre du Chevalier de la Tour Landry pour l'enseignement de ses filles*, written in 1371–1372, is the tract of a provincial aristocrat who has sought the assistance of two priests and two clerks in writing a book that will instruct his young daughters in reading and discerning good from evil, so that they may protect their chastity from ill-intentioned men.[35] The Chevalier's paternal asides to his "belles filles" punctuate his personal anecdotes and exempla, which are derived largely from the thirteenth-century Franciscan *Miroir des bonnes femmes*, presenting good and evil women.[36] Female dress is a major topic of the Chevalier's moral counsel, one that intersects broadly with his advice on marriage, sexual and social mores, and ethical values. In a series of chapters leading to the exemplum of Eve (drawn from the *Miroir*) and then extending to the exemplum of Lot's daughters (chapters 21 to 45), the Chevalier returns repeatedly to the subject of women's inappropriate dress, which he alternately condemns, ridicules, and demonizes. His sartorial conservatism is bolstered by negative exempla of women who were chastised or more severely punished for using clothing to transgress moral or ethical norms: by refusing to dress in good clothes for Sundays and holidays (chapter 25); by owning too many dresses, whose value would be better shared with the poor (chapter 26); by taking too long to dress and missing church (chapter 31); by flaunting "cointise" (finery) and outrageous styles that shout their defiance of modesty and decorum (chapter 47); by rushing to adopt the new fashions (chapters 48 and 49); by hoarding an extravagant wardrobe (chapters 50 and 51);

by dressing up in finery out of pride and falling into sin (chapter 54). Toward the book's end, the Chevalier revisits the dress question and stresses a particularly fatherly concern: the necessity of wearing warm clothes in cold weather and not going about clad only in a fashionable "cotte hardie" (fitted dress), as did the young lady who lost her suitor because she was cold and pale (chapter 120), as did the young man, Foulque de Laval (chapter 121), and, most curiously, as did the foolish and long-departed "Gaulois and Gauloises" who lived backwards, wearing warm clothes in summer and light clothes in winter, who made a rule of infidelity, and literally froze to death in their amorous embraces.[37]

The Chevalier de la Tour Landry's views on dress thus encompass spiritual, moral, ethical, and practical concerns. His advice can be summed up by the maxim that heads chapter 49, "Tenir moyen estat," which can be translated as meaning "uphold the middle station by your way of dressing," "dress moderately or conservatively," or "track a middle course in the fashion race." As does Christine in the *Livre des Trois Vertus,* the Chevalier uses the term "estat" to refer to social "estate," or station in life, and to the wardrobe that symbolically embodies class.[38]

In keeping with his concern for the chastity of unmarried maidens and the fidelity of wives throughout the book, and in concert with his avowedly clerical sources, the Chevalier de la Tour Landry presents the most sexualized depiction of women's dress and illustrates his points with the most punitive exempla. The tension between proper dress and ostentatious fashion is portrayed as a moral division between social order and sexual and social disorder, a topic rehearsed in numerous medieval sermons on the subject, which in the Chevalier's retelling takes on the quality of an obsession.[39] In the chapter entitled "D'un esvesque qui prescha sur les cointises" [On the bishop who preached against finery] (chapter 47), the Chevalier's young daughters learn on the high authority of a holy bishop and "grant clerc" that the Flood was caused by "l'orgueil et les desguiseures des hommes, et espécialement des femmes, qui se contrefaisoient de atours et de robbes" [the pride and the dressing-up of men, and especially of women, who made themselves over with headdresses and gowns] (98), since such dress led to the "vil pechié de luxure" [vile sin of luxury/debauchery]. As the Chevalier reports on the bishop's condemnation of his parishioners' costume, colorful sexual expressions and animal comparisons prevail: the men are in short cloaks that show their "culz et leurs brayes et ce qui leur boce devant" [their ass and their breeches and what bulges in front] (98); the ladies wear headdresses resembling "limas cornus" [horned snails], "licornes" [unicorns] (98), and "cerfs branchus" [stags with antlers], whose horns and branches are compared to the devil's nets in which he lurks for his prey like a spider (99). Although the Chevalier recognizes that styles will inevitably change, he insists that those who rush to the forefront in the fashion race are the ones who fall the most certainly into danger, like the young ladies who fell in the mud as they rushed ahead of the others (chapter 48).

But the Chevalier's vivid evocation of the new styles, which provides lively descriptions of fashionable gowns and accessories and of the women who wore them, accentuates the desirability of the very items he decries. Even as he warns against strange and foreign ways of dressing and laments the spread of "nouveaulx estats," the Chevalier acts as a commentator of the fashion scene who broadcasts the latest styles and unwittingly enhances their value. The first exemplum in this series (chapter 21) launches the discursive circulation of fashion into motion. Here the Chevalier describes a conversation overheard between the Sire de Beaumanoir and his female cousin, who has chided the Sire for not allowing his wife to wear the latest fashions in Brittany, namely large fur-lined sleeves and hoods. Retorting that he could provide his wife with a cloak and hood completely covered in fur if he so wished, the Sire de Beaumanoir explains the real reason that he eschews such newfangled styles: he maintains that slit dresses and fur-lined sleeves were brought over to France by the prostitutes who accompanied the English troops (in the skirmishes of the Hundred Years' War) and that, therefore, decent women should not associate themselves with such "nouveaultez": "les plus saiges sont celles qui derrenièrement prennent telles nouveaultez" [the wisest women are those who adopt such new fashions last] (47). The Chevalier's reported speech between two persons who talk about styles from elsewhere and the Sire de Beaumanoir's account of himself as an eyewitness ("car je suy du temps et le vy" [for I was there at the time and I saw it] [47]) demonstrate the dynamic intersection between fashion and commentary in late fourteenth-century culture. As the style circulates from England to France, as the mode travels back and forth between prostitutes and noble ladies, so the talk about fashion circulates among the Sire and his cousin and the Chevalier who overheard the conversation and reports it to his daughters, attempting to make slit robes and fur linings sound as reprehensible and as ridiculous as possible.

Although the Chevalier attempts to equate fur linings with the "low" style of prostitutes, illuminations and sumptuary legislation attest that fur linings were highly prized among male and female members of the nobility and the wealthy bourgeoisie. Piponnier and Mane speak of the "consommation effrénée de pelleteries" [runaway consumption of skins], which were used to line boots, hoods, sleeves, gloves, and cloaks (33). According to Ruth Karras, English ordinances repeatedly forbade "common women" from wearing furs or "noble lining", both so that they might be distinguished from respectable women, who would then not be harassed on the streets, and so that the expensive styles of fur-lined clothes did not become so prevalent that "honest" wives and daughters would demand them as a part of their wardrobe.[40] If the Chevalier's story is true, then prostitutes openly defied attempts to regulate their dress, with the result that successful whores could adopt the fashion of the most elegant, thus blurring the distinction between "common" and "respectable" ladies, who would desire the same fashions as the prostitute.

By the end of chapter 21, the desire for fur trim has traveled from the nobility to "femmes servantes" and "femmes de chambres, clavières et aultres de mendre estat" [female servants, chamber maids, servants, and others of low station] whom the Chevalier mocks for wearing linings that become soiled with mud and attract fleas (49). Although he would not presume to dictate the styles that greater ladies might adopt ("qui bien le pevent faire à leur plaisir et à leur guise" [who can well do what they please as they wish] 49), the Chevalier insists on the authority of his word among his daughters and his female servants, "à qui je puis dire et monstrer ce que je vueil et il me plaist" [to whom I can speak and show what I like and as it pleases me]. Attempting to prevent the spread of "nouveaulz estats" across national boundaries, between classes, and within households, the Chevalier seeks to control the discourse on dress in his own domain, that of a provincial, midlevel aristocrat.[41]

Yet, as the Chevalier laments on several occasions, fashion's discursive circulation at the current moment ("aujourd'huy") is impossible to stop: as soon as any woman hears about another woman's new gown or headdress, she won't stop talking about it until she has successfully badgered her husband for a copy (48–49). In such a climate, even a condemnation of new styles could promote envy and foster imitation. The Chevalier continues to publicize the latest fashions as he attacks them. In chapter 49, he complains again that hearsay and women's rhetorical skills prevail in the struggle to maintain "moyen estat": in his "meschant siècle" [evil time] any report of a "nouveaulté" inspires such a tirade within the household that husbands inevitably give in to their wives (102–3). Yet, in the same passage, the Chevalier furthers the discursive circulation of a new accessory—in this case a ridiculous gallows-shaped headdress—by insisting on its timeliness (he has learned about it just this year, in 1372) and by describing it in concrete terms, even if not precisely as his source described it: "maiz en bonne foy je le retins petitement" [but, in good faith, I only remember a little (of what she told me)] (104). The fact that the bearer of the "gibet" was mocked at the time did not prevent the style from being imitated.

That the Chevalier devotes so much attention to hats and gowns attests to the enormous symbolic power that clothing represented for women in late medieval culture. New styles visually challenged the old order. This section's final exemplum on the pitfalls of fashion ends with the brutal punishment of a lower-class transgressor whose sartorial desires compromise aristocratic honor. In chapter 55, following the tale of Lot's daughters, whose sin in dressing up led them to accept bad advice, the Chevalier tells how a servant betrays her mistress for the sake of a new *chapperon* (hood) by arranging for a meeting between the married lady and the dishonest knight who has bribed her. When the husband learns the ultimate cause of his wife's infidelity (115–17), he insists that the girl put on the hood before he beheads her, "si luy fist vestir et coupper le col et le chapperon tout ensemble" [so made her dress and had the neck and the hood cut together] (116). The Chevalier's insistence on the husband's cutting of head and hood (which is repeated twice, first as a direct-speech command) seems to underscore the moralist's own frustrated struggle to control the sexual and social transgressions embodied in "nouveaux estats."

Whatever the views of their moralizing narrators, conduct books participated in an ongoing commentary about style that must have kept fashion in the forefront as a lively topic for debate in courts and households. Illuminations that portray the opening scene in many copies of these books reinforce the book's participation in the symbolic workings of fashion. Illustrated manuscripts of the *Livre du Chevalier de la Tour Landry* usually portray the Chevalier with his daughters, who are attired in different styles of appropriately attractive dress, with varied cuts, colors, fabrics, styles, and headdresses. As is characteristic of manuscripts of this period, styles are portrayed as up-to-date if not positively fashionable, as in the case of Bibliothèque Nationale ms. fr. 1190 (formerly 7403). See Figure 3.1. In this fifteenth-century manuscript, thought by the editor to be the earliest extant,[42] the knight wears a stylish blue *houp-*

Figure 3.1. Opening illustration for Geoffroy de la Tour Landry, *Le livre du Chevalier de la Tour Landry pour l'enseignement de ses filles*. Bibliothèque Nationale, ms. fr. 1190, fol. 5. Courtesy of Bibliothèque Nationale de France, Paris.

pelande, with dagged sleeves, scarlet hose, and an extravagant lavender headdress whose cut, as Montaiglon remarks, is diametrically opposed to the moderate styles advocated in the book.[43] The daughters wear, respectively, an embroidered gown with scalloped, lined sleeves and red *bourrelet;* a red dress with long, trimmed sleeves and a blue headdress; and, for the youngest, a gray dress with a simple collar and no headdress. The family's enclosure within a walled garden echoes the Prologue and may mirror the aspirations for aristocratic leisure, prosperity, and fertility (as suggested by the flowering trees in the background) of the readers for whom this well-worn and stylish manuscript was designed.

In contrast to the lavish dress and aristocratic garden of B.N. ms. fr. 1190, Bibliothèque Nationale ms. fr. 12477, one of three copies of the *Ménagier de Paris,* presents an orderly, bourgeois interior in an opening miniature. See Figure 3.2. The wealthy husband and his conservatively but richly dressed wife appear contained within a domestic interior whose furnishings and decor are carefully depicted. His fashionable, draped hat and long, fur-timmed *houppelande* attest to his prosperity and social prominence; her neat collar and headdress convey appropriate decorum; the careful draping and pillows of the couch enclose the couple in a vignette of domestic harmony. This contained, yet detailed, image provides a fitting introduction to the Prologue, in which the elderly narrator engages to instruct his young wife within the privacy of their bedchamber.[44] The Ménagier's book is a hefty compendium of texts for household use (including a treatise on falconry, a cookbook with hundreds of recipes, and numerous exempla) that recasts aristocratic views on decorous clothing within the framework of a busy, urban household.

The Ménagier is less preoccupied with fashion than the Chevalier, and he devotes no separate chapter to dress. Nonetheless, the prominent placement of his instructions to his wife on how to dress each day, which appear at the end of the First Distinction, highlights the centrality of clothing as a mark of the wife's social standing (I, 10). Dress is the first "material" item of the wife's life, and it appears seamlessly inserted into a chapter on prayer, as if, indeed, cleanliness were next to godliness. A woman's duty is to arrange herself carefully, in keeping with her station, without introducing "nouvelles devises," and with neither too little nor too much *beuban* or adornment (9). Her collar, gown, and overgown should all lie neatly in place: "Et avant que vous partiez de vostre chambre ou hostel, ayez par avant avisé que le colet de vostre chemise, de

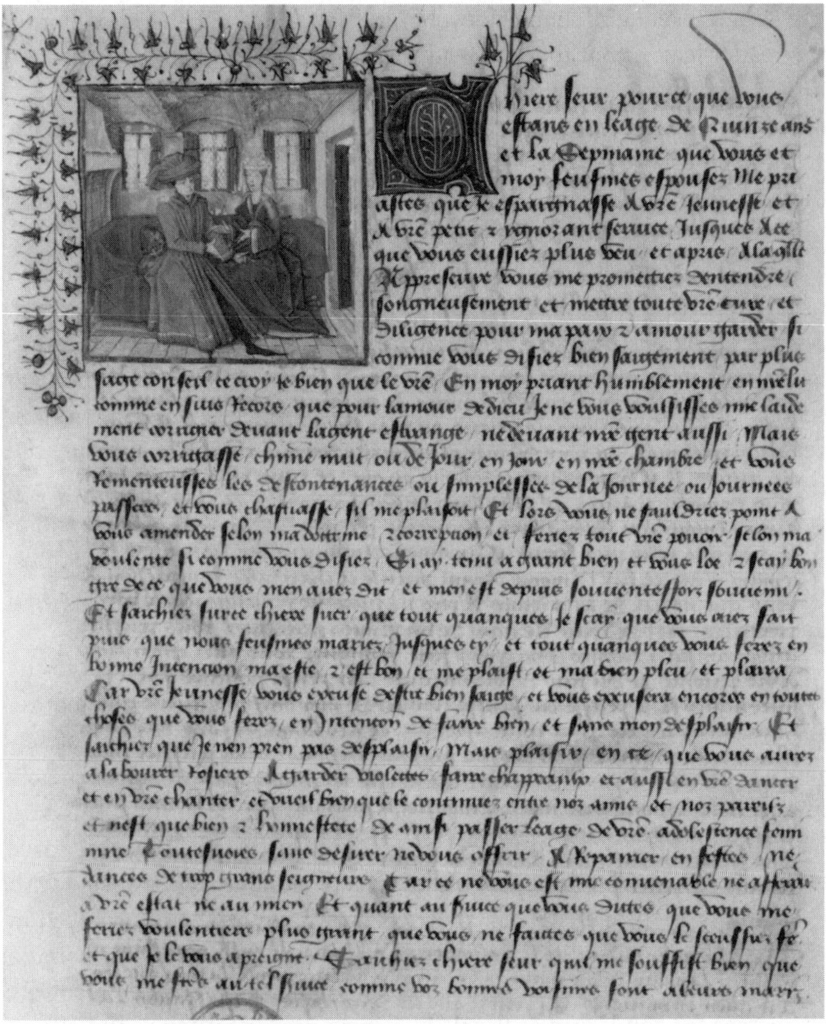

Figure 3.2. Opening illustration for the *Ménagier de Paris*. Bibliothèque Nationale, ms. fr. 12477, fol. 1. Courtesy of Bibliothèque Nationale de France, Paris.

vostre blanchet, ou de vostre coste ou seurcot ne saillent l'un sur l'autre" (9). Perhaps because a wife as busy and confined to her house as the Ménagier's would have no time for fancy dress and no place to flaunt the latest styles, the Ménagier does not fulminate against fashion. Rather, he stresses the wife's neatness, which should reflect the order of a well-kept household.

In a subsequent chapter devoted to the creation of the ideal home, the reader learns that the husband's clothing and household linens are just as important as the wife's attire, for his dress is a reflection of her own character: "Et vous pry que vous le tenez nectement de linge, car en vous en est" (99). Fresh linens and clean clothes are key features of the comfortable home that the wife must provide for her hardworking husband, whose business forces him to travel through rain, wind, snow, and hail and to live a miserable existence away from home. The woman will make sure that he finds a warm hearth where he will be "bien couché en blancs draps et cueuvrechiez blans, bien couvert de bonnes fourrures, et assouvy d'autres joyes et esbatemens, privetez, amour et secretz dont je me taiz. Et l'endemain robes-linges et vestemens nouveaulx" [sleeping comfortably in white sheets and white headdress, well covered in good furs, and satisfied with other joys and distractions, private pleasures, love and secret things about which I will remain silent. And the next morning he will have clean undergarments and new clothes] (I, vii, 20–24). The physical comforts of clean linens and the sensual delights of marriage are seamlessly interconnected in this passage.

More than the Chevalier or Christine, the Ménagier attends to the practical details of wardrobe maintenance. In two chapters devoted, respectively, to care of the husband and household and the hiring of servants (I, vii, and II, iii, 11–13), the Ménagier reminds the reader how much physical work and logistical ingenuity are entailed in combating the impending disorder, dirt, and decay that threaten the physical space of the household. Clothing and bedding become filthy and infested with fleas unless the proper steps are taken. Accordingly, in the central section of the chapter instructing the wife to make the household "un paradiz de reppos" [a restful paradise] for the husband, the Ménagier recounts six recipes for getting rid of fleas: "Et en esté gardez que en vostre chambre ne en vostre lit n'ait nulles puces: ce que vouz pouez faire en six manieres, sicomme j'ay oy dire" [In summer make sure neither your room nor your bed have fleas, which you can do in six ways, as I've heard] (I, vii, 3, ll. 4–6). These include spreading alder leaves in the room to attract the pests; enticing them with sticky bread and burning them; luring them to rough cloth or sheepskin and carrying them out of the room; spreading out a white cloth over the bed onto which the fleas will jump, so that they can be more easily killed; and suffocating the fleas by wrapping up the bedclothes in a space without air (I, vii, 3, ll. 7–26). In the chapter on hiring servants, the Ménagier provides detailed instructions on how the wife and her "beguine" [female servant] should maintain "draps, couvertures, robes et fourrures, pennes et autres telles choses" [sheets, covers, robes and furs, skins, and other such things]. Clothing must be aerated often to prevent vermin, especially in the damp winter months (II, iii, 11). Spots may be removed with a variety of substances, including "pissat" [animal urine], "fiel de beuf" [beef gall], "terre de robes" [earth], "vertjus" [verjuice] and water (II, iii, 12) depending on the types of material and kind of stain.

That so many methods of flea and spot removal need be enumerated points to the intractability of these domestic problems and to the ingenuity, perseverance, and patience that were involved in keeping up bourgeois appearances.[45] It is no wonder that the Ménagier insists so often on obedience and devotion in marriage, which he underscores with the tale of Griseldis, among other positive and negative exempla of wifely devotion. As Brereton and Ferrier have shown, among the most significant changes that the Ménagier makes to his source is his emphasis on Griseldis's efficient household management.[46] We also note that the Ménagier's version of the passage in which Griseldis commands the servants to arrange the household for Walter's new wife amplifies in particular the description of household textiles, the tapestries, the embroideries, and the monogrammed wall hangings: "et elle emprist a *drecier* et a ordener les litz et les chambres, tendre *les tappis de haulte lice* et toutes choses *de broderie et devises* qui appartenoient aux paremens du palais" [and she undertook to arrange and order the bed and rooms, to hang the tapestries from high-warped looms and everything with embroidery and devises that belonged to the decorations of the palace] (*Menagier,* 333; emphasis added).[47] Griseldis's symbolic association with clothing and her management of her own wardrobe are, of course, inseparable from the virtue that she embodies: when the poor girl is chosen to marry Walter, female servants adorn Griseldis head to toe with "riches draps et paremens de nopces," thus making her so "soudainement transformée" by her clothes that others do not recognize her (Lettres Gothiques ed., 202). Later, when Walter banishes her, she chooses to return the sartorial trappings of their marriage and to strip herself naked, save for a simple *chemise,* emblem of the virginity she brought to the marriage and a mark of his "honneur" (Lettres Gothiques ed., 220). What the editors refer to as the "fashionable tale" of Griselda (which, as we've seen, circulated widely with these conduct books) thus highlights women's practical, moral, and symbolic relation to clothing.[48]

Women's work with cloth is also key in the tale of Jehanne la Quentine, which is significantly placed as the last exemplum of the First Distinction.[49] When Jehanne's husband, Thomas, has an affair with a "povre fille qui estoit fillerresse de layne au rouet" [poor girl who was a spinner of wool at a wheel] in the woman's hovel, the wife upholds the marital duty of providing for her husband's material needs by outfitting the bare space, where there was "rien fors ung lit et une couverture, son thouret et ung pou d'autre mesnage" [nothing but a bed, a cover, her spinning wheel, and a few other household items], with all the comforts of a bourgeois home. Among the items she gives to the girl are "ung bon lit, et duvet, draps et couverture selon son estat, cueuvrechiefs, orilliers, chausses et robes-linges nectes" [a good bed, a quilt, sheets and cover appropriate to his station, headcovers, pillows, hose, and clean shirts] (I, ix, 4), which she offers to clean whenever they are dirty. When the husband learns from his mistress that his wife has so dramatically improved his surroundings, he confesses his sins and returns to the wife, whom he loved "humblement et cordieusement" [humbly and warmly] ever after. Aside from the Ménagier's intended lesson of wifely devotion, this exemplum demonstrates how their material relationship to textiles determines the lot of women, condemning some to a servile existence and allowing others to manipulate cloth to their social advantage.

Christine de Pizan combines both clerical objections to fashion voiced by the Chevalier and the practical concerns with household linens and wardrobes recorded by the Ménagier within a new, more comprehensive vision. As critics have noted, Christine's approach to women's dress is both more complex and more conflicted than that of her male predecessors.[50] In the *Cité des dames,* as Hicks has shown, Christine dismantles the clerical notion that love of finery is a female trait attribute by assigning it to a male saint.[51] In the *Livres des Trois Vertus,* although she echoes the Chevalier's condemnation of "oultrage" and "desguiseures" in female dress, her denunciation of fashion is only one thread of a rich tapestry that portrays women's relationship to cloth, clothing, adornment, and household linens in every social class: in book I, for the Princess; in book II, for ladies-in-waiting and ladies on the manor; and in book III, for bourgeois women (wives of administrators, merchants, artisans, laborers), prostitutes, and the poor. Remarks on women's attire, expenditures for wardrobes, choice of servants' dress, management of household linens, and the production of cloth and clothing are so closely woven into each section that clothing becomes inseparable from the fabric of life.

Paying greater attention to the fine details as well as the moral value of textiles than her predecessors, Christine depicts the dynamic intersection of clothing with women's social, economic, ethical, and spiritual lives. Her pedagogical methods are less prescriptive than either the Chevalier's or the Ménagier's; her rhetorical strategies are subtle and indirect. Exempla and doctrinal teachings—the staple of the *Chevalier de la Tour Landry* and the *Ménagier de Paris*—are sparse.[52] Tailoring her rhetorical strategies and the content of her advice to each social class,[53] Christine offers astute observations and analyses of women's social conditions. In a complex interweaving of allegorical voice, personal intervention, and reported speech that sometimes portrays the imagined inner thoughts of its reader,[54] Christine observes women's condition. Even as the *Livre des Trois Vertus* provides the most extensive arguments against luxury and fashion, its moralist also provides the most vivid account of the inexorable tide of fashion, as her representation of "oultrages" intensifies from book I to book III.

The frontispiece illumination that accompanies Boston Public Library ms. 1528 reflects the sophistication of Christine's narrative strategies and her more complex vision of women's dress. See Figure 3.3. In this manuscript, which is thought to emerge from Christine's workshop, the author appears on the left in bed in her signature dress—a modest but fine blue dress with moderate sleeves and a simple, neat white starched headdress—pulled to her feet by the more richly attired Virtues. Her bedclothes and hangings are carefully depicted. On the right appear ladies of different social classes, attentively portrayed in different styles, colors, fits of dress and headdress, who sit at the feet of the royally clad Prudence Mondaine, who reads from a book, just as her allegorical voice will soon address the reader. The variety of clothing—simple gowns, costlier *houppelandes,* starched headdresses, liripipes, an elaborate *bourrelet,* and crowns—reflects the royal, noble, bourgeois, and common readers whom Christine addresses and underscores the importance of the topic of dress throughout the book. As Laura Rinaldi Dufresne has shown, subsequent manuscripts throughout the fifteenth century portray the Virtues and the author dressed in ever more elaborate garb, in careful imitation of contemporary styles.[55] However forceful their condemna-

Figure 3.3. Opening illustration for Christine de Pizan, *Le livre des Trois Vertus.* Boston Public Library ms. 1528, frontispiece. Courtesy of the Trustees of the Boston Public Library.

tion of "nouveaux estats," neither the Chevalier de la Tour Landry nor Christine de Pizan could prevent future copies of their books from portraying changing styles, even high headdresses that were once considered outrageous.

In book I of the *Livre des Trois Vertus,* which presents an interlacing of allegorical voices speaking to the Princess, Christine launches a circumspect, yet trenchant, attack on luxury. The initial portrait of the Princess depicts her lying lazily in bed, where she is beset by the voice of Temptacion to indulge in idleness and luxury. She reclines between sweetly smelling sheets in a richly decorated bed, "en son lit entre souefs draps, avironnee de riches paremens et de toutes choses pour aise de corps" [in her bed between sweet/soft sheets, adorned with rich attire and with all things for the comfort of her body] (12). This vignette recalls the author's Prologue, which portrays her as exhausted from writing the *Cité des dames* and lying in idleness, "oyseuse et querant repos" (7), presumably in bed (where many miniatures portray her), as she is roused by voices of the allegorical figures Reason, Rectitude, and Justice to continue her work. But the voice that speaks to the Princess is that of Temptacion, inciting the Princess to think only of her own pleasures. By means of an internal monologue that rehearses her selfish, proud, and avaricious desire, Christine portrays a woman obsessed with material "tresors," who believes she may command whatever gowns, accessories, jewels, or clothes she wants "tieulx robes, tieulx paremens, tieulx joyaulx, tieulz abillemens," in the manner she desires "ainsi et ainsi fais et de tel devise," simply because she has none in the latest fashion "tu n'en as nulz de si nouvelle façon" (13). Christine's disdain for the sartorial extravagance of the ruling family is cloaked in allegory, but her contempt for self-indulgence is evident.

Temptacion's reasoning is soon countered by the voice of "l'amour et craintte de Nostre Seigneur," which describes such riches as a "doloreux tresor" because they are only amassed at the expense of the labor and sweat of others "le prejudice de plusieurs, a leur grant grief et extorcion . . . la sueur de plusieurs gens et contre leur voloir" (16). The contrast between the pleasure of luxuries and the work that has gone into making them is repeated at several points in this passage: when this voice explains how "orgueil" makes the Princess believe that her sole occupation should consist of visiting her trunks of jewels and clothing (17), and later when the speaker explains that "orgueil" makes the Princess so desirous of "superflus habis" that she thinks neither of their cost nor their origin and makes her so "desdaigneuse" of what she owns that no "superflus habis, joyaulx, et paremens" [superfluous clothes, jewels, and adornments] can satisfy her (18).

When the voice of Prudence Mondaine replaces that of Temptacion, however, clothing remains a matter of high regard, the subject of several lengthy exhortations. The Princess's rich wardrobe of jewels, clothing, and other accessories must reflect the honor of her God-given station, and extravagant clothing or new styles should be avoided (43–44). The Princess should content herself with what was worn by her "nobles devanciers" [noble ancestors] and should not desire "nouvelles choses" (44). Her ladies should be similarly attired, without "desguiseure / ne deshonnesteté de trop grans colléz ou d'autres oultrages," so that they will not stir up rumors in foreign courts or in town (73). The material attributes of a rich wardrobe embody spiritual, moral, and political order and project that order visually; any deviation—novelty, extravagance, or seductiveness—reflects dangerous change or dissolution.

Christine portrays the Princess as an agent of social control, responsible for her own self-government and for the regulation of those around her—a feature that no doubt ensured the book's popularity with royal circles throughout the early modern period.[56] Always shrewdly cognizant of the financial aspects of material conditions that determine social life, Christine pegs the desired value of the appropriate sartorial "treasure" at one-fifth of a princess's total wealth: the other four parts should be devoted to alms, housekeeping, salaries for her retinue, and gifts to foreign visitors or others (76–77).

Christine's objections to extravagance and novelty in book I are cloaked in allegory, and, although they reveal an astute understanding of court politics and finances, they levy no specific charges. It would have been unseemly for Christine to criticize the particular styles of her patrons. But in book II, as Christine turns from the court to speak to ladies-in-waiting and ladies on the manor, she adopts a direct manner of address and portrays women's relationship to cloth and clothing much more concretely.

Because the dress of ladies-in-waiting is the purview of the Princess (as elaborated in book I), Christine's remarks on dress in book II concern only ladies on the manor, who are responsible for all the details of estate management—finances, defense, supervision of workers, and household work. Our first glimpse of the relation of these women to cloth is a description of the lady and her servants working at home, to produce wool and then fabric to be made into clothing:

> Elle, ses filles et ses damoiselles s'embesoignera de draper, de trier celle laine et sortir et mettre les colléz de celle fine laine a part pour faire les fins draps pour son mary et pour elle et pour vendre, se mestier est: des gros pour les petiz enfans, pour ses femmes et maignees. Fera couvertures de gros bourdons de la laine, et des fermiers fera coultiver des chanvres que toilleront et fileront a ces soirs en yver ses chamberieres pour faire des grosses toilles. (156)
>
> [She and her girls and young women will occupy themselves in making clothing. They will select the wool, putting the best quality to one side to make fine garments for her and her husband or to sell if she needs to do so. She uses the coarse wool for little children and for her women and household. She will make heavy table covers from the wool, and from the scraps she will

have the linens trimmed that her chambermaids will spin and weave on winter evenings.] (Trans. Lawson, 132)

The contrast of this industrious woman who makes her own "fins draps pour son mary et pour elle et pour vendre" with the Princess who merely reclines in "souefs draps" and whose only "ouvrage" consists of visiting her jewels is obvious. Christine tells us that by astutely managing the production of household woolens and linens, as well as other household work, the lady on the manor may well bring in more profit than is accrued from the "revenues de terre," as did the Countess of Eu, a historical personage. The reader understands that a good lady's virtuous labor not only enhances her moral "tresor," and thus leads to spirtual salvation; it also enhances her financial "tresor," her personal coffers.

Immediately after this positive vignette of homespun virtue, Christine turns to denounce, by contrast, "celles qui son oultrageuses en leurs abiz, atours, et abillemens" (157). At greater length than in book I, Christine launches into an attack on "oultrageux attours et abiz." For nearly eighty lines, she laments the loss of "anciennes coustumes," when queens, duchesses, countesses, and ladies did not attempt to adopt the costumes of their superiors, and she complains about the disquieting lack of order and decorum at the moment: "mais a present pareillement que tout est desordonné . . . n'y a es abiz ne es attours regle tenue" (157–58). With deeper social analysis than the Chevalier de la Tour Landry or the Ménagier de Paris, Christine locates the source of this disorder not in women's sexuality, but rather in the desire of men and women to assume a social position higher than the one they have, like sheep who must follow the leader: "et tout ainsi que les berbis suivent l'une l'autre" (158, l. 27). Christine chides the social climber on two counts: first, that anyone who attempts to dress above his or her station incurs ridicule, and second, that such practices often lead to indebtedness.

Thus, as she did for the Princess, Christine adduces social, moral, and economic arguments to support decorum in dress and denounce fashion. But she goes much further than she did in book I when she criticizes the fashion choice of a "simple dame" from the provincial region of Gastinois who tried to rise above her station. In concrete terms and in close detail, Christine describes how the lady ordered a "cote hardie" (fitted gown) sewn with "v. aulnes de drap a l'aune de Paris de drap de Bruisselles de la grant moison, et traine bien par terre trois quartiers, et aux manches a bombardes qui vont jusques aux piéz" [five Paris measures of Brussels cloth from the great harvest, with a three-quarters train, and with huge sleeves going down to her feet] (159). Christine emphasizes that this is the latest news, heard just "l'autre jour" [the other day] from a "taillandier de Paris" [Parisian tailor]. Like the Chevalier who acts as a fashion reporter as he tells what he heard from the Sire de Beaumanoir, Christine advertises the style even as she pronounces it inappropriate. By insisting on the precise measure of cloth and the origin of the fabric, Christine affirms a system in which quantity, quality, and origin of fabric symbolize social aspirations. Her description of the "simple dame" from the provinces who wears fancy city clothes that look ridiculous on her has precisely the effect of making the lady an object of fashion, one who asserts her position—and puts herself into circulation—by her manner of dress. As she trains her observant, Parisian eye on the cut and fabric and condemns the style of a provincial visitor, Christine and her book help to construct the discourse that assigns social and moral value to the material world of women's clothing.

Book III, addressed to "femmes d'estat," "bourgeoises," "femmes de marchans," "femmes veuves," wives of artisans, and servants, prostitutes, laborers, and the very poor, has the most varied remarks about dress, and the section on "femmes d'estat," "bourgeoises," and merchants' wives contains the most extensive observations and detailed critiques of fashion. As in book II, a positive portrait of women's relation to cloth and clothing precedes a negative attack on fashion. In a passage that recalls the description of the good housewife in the *Ménagier de Paris*,[57] Christine describes the extensive domestic duties of the "sage mesnagiere" (173–77), a major portion of which involves the production and maintenance of textiles. First, the *mesnagiere*'s husband should have an impeccable wardrobe, since his neatness is a reflection of her honor: "Doit estre soingneuse que son mary soit nettement tenus en robes et toutes choses, car le net aournement du mary est l'onneur de la femme" [She must be careful that her husband is neatly supplied with robes and all things, since a husband's neat appearance is the honor of the wife]. Then, Christine describes how the *mesnagiere*'s "bonne oeuvre" might consist of spinning or sewing, how she should keep her chambermaids busy after their regular tasks are done (presumably in sewing), and how she should buy hemp in the market and have it spun by "povres femmes," whom she must not exploit by virtue of her position. Christine exhorts the housewife to take care and pleasure in having quality household linens, which she defines as the "plaisir naturel" [natural pleasure] of women. When Christine describes how the housewife should maintain her trunks of "tres beau lin" [very fine linen]—"si le tendra blanc et souef flairant, bien ployé en coffres" [and so she will lay it out white and sweetly smelling, neatly folded in trunks]—she offers another striking contrast with the earlier portrait of the Princess, whose "souefs draps" were arranged by others and whose principal work consisted of visiting her "coffres" of jewels. Like the Princess, the good housewife should perform acts of charity; these consist of giving clothing to the poor before it becomes infested with worms (176) and of giving up some of the food and drink of her table. Through frugal, efficient household management that also provides for others less fortunate—which includes the appropriate management of clothing—the housewife can earn lasting "tresor." The relationship between women and clothing has material, economic, social, and moral effects.

As she did in book II, Christine immediately counters a positive portrait of domestic equilibrium with denouncements on the pitfalls of fashion. In chapter 2, Christine warns "femmes d'estat et bourgeoises" against the perils of outrageous dress, and in chapter 3 she devotes a special section to "femmes de marchans" (merchants' wives). To the first group, Christine offers a clear outline of her objections to "vestemens oultrageux," which she categorizes in terms of sexuality (it is a sin to care too much for one's body), social standing (one will be less prized, not more so), finances (a waste of money), futility (since everyone copies everyone else, and new styles multiply, this only leads to general impoverishment), and general moral depravity (such styles incite "convoitise" and sin in others). The most extensive argument that Christine adduces against showy dress in this chapter is that it causes men to think of women as objects to be pursued. In a lengthy passage that repeats objections raised by the Chevalier, Christine explains how tight clothing and low-cut dresses, as well as "choses nouvelles" (179), might incite men to think of "fole amour" even if the lady has dressed that way only for her own pleasure. Rather than describe the harsh punishments suffered by women who dress up, as does the Chevalier, Christine provides her readers with a twelve-line verbal retort that the naive young woman might use against a young man who approaches her with suspicious purpose (180). Fashion commentary in this section blends gradually into a critique of gender roles.

Chapter 3 of book III, addressed to wives of merchants, contains the longest commentary on female sumptuary habits in the *Livre des Trois Vertus* (if not in Christine's entire oeuvre) and the longest physical description of textiles in the book. Once again, Christine tailors her treatment to suit her subject: she speaks to the merchants' wives in commercial terms. Rather than frame her remarks in a Boethian dialogue or within abstract moral dicta, Christine begins with a very concrete description of the social and economic context of fashion in the urban centers of Europe. She describes the wives of those men "qui se meslent des marchandises" as wearing "grant et cousteux estat," not only in Paris, but even more so in Venice, Genoa, Florence, Lucca, and Avignon. Recognizing the economic factors that have created the vogue for fashion in Europe, Christine reminds her readers that the breakdown of social boundaries through dress is a recent phenomenon, as one can see by consulting the "croniques et anciennes hystoires" (184). Although she acknowledges that Italian women dress even more extravagantly, she insists that they do not have the reputation of France to uphold, and that their wardrobes are not as expensive (184). Such material considerations lead Christine to disgress on the "grant oultrage" recently committed by a "femme de marchant" who has lavishly outfitted her chambers for the lying-in of her child, "en la gesine d'un enfant qu'elle eut."

Before she launches into her description, Christine questions even whether the woman in question deserves the title of merchant's wife—"Est vivre voire comme marchant?" (184, l. 38) Unlike the great international wholesale traders of Venice and Genoa, the husband of this Parisian woman is merely a retail merchant, who buys "en gros" and sells "a detail pour iiii. solz de denrees" (184, l. 44). Christine's astute account of the origins of this family's capital points to a significant economic transformation: in a society where a noble title no longer necessarily indicates wealth, and where even a trader can become a "noble merchant," a prosperous bourgeois can imitate a noble lifestyle. Despite the fiscal crises of the Crown and the decline in rents, some sectors of the late medieval European economy were evidently robust enough to permit even a petty merchant such as this Parisian retailer to display his wealth. Christine's choice of the merchant's wife as the key description in her third triptych points with almost uncanny prescience to the power of the mercantile economy to transform European culture.

Given the fertile growth of the merchant class, it is perhaps no accident that the scene Christine describes is that of the lying-in of an expectant mother (a *gisant*), an event attended by much ceremony and conspicuous display of fabrics in the Middle Ages. By choosing to depict a woman who reclines in her bed, Christine underscores the contrast of this vignette with that of the Princess, who reclines indolently in book I, and with the self-portrait of the author, who rested from her labors in the Prologue. The tertiary nature of this bed scene is highlighted not only by its placement in chapter 3 of book III, but also by the descriptive approach to the bed, which is encountered after the observer passes through two other rooms, each of which contains "un grant lit de parement bien et richement encourtiné" [a large bed well draped and enclosed by rich curtains] (185). The bed of the *gisant* in chapter 3, book III, is the third bed in the wife's house and the third description of a woman reclining in Christine's book.

As she did for the costume of the "simple dame" of Gastinois, Christine renders the portrait of the room with careful attention to the quality, origin, dimensions, and cost of the wallhangings, bedcurtains, rugs, sheets, coverlets, furniture, and costume displayed by the bourgeois *gisant,* who is decked out like a lady:

> Et puis de celle on entroit en la chambre de la gisant, laquelle esoit grant et belle, toute encourtinee de tapisserie faicte a la devise d'elle ouvree tres richement de fin or de Chipre, le lit grant et bel encourtiné tout d'un parement et les tapis d'entour le lit mis par terre sur quoy on marchoit, tous pereilz a or ouvréz, les grans draps de parement qui passsoient plus d'un espan par soubz la couverture de si fine toile de Raims que ilz estoient prisiéz a .ccc. frans; et tout par dessus le dit couvertoir a or tyssu avoit un autre grant drap de lin aussi delié que soye, tout d'une piece est sans cousture—qui est chose nouvellement trouvee a faire et de moult grant coust—que on prisoit deux cens frans et plus, qui estoit si grant et si large que il couvroit de tous lez le tres grant lit de parement et passoit le bourt du dit couvertoir qui trainsnoit de tous lez; et en celle chambre avoit un grant

dreçoir paré, tout couvert de vaisselle doree. En ce lit estoit la gisant, vestue de drap de soye taint en cramesy, appuiee de grans oreilliers de pareille soye a gros boutons de perles, atournee comme une damoiselle... (185, 51–69)

[And then from that chamber one entered the chamber of the woman in childbed, a large and well-appointed room hung from floor to ceiling with tapestries made with her device worked very richly in fine Cyprus gold. In this chamber was a large, highly ornamented dresser covered with golden dishes. The bed was large and handsome and hung with exquisite curtains. On the floor around the bed the carpets on which one walked were all worked with gold, and the large ornamented hangings, which extended more than a hand span below the bed-spread, were of such fine linen of Rheims that they were worth three hundred francs. On top of this bedspread of tissue of gold was another large covering of linen as fine as silk, all of one piece and without a seam (made by a method only recently invented) and very expensive: it was said to be worth two hundred francs and more. It was so wide and long that it covered all sides of this large, elaborate bed, and extended beyond the edge of the bedspread, which trailed on the floor on all sides. In this bed lay the woman who was going to give birth, dressed in crimson silk cloth and propped up on big pillows of the same silk with big pearl buttons, adorned like a young lady.] (Trans. Lawson, 154)

With an eye for the moral character of the material world and an attention to precise physical and economic detail that rival those of Balzac, Christine presents the *gisant* as an extension of her chambers, in which she appears like another decoration. The hangings of the room contain her *devise,* worked in gold, and she is dressed like her room in richly embroidered "draps." The accumulation, overlay, and variety of fabrics in this description, which come from as far away as Cyprus and as close as Rheims, and which include linen woven in large spans by new techniques of fabrication—"qui est chose nouvellement trouvee a faire et de moult grant coust"—attest to the vitality and ongoing innovation of the European textile trade, whose growth was spurred by the creation of rooms like the one Christine recounts.

Indeed, even as she condemns this "oultrage," Christine confirms the value of the *gisant*'s production. When the moralist tells us that this "oultrage" is so extraordinary that it is "digne d'estre mis en livre" [worthy of being put in a book], she confers a singular honor to the wife's costume and chambers: she describes these in a book that will circulate among the courts and households of Europe. Furthermore, Christine's editorial choice confirms the symbolic capital that has already accrued to this sartorial display. News of it has traveled to the chamber of the queen, "Si fut cest chose raportee en la chambre de la royne" (186, l. 75), where the nobles present, jealous of the "habondance des richeses," suggest that Parisians with so much wealth be taxed so that their wives not go about comparing themselves to the queen (186). The splendor of the *gisant*'s bedchamber vies dangerously with Isabeau's royal chambers. The rich bed and sumptuous hangings with fleur de lis in the famous frontispiece of the Harley ms. 4431 (from Christine's workshop, c. 1410–1415), which depicts Christine presenting her work to the queen, bear remarkable similarity to this bourgeois bedroom.[58]

Christine joins her courtly patrons in condemning the social, economic, and moral "disorder" emblematized by the sumptuary "disguise" of this scene: a fifty-line moral lamentation follows the portrait in which Christine enjoins such women not to attempt to shun the honor of their rightful state by hoarding and displaying material wealth, but rather to store up spiritual riches; as she has in the other books, Christine asks women to seek their "tresor" in paradise, not on earth (187).

Yet, as in other instances of fashion bashing by the Chevalier de la Tour Landry and earlier by Christine, this remarkable passage has the effect of putting the wife's extravagant creation into discursive circulation and ensuring that a vivid portrait of her chamber will travel beyond the chambers of the queen, to other courts and households. Through her artful display, the merchant's wife attracts the queen's attention. The *gisant*'s ostentatious bedroom, within which the bourgeois family is literally reproduced and displayed, provides an arresting counterpart to the Princess's bed of idleness, which Christine denounced in book I. Whatever disapproval Christine may wish to express, this bourgeoise is neither lazy nor morally dissolute. She is rather socially ambitious and successful; her splendid chambers attest to the successful business of her retail-textile-merchant spouse and, presumably, to her own ability to employ many of the precepts of household management that Christine has laid forth. Although the bourgeoise's bed is intended as a negative exemplum (an extreme extrapolation of the royal bed of indolence and a perversion of the author's bed of virtue), the narrator's lavish description of covers, hangings, and clothing advertises and promotes their undeniable appeal.

The bourgeoise who catches the attention of an astute observer of urban life has her room immortalized in Christine's prose. Christine's book, like that of the Chevalier de la Tour Landry and the Ménagier de Paris, not only registers changing fashions, but also promotes a system of self-improvement that undermines the steady relationship between the estates. As Norbert Elias has observed of Erasmus, the Renaissance moralist's observation of particular details and of individual distinctions marks a break with earlier didactic tracts.[59] Here, well before the advent of the Renaissance with its much-touted "self-fashioning," Christine not only observes the particular details of dress, costume, and sumptuary display, but also promotes the active participation of subjects in shaping the material, economic, social, and moral conditions of their existence.

If the remaining ten chapters of book III speak sparsely of fashion, it is because women of lesser wealth and social prominence are more restricted in the ways they can dress. Accordingly, Christine tells young maidens to be honestly and neatly dressed (195, ll. 41–43), warns chambermaids never to accept a "chapperon" or "robe" from a man who would have her convey a message to her mistress (which recalls the scene analyzed earlier in the *Livre du Chevalier de la Tour Landry*), urges prostitutes to give up their "tres deshonneste habit et se veste et affuble de cote large et honneste" [very dishonest clothing and dress and cover themselves with ample and respectable clothes] (213, ll. 59–60), and suggests that, among other honest occupations, they take up "lessive" [washing clothes] for large estates or spinning. Christine recognizes that laborers' wives need not be warned about fashion, for they lack the means to buy "grans paremens ne oultrageux abiz" [grand accessories or outrageous clothes] (218, ll. 4–5). By the time she reaches poor women, Christine ceases to offer advice about management of the material world at all, since the poor possess nothing. But the topic of clothing continues to prevail as a metaphor for spiritual status or "estat." In a prayer that she offers to God on their behalf, Christine reminds poor women that the rich are burdened by their "richeses" and "boubans" and that the unfortunate creature who is "vestue de povreté" has taken on the livery of the holy King: "He! mon Createur! tout poissant Roy sur tous roys, et moy ta povre creature, qui suis revestue de tes robes en ame et en corps: n'ay pas souffissance en ame, en tant que tu l'as faicte a ton ymage? En corps que j'ay char humaine, si que tu volz avoir, et vestue de povreté, laquelle robe tu volz avoir toute ta vie; et bien monstras que tu auctorisoies plus l'estat de cest perphecion de povreté que nul autre, quant pour toy meismes l'esleus" [Ah! My Creator! All powerful King of kings, and I, Your poor creation, dressed in Your robes in soul and body: am I not fulfilled in my soul, since You have made it in Your image? My body is of human flesh, as You chose to have, and clothed in poverty, whose garments You desired Your whole life. You demonstrate that You esteem the state of poverty more than any other, since You Yourself have chosen it] (222). She also reminds us that Christ, God's chosen son, had tastes very different ("jugemens") from those of other men, since he sent his son to be born in a stable, "en povres drapelléz" [in the poor shreds of cloth].

From the "souefs draps" of the Princess, to the clean "draps" of the industrious housewife, to the poor but noble "drapelléz" of the Christ child, the representation of clothing in Christine's *Livre des Trois Vertus* is woven throughout Christine's practical allegory, conveying social, economic, moral, and spiritual values. Christine's careful attention to the very fabric of sartorial display betrays her own unwitting complicity with a system in which women can literally fashion their "honneur" out of cloth. Although the author attempts to fix the social meaning of textiles in a stable economy, where the social "estat" and the material "estat" would perfectly coincide, her book provides stunning examples, as do the books of the Chevalier de la Tour Landry and the Ménagier de Paris, that "nouvelles choses" have ushered in a new social order.

The persistence and intensification of antifashion discourse from 1372 to 1405 in these three books confirm what other historical sources amply demonstrate: sumptuary laws and didactic denouncements of sartorial extravagance failed to dampen the desire for "nouveaux estats" in dress and household accoutrements for those women and men who could afford them. Even as they attack women's fashion, the *Livre du Chevalier de la Tour Landry*, the *Ménagier de Paris*, and the *Livre des Trois Vertus* join in the discourse that draws attention to women's ways of managing clothing and household linens and so enhance the symbolic power of dress. Furthermore, as texts that will be *copied* for future readers (just as styles are copied for wearers), as precious objects whose ownership brings distinction to their readers, these books appear as fashionable "nouvelles choses" within courts and households. Christine herself states her desire that her book should "multiply" in numerous copies, whatever it may cost, and that it circulate among "roynes, princesses et haultes dames" and be disseminated among "les autres femmes," in "tous pais" (225). The widespread distribution of her texts and other conduct books thus followed the pan-European journey of stylish textiles, through whose changing designs elite women and men attempted to negotiate the instabilities of late medieval culture.

NOTES

I would like to thank Bonnie Erwin and Scott Hiley for their thoughtful comments on earlier drafts of this essay. A debt of gratitude is also due to E. Jane Burns and Nancy A. Jones for graciously sharing their thoughts and bibliography about women and clothing in the Middle Ages as we prepared a panel on "Textiles and the Regulation of Gender" for "Attending to Early Modern Women: Crossing Boundaries," a conference held at the University of Maryland, College Park, in November 1997.

1. Andrew Ross, ed., *No Sweat: Fashion, Free Trade, and the Rights of Garment Workers* (New York: Verso, 1997).

2. See, for example, Leslie Rabine's analysis of the contradictory messages about women's autonomy and women's exploitation conveyed by contemporary fashion magazines, "A Woman's Two Bodies: Fashion Magazines, Consumerism, and Feminism," in *On Fashion*, ed. Shari Benstock and Suzanne Ferriss (New Brunswick, N.J.: Rutgers University Press, 1994), 59–75.

3. Recent critiques and analyses of fashion and clothing include Fred Davis, *Fashion, Culture, Identity* (Chicago: University of Chicago Press, 1992); Benstock and Ferriss, eds., *On Fashion;* Christopher Breward, *The Culture of Fashion: A New History of Fashionable Dress* (Manchester: Manchester University Press, 1995); Annette B. Winer and Jane Schneider, *Cloth and Human Experience* (London: Smithsonian Institution Press, 1989); Elizabeth Wilson, *Adorned in Dreams: Fashion and Modernity* (London: Virago Press, 1985).

4. As demonstrated by Fred Davis, *Fashion, Culture, Identity.*

5. For a fine overview of the reactions of legislators, clerics, and moralists to women's dress, see Diane Owen Hughes, "Regulating Women's Fashion," in *A History of Women in the West*, vol. 2, *Silences of the Middle Ages*, ed. Christiane Klapisch-Zuber (Cambridge: Harvard University Press, Belknap Press, 1992), 136–58.

6. For example, Joan Evans adduces examples from both the *Livre du Chevalier de la Tour Landry* and *Le livre des Trois Vertus* to describe the evolution of fashion in France; see Joan Evans, *Dress in Medieval France* (Oxford: Clarendon Press, 1952), 36, 53.

7. On the semiotics of fashion, see Roland Barthes, *Le système de la mode* (Paris: Seuil, 1967); on the idea that choice of clothing in contemporary Western society indicates the "material or symbolic profit" that subjects can expect to obtain from what they wear, see Pierre Bourdieu, *Distinction: A Social Critique of the Judgement of Taste* (Cambridge: Harvard University Press, 1984), 202.

8. In Bourdieu's terms, the conduct book is not only a material object, or cultural good, that enhances the social space and reveals taste, as would a fine piece of furniture, but also a means by which its owner may engage in the process of acquiring cultural competency.

9. *Le livre du Chevalier de la Tour Landry pour l'enseignement de ses filles,* ed. Anatole de Montaiglon (Paris: Jannet, 1854; reprint, Millwood, N.Y.: Kraus Reprint, 1982). Caxton's Middle English translation has been edited by M. Y. Offord, *The Book of the Knight of the Tower,* Early English Text Society (London: Oxford University Press, 1971).

10. *Le Menagier de Paris,* ed. Georgine E. Brereton and Janet M. Ferrier (Oxford: Clarendon Press, 1981). A facing-page French translation of this edition that includes the tales of Griseldis and of Melibee as well as "Le chemin de povreté et de richesse" (omitted from the Oxford edition) is *Le mesnagier de Paris,* ed. Brereton and Ferrier, trans. Karin Ueltschi, Lettres Gothiques (Paris: Livre de Poche, 1994).

11. Christine de Pizan, *Le livre des Trois Vertus,* ed. Charity Cannon Willard and Eric Hicks (Paris: Champion, 1989). A translation is provided by Sarah Lawson, *The Treasure of the City of Ladies, or The Book of the Three Virtues* (New York: Penguin Books, 1985). Translations in the article are mine, unless otherwise indicated.

12. Anne Marie De Gendt, "'Plusieurs manières d'amours': le débat dans *Le livre du Chevalier de la Tour Landry* et ses échos dans l'oeuvre de Christine de Pizan," *Fifteenth-Century Studies* 23 (1996): 121–37.

13. See the inventory of the library at Molins, in A.-M. Chazaud, *Les enseignemens d'Anne de France, duchesse de Bourbonnois et d'Auvergne à sa fille Susanne* (Moulins: Desrosiers, 1878; reprinted Marseilles: Laffitte, 1978), 231–58, items 89, 129, 133, 252.

14. Both the Ménagier and Christine draw upon Philippe de Mézières' *Livre de la vertu du sacrement de mariage,* as Elie Golentischeff-Koutouzoff has shown in *L'histoire de Griseldis en France au XIVe et au XVe siècle* (Paris: Droz, 1933), 123–31.

15. These are the Paris mss. B.N. fr. 24398; B.N. fr. 24397; B.N. 1190; Arsenal 2687; and British Library, 19 Cotton VII. For a description, see Elie Golentischeff-Koutouzoff, *L'histoire de Griseldis,* 87–114.

16. For an account of the twenty-one manuscripts of the *Livre du Chevalier de la Tour Landry,* see Offord, ed., *The Book of the Knight of the Tower,* xviii–xxvi; on the *Ménagier de Paris,* see Brereton and Ferrier, eds., *Le Menagier de Paris,* xii–xvii; on the twenty-one manuscripts of the *Livre des Trois Vertus,* see Willard and Hicks, eds., *Le livre des Trois Vertus,* xix–xxv.

17. As has been emphasized for Christine's work by Charity Cannon Willard, "The Manuscript Tradition of the *Livre des Trois Vertus* and Christine de Pizan's Audience," *Journal of the History of Ideas* 27 (1966): 433–44.

18. On this change, in addition to Hughes, see Françoise Piponnier and Perrine Mane, *Se vêtir au Moyen Age* (Paris: Biro, 1995), 70–117; Breward, *The Culture of Fashion,* 7–40;

Stella Mary Newton, *Fashion in the Age of the Black Prince: A Study of the Years 1340–1365* (Woodbridge, Suffolk, England: Boydell Press, 1980); Evans, *Dress in Medieval France,* 26–58; Mary G. Houston, *Medieval Costume in England and France: The 13th, 14th, and 15th Centuries* (London: Adam and Charles Black, 1950), 159–98.

19. On the sexual ambivalence of courtly clothing in twelfth- and thirteenth-century literature, see E. Jane Burns, "Refashioning Courtly Love: Lancelot as Ladies' Man or Lady/Man?" in *Constructing Medieval Sexuality,* ed. Karma Lochrie, Peggy McCracken, and James A. Schultz (Minneapolis: University of Minnesota Press, 1997), 111–34.

20. Davis, *Fashion, Culture, and Identity,* 15.

21. A precise and nuanced account of the fashion changes in this period, which I have summarized broadly, is offered by Stella Mary Newton, *Fashion in the Age of the Black Prince.*

22. As noted by Hughes, "Regulating Women's Fashion," 141–42. On the end of the rectangular tunic as the beginning of "conspicuous waste," see Newton, *Fashion in the Age of the Black Prince, 3.*

23. On the visual and textual representation of social order in Oresme's work, see the excellent study by Claire Richter Sherman, *Imaging Aristotle: Verbal and Visual Representation in Fourteenth-Century France* (Berkeley: University of California Press, 1995).

24. On Christine's work for royal and ducal patrons, see Charity Cannon Willard, "Christine de Pizan as Teacher," *Romance Languages Annual* 2 (1992): 132–36.

25. See Etienne de Fougères, *Le livre des manieres,* ed. R. Anthony Lodge (Geneva: Droz, 1979), stanzas 244–313; Vincent of Beauvais, *De eruditione filiorum nobilium,* ed. Arpad Steiner (Cambridge, Mass.: Medieval Academy of America, 1938), chap. XLII–LI; Egidio Colonna, *Li livres du gouvernement des rois,* ed. Samuel Paul Molenaer (New York: MacMillan, 1899), book II, pt. I, chap. I–XXI, and pt. II, chap. XIX–XXI.

26. See *Robert de Blois: Son oeuvre didactique et narrative,* ed. John Howard Fox (Paris: Nizet, 1950). On other didactic works for women, see Alice Hentsch, *De la littérature didactique du moyen âge s'adressant spécialement aux femmes* (Halle, 1903; reprint, Geneva: Slatkine, 1975), and Diane Bornstein, *The Lady in the Tower: Medieval Courtesy Literature for Women* (Hamden, Conn: Archon Books, 1983).

27. See the spirited description and moralistic condemnation of sartorial extravagance in this period provided by H. Baudrillart in a chapter entitled "La démence du luxe," in his *Histoire du luxe privé et public depuis l'antiquité jusqu'à nos jours,* vol. 3, *Le Moyen Age et la Renaissance* (Paris: Hachette, 1881), 280–319; see also Pierre Kraemer-Raine, *Le luxe et les lois somptuaires au Moyen-Age* (Paris: Sagot, 1920), 50–102.

28. For an account of Isabeau de Bavière's treasury and opulent wardrobe, see Jean Verdon, *Isabeau de Bavière* (Paris: Tallandier, 1981), 79–105.

29. On the disastrous social consequences of royal expenditures as chronicled by moralists of the time, see Mathilde Laigle, *Le livre des Trois Vertus de Christine de Pisan* (Paris: Champion, 1912), 266–83.

30. On French regulations from 808 onwards, see Kraemer-Raine, *Le luxe et les lois somptuaires.* For a thorough consideration of the rise of sumptuary legislation in the midst of late medieval and early modern socioeconomic transformations in Europe (with a focus on England), see Alan Hunt, *Governance of the Consuming Passions: A History of Sumptuary Law* (New York: St. Martin's, 1996).

31. See "L'ordonnance de 1294" in Kraemer-Raine, *Le luxe et les lois somptuaires,* 106–16.

32. Hunt provides a thorough consideration of these arguments and others that attempt to discern the social effects of sumptuary law throughout *Governance of the Consuming Passions.*

33. See "The Paradox of Enforcement and Non-Enforcement," *Governance of the Consuming Passions,* 354–56.

34. See, for example, Hughes, "Regulating Women's Fashion"; Newton, *Fashion in the Age of the Black Prince;* Hunt, *Governance of the Consuming Passions;* Baudrillart, *Histoire du luxe privé et public,* 632–64.

35. On the moralist's stated aims, see Anne Marie De Gendt, "Sens et fonction du Prologue dans *Le livre du Chevalier de la Tour Landry," Neuphilologische Mitteilungen* 95, 2 (1994): 193–206.

36. See John L. Grigsby, "A New Source of the *Livre du Chevalier de la Tour Landry," Romania* 84 (1963): 171–208.

37. On this last example, see Danielle Regnier-Bohler, "Galois, Galoises et la nature du temps: Le monde *Bestourné* chez le Chevalier de la Tour Landry," in *Et c'est la fin pour quoy sommes ensemble: Hommage à Jean Dufournet: Littérature, histoire, et langue du Moyen Age* (Paris: Champion, 1993), 1187–91.

38. Under the first meaning of "estat," Godefroy provides both "condition" and "coiffure somptueuse"; Frédéric Godefroy, *Dictionnaire de l'ancienne langue française,* vol. 3 (Paris: 1884), 602–3; the *Complément* also defines *gens d'estat* as "gens de condition élevée" and includes "condition politique de l'ancienne France," as in "les gens des trois estaz" (Godefroy, *Complément au dictionnaire de l'ancienne langue française,* vol. 9 [Paris: 1898], 558–59). Both the Chevalier de la Tour Landry and Christine de Pizan seem to use the term to refer not only to headdresses but also to the totality of women's wardrobes.

39. Other aspects of the Chevalier's moral project are discussed by Anne Marie De Gendt, "'Pour cy a cy bon exemple': Morale et récit dans *Le livre du Chevalier de la Tour Landry,"* in *Non nova, sed nove: Mélanges de civilisation médiévale dédiés à Willem Noomen,* ed. Martin Gosman and Jaap van Os (Groningen: Bouma's Boekhuis, 1984), 67–79; Danielle Regnier-Bohler, "Femme, faute, fantasme," in *La condición de la mujer en la Edad Media: Actas del coloquio celebrado en la casa de Velásquez, del 5 al 7 de noviembre de 1984* (Madrid: Universidad Complutense, 1986); Danielle Regnier-Bohler, "Un traité pour les filles d'Eve: l'écriture et le temps dans *Le livre du Chevalier de la Tour Landry pour l'enseignement de ses filles,"* in *Education, apprentissages, initiation au Moyen Age,* Cahiers du C.R.I.S.I.M.A., 1 (Montpellier: Centre de recherche interdisciplinaire sur la société et l'imaginaire au Moyen Age, 1993), 449–67; Roberta L. Krueger, "Intergeneric Combination and the Anxiety of Gender in *Le livre du Chevalier de la Tour Landry pour l'enseignement de ses filles," Esprit créateur* 33 (1993): 61–72; Anne Marie De Gendt, "'Gens qui ont le siècle à la main': Les grands de ce monde dans le *Livre du Chevalier de la Tour Landry," Fifteenth-Century Studies* 21 (1994): 1–15.

40. Ruth Mazo Karras, *Common Women: Prostitution and Sexuality in Medieval England* (New York and Oxford: Oxford University Press, 1996), 21–22.

41. On the social milieu of the author, Geoffroy de la Tour Landry, see "La vie intellectuelle de la noblesse angevine à la fin du XIVe siècle d'après le Chevalier de la Tour Landry," in *La littérature angevine médiévale: actes du colloque du samedi 22 mars 1980,* Cen-

tre de Recherche de Littérature et de Linguistique de l'Anjou et des Bocages, Université d'Angers (Maulévrier: Hérault, 1981), 135–54.

42. Montaiglon, ed., *Le livre du Chevalier de la Tour Landry,* xxxviii.

43. Ibid., xxxviii.

44. On the personal interjections of the Ménagier throughout the compilation, see Janet M. Ferrier, "A Husband's Asides: The Use of the Second Person Singular in *Le Ménagier de Paris,*" *French Studies* 31, 3 (1977): 257–67.

45. On the moral and economic importance of women's work as a theme in didactic literature of this period, see Mireille Vincent-Cassy, "Quand les femmes deviennent paresseuses," *Femmes, mariages-lignages, XIIe–XIVe siècles: Mélanges offerts à Georges Duby* (Brussels: De Boeck Université, 1992), 430–47.

46. Brereton and Ferrier, Appendix I, *Menagier de Paris,* 332–35.

47. The high-warped loom was used for making superior quality tapestries, according to John Hayes, "Tapestry and Its Relation to Decorative Art," *Bulletin of National Association of Wool Manufacturers* (Boston, 1879), 5. I would like to thank Scott Hiley for bringing the significance of this detail to my attention.

48. For a very different perspective on the integral relation between women and cloth work in thirteenth-century romance that also emphasizes how women's agency can be expressed through textiles, see Nancy A. Jones, "The Uses of Embroidery in the Romances of Jean Renart: Gender, History, Textuality," in *Jean Renart and the Art of Romance: Essays on "Guillaume de Dole,"* ed. Nancy Vine Durling (Gainesville: University of Florida Press, 1997), 3–44.

49. See the discussion of this contemporary exemplum in Janet M. Ferrier, "Seulement pour vous endoctriner: The Author's Use of Exempla in *Le Ménagier de Paris,*" *Medium aevum* 48 (1979): 77–89.

50. Critics who have analyzed Christine's counsel on female dress in *Le livre des Trois Vertus* include Mathilde Laigle, *Le livre des Trois Vertus de Christine de Pisan* (Paris: Champion, 1912), 205–14; Marie-Thérèse Lorcin, "Les echos de la mode dans *Le livre des Trois Vertus* de Christine de Pizan," *Razo* 7 (1987): 89–94; Eric Hicks, "Discours de la toilette, toilette du discours: De l'idéologie du vêtement dans quelques écrits didactiques de Christine de Pizan," *Revue des langues romanes* 92, no. 2 (1988): 327–41; Laura Rinaldi Dufresne, "A Woman of Excellent Character: A Case Study of Dress, Reputation, and the Changing Costume of Christine de Pizan in the Fifteenth Century"; Josette Wisman, "Aspects socio-économiques du *Livre des Trois Vertus* de Christine de Pizan," *Le moyen français* 30 (1992): 27–44; Roberta L. Krueger, "Chascune selon son estat: Women's Education and Social Class in the Conduct Books of Christine de Pizan and Anne de France," *Papers on French Seventeenth-Century Literature* 24, no. 46 (1997): 19–34.

51. See Eric Hicks, "Discours de la toilette."

52. For a comparison of methods and subject matter in the three books, see Marie-Thérèse Lorcin, "L'école des femmes: Les devoirs envers le mari dans quelques traités d'éducation," *Education, apprentissages, initiation au Moyen Age,* 233–48.

53. See Marie-Thérèse Lorcin, "Le *Livre des Trois Vertus* et le *Sermo ad status,*" in *Une femme de lettres au Moyen Age: Etudes autour de Christine de Pizan,* ed. Liliane Dulac and Bernard Ribémont, Medievalia, 16, Série "Etudes christiniennes" (Orleans: Paradigme, 1995), 139–48.

54. For various approaches to Christine's complex blending of allegorical and personal narrative voices in the *Livre des Trois Vertus,* see Liliane Dulac, "The Representation and Functions of Feminine Speech in Christine de Pizan's *Livre des Trois Vertus,*" in *Reinterpreting Christine de Pizan,* ed. Earl Jeffrey Richards (Athens: University of Georgia Press, 1992), 13–22; Maureen Quilligan, *The Allegory of Female Authority: Christine de Pizan's "Cité des Dames"* (Ithaca, N.Y.: Cornell University Press, 1991), 255–57; Andrea Tarnowski, "Autobiography and Advice in *Le Livre des Trois Vertus,*" in *Une femme de lettres au Moyen Age,* ed. Dulac and Ribémont, 151–59. On the complexity of Christine's pedagogical strategies, see Roberta Krueger, "Christine's Anxious Lessons: Gender, Morality, and the Social Order from the *Enseignemens* to the *Avision,*" in *Christine de Pizan and the Categories of Difference,* ed. Marilynn Desmond (Minneapolis: University of Minnesota Press, 1998), 16–40.

55. Laura Rinaldi Dufresne, "A Woman of Excellent Character."

56. The book was the source of Anne de France's *Enseignemens* for her daughter and was translated into Portuguese for Isabelle of Portugal. See Charity Cannon Willard, "Anne de France, Reader of Christine de Pizan," in *The Reception of Christine de Pizan,* ed. Glenda K. McLeod (Lewiston: E. Mellon Press, 1991); Robert B. Bernard, "The Intellectual Circle of Isabel of Portugal, Duchess of Burgundy, and the Portuguese Translation of *Le Livre des Trois Vertus* (O Livro dos Tres Vertudes), in ibid., 44–56. On how Anne de France has adopted Christine's precepts of management of court life, see Krueger, "Chascune selon son estat."

57. Hicks and Willard note the parallels with the Ménagier in the *Livre des Trois Vertus,* 241, n. III/I/65.

58. For a description of this portrait and details on Isabeau de Bavière's chambers, see Sandra Hindman, "The Iconography of Queen Isabeau de Bavière (1410–1415): An Essay in Method," *Gazette des beaux arts* 102 (1983): 102–10.

59. "The increased tendency of people to observe themselves and others is one sign of how the whole question of behavior is now taking on a different character: people mold themselves and others more deliberately than in the Middle Ages" (Norbert Elias, *The History of Manners,* trans. Edmund Jephcott, vol. 1, *The Civilizing Process* [New York: Urizen Books, 1978]).

4

The *Miroir des bonnes femmes*

Not for Women Only?

Kathleen Ashley

Over the past twenty years and from a variety of contemporary theoretical perspectives, we have learned to read meaning as deriving from more than the contents of the isolated text. Whether we look to structuralism and semiotics generally, with their insistence that place within a whole system governs the meaning of the part, or to Bourdieu and de Certeau, with their particular interest in how cultural practices produce meaning, the autonomy of the verbal text is called into question. De Certeau, for example, insists that "the presence and circulation of a representation (taught by preachers, educators, and popularizers as the key to socioeconomic advancement) tells us nothing about what it is for its users. We must first analyze its manipulation by users who are not its makers."[1] Claire Sponsler has articulated this insight slightly differently in discussing what she calls "medieval ethnography." She says that

> anthropology has offered models for thinking about and interpreting texts not as isolated moments of aesthetic practice nor as inert documents pointing to historical events, but rather as events, incidents, and activities within a complex dynamic of the production and consumption of culture. (1–2)[2]

This essay will pose for our consideration those issues that arise at the intersection of the production and the reception of medieval conduct literature. I'll first trace what I take to be the reigning "party line" on conduct books addressed to women. Then I will use for my case study a little-known and still unedited French work, the *Miroir des bonnes femmes,* which was composed circa 1300 and exists in only three copies. One incomplete version appears to have been produced around 1300, another now in Paris can be dated around 1360, and the third—the one that particularly interests me—was copied into a Burgundian manuscript at the beginning of the fifteenth century.[3] The Burgundian manuscript, which is now in Dijon, contains two other didactic works: the *Doctrinal aux simples gens* and the *Mireour de l'eglise.* Both are vernacular explanations of ecclesiastical doctrine and ritual not specifically addressed to women, although Geneviève Hasenohr has shown that this kind of compilation was typical of the libraries of literate laywomen in the later Middle Ages.[4]

What I have been able to discover about the manuscript and its owners, through my research in various Burgundian archives and libraries as well as through the discovery of material cultural remainders, will help us to define a number of problems with the usual approaches to women's conduct books, approaches that may rely on a too literal reading of the work itself and may ignore the meanings that emerge from its specific and located uses.

The *Miroir des bonnes femmes* offers a model that differs from those often employed to interpret didactic texts addressed to women. The first and most common model is based on gender. According to this view, conduct books were written by men to discipline women. It is a model that derives its support from a reading of the texts themselves and privileges the implied authorial intentions at the time of production. The *Miroir* appears to be no exception since it is addressed to women readers in the voice of a clerical authority figure, a Franciscan friar, as John Grigsby, who first studied the *Miroir* thirty-five years ago, pointed out.[5]

Rabelais in his comic narrative *Gargantua* describes the methods employed by an old and jealous husband to control his young wife—above all by reading her conduct literature about chaste and unchaste women![6] Rabelais's satirical suggestion that conduct books are primarily designed to be used by desperate male authorities to subjugate women is echoed seriously in much scholarly analysis. Whether the male is husband or cleric, it is *his* power that is bolstered through containment of female freedom and agency. Or so the argument goes.

However, the Dijon version of the *Miroir* demonstrates clearly that one cannot use gender alone as an analytic tool, since male as well as female ownership is indicated by the names written on the manuscript. The *Miroir* is rhetorically addressed to women, but the owners whose names are inscribed at the beginning and end of the text or on blank pages include both males (Jacques and Aymé de Beaumont and Jacques de Thésut) and females (Loyse de Beaumont and Jacquette and Huguette de Thésut). Obviously, gender must be combined with other social variables in order to interpret the reception of this specific conduct text.

A corollary to this methodological principle is that one cannot deduce the ownership or readership of a medieval text *solely* from its contents. The Dijon version of the *Miroir* is part of a selection of moral/religious works presumably aimed at nonaristocratic lay readers, both male and female. Furthermore, medieval manuscripts had a long afterlife, and medieval writings were copied and used in ways never envisaged by their authors. Gerald Bruns has identified this characteristic as the "openness" of manuscript culture; the text seems to open outwards "in the sense that it seems to a later hand to require collaboration, amplification, embellishment, [and] illustration."[7] Kate Harris, too, has argued, in her examination of the role of book owners in book production, that it was not uncommon for a manuscript to be in use for several centuries, with resulting programs of "embellishment, addition, modification," and so on suggesting a "dynamism fitting uneasily into the constraints of 'period.'" Harris concludes that we need "an *interpretation of use* [my italics] as well as a study of production."[8] As material objects, conduct books may even be employed for purposes at odds with, or substantively unrelated to, their textual contents or the intentions of their original producers.

Beyond the gender of the addressees, conduct book ownership has more recently been linked with class. This model, which privileges reception over the intentions of producers, posits such books circulating primarily among the upwardly mobile middle classes. Claire Sponsler, in her recent book on the production of subjects in late medieval commodity culture, notes that conduct books proliferated as commercial publishing responded to the demands of bourgeois readers.[9] The extant evidence for England suggests that in the fifteenth and sixteenth centuries both printed and manuscript books of conduct were largely owned by the merchant classes, and Sponsler argues that "Conduct books sold themselves by selling decorum as a useful tool for socioeconomic mobility and personal happiness."[10] As we will see shortly, the owners of the Dijon *Miroir* certainly epitomize the upward mobility of urban bourgeois elites. However, I think neither gender nor class alone can be taken as an adequate explanation for the ideological role played by the *Miroir des bonnes femmes* in the fifteenth and sixteenth centuries.

Felicity Riddy's recent *Speculum* article on the poem "What the Goodwife Taught Her Daughter" hypothesizes that this conduct work had an ideological role within the late medieval urban setting, as part of the process of bourgeois self-definition and "one of the means whereby this group articulated a set of values that endorsed worldly and material success."[11] But Riddy goes beyond her class-based analysis to incorporate gender. The "household ideology" of the poem she discusses derives from the crucial function of the household in the bourgeois ethos; since female domesticity was central to the household, these texts represented the woman as "repository and maintainer of bourgeois values." Both the terms "goodwife" and "goodman" indicate urban bourgeois status, and Riddy argues that the bourgeois ethos seeks to conflate the meanings of virtuous woman and citizen's wife.[12]

Riddy's insight that female gendering is central to the formation of a distinctively bourgeois ethos is one that applies equally to the *Miroir des bonnes femmes* as it appears to have been received in the fifteenth century. Riddy, however, based on her analysis of the poem "What the Goodwife Taught Her Daughter," argues that conduct books were primarily used in the socialization of young female servants and apprentices by the "goodwife" to produce the regulated bourgeois household. The *Miroir* appears to have been used for a different purpose, one involving not just household identity but specifically *family* identities. The male and female names on our manuscript suggest that family members of both sexes took an interest in and found relevant a work nominally addressed just to women.

The theorist Gérard Genette has used the term "paratext" to indicate the various commentaries and notations that surround any text—including titles, subtitles, illustrations, and marginalia, as well as official commentary.[13] According to Genette, the paratext frames the interpretation of the text and shapes the implicit contract involved in its reading. He was not, of course, thinking of medieval manuscripts, but his theoretical insight provides a way of approaching earlier writing. In the case of the *Miroir des bonnes femmes,* the names inscribed at significant places in the manuscript and the written comments of its owners indicate how the book was used within the family context in the fifteenth and sixteenth centuries.

Speaking from the margins of the *Miroir* are voices insistently claiming ownership: "ce livre est a moy Jacques de beaumont" (This book is mine . . .) is written on the last page of the *Miroir* text, underneath the scribal conclusion and date of 1406 (f. 139). The same hand has written on an earlier blank page after the *Doctrinal* (f. 32v), "ce present livre est a moy de beaumont." On the two pages after the end of the *Miroir* text are more claims of ownership—"Ce present livre est a moy Loyse de Beaulmont" (on 139v) and, at the top of the page in a large sixteenth-century hand, "A Jacquette et Huguette de Theseut." Loyse de Beaumont's name is also written and smudged out on these final pages, as if she were practicing her signature. This is a manuscript appropriately owned by literate women of both the Beaumont and Thésut families, but it also contains the ownership claims of their fathers, so that we cannot assign the work a function solely in connection with female readers.

Instead, we need to revise our model to include "familial" functions, which are evident if we look at the marginalia. On f. 140 after the copying of the three didactic texts are two dated entries. The first one says that in 1483, on the Sunday after Saint Martin's, on the 16th day of the month of November, the unnamed male writer, who was then living in his house on the rue de la Poulayerie, prepared the *pain benys* (the blessed bread for the church service), and at that time his wife was pregnant with their daughter Philiberte, who was born in April 1484.[14] Below this entry is another asking God's forgiveness of the sins and blessing on the soul of her father, Aymé de Beaumont, who died on the feast of St. Maurice, the 22d of September in 1513.[15]

The marginalia on the *Miroir* manuscript therefore disrupt any simple binary system that separates male from female reading; they also suggest that the manuscript functioned at least partially as a *livre de raison.* This is the term for a whole category of late medieval and early modern books used by families to record significant family events. Typically they note births, deaths, and marriages, but they may also include other kinds of data important to the family, such as participation in public rituals or the depredations of war and plague. Loyse's entry, written in 1513 at her father's death, immediately below Aymé's entry of the late fifteenth century, allows us to hypothesize that the manuscript had a particular meaning to the Beaumonts, a meaning connected to their family identity.

The most common type of book chosen to function as a *livre de raison* in this period was the Book of Hours.[16] The Dijon *Miroir* manuscript would thus be an unusual but not unlikely choice for a family memory book; the entries by Aymé and his daughter Loyse are enough to suggest that for the Beaumonts, at least, the manuscript was not just the property of an individual owner but also embodied their sense of being part of an ongoing lineage. Typically, too, it was the male head of household who owned the *livre de raison* and was expected to maintain its record of family history. In this case, however, Loyse rather than her eldest brother François inherited the manuscript, and it then passed to the Thésut sisters, Jacquette and Huguette. Claims of book ownership by fathers and sons and daughters suggest that works of female conduct played a role in articulating bourgeois family ideologies that were in the process of formation during the late medieval and early modern periods.

Families Who Owned the *Miroir*

Though it is now in the Dijon municipal library, the manuscript was originally in and around the city of Chalon on the Saône river, fifty miles to the south. Its owners for at least its first one hundred years—from the early fifteenth into the early sixteenth century—were members of the Beaumont family. References to Jacques de Beaumont, whose two signatures are the earliest on this manuscript, may be found in the archives from Chalon for several decades of the early to mid–fifteenth century. He is almost always identified as *licencié en lois* (trained in the law), and his position is given as lieutenant and *avocat* (lawyer) for the *bailli* (fiscal administrative unit) of Chalon and *conseiller* for the Duke of Burgundy.[17] Jacques is thus a member of the professional middle class and a civil servant, a member of the central administration of Burgundy that was replacing the judicial, financial, and military powers of the landed nobility.

Jacques de Beaumont appears to have married well. His wife, Ymbelette, was the daughter of Jean Perrier, referred to as *honorable homme* and *saige maistre*—terms for an educated member of the middle classes.[18] The eminence of the Perriers relative to the Beaumonts is evident in the last will and testament of Jacques's son Aymé, the manuscript owner who died in 1513.[19] Aymé only briefly mentions his father Jacques in his final testament, but his mother, Ymbelette Perrier, and her father, Jean Perrier, are significantly linked in the document to several donations in the town of Tournus, south of Chalon. Aymé orders memorial masses to be said at the abbey church of Tournus in the chapel founded by his grandfather Jean Perrier, and a large stone inscribed with the foundation narrative was to be placed there. In honor of his mother, Aymé also has inscribed stones placed in the Tournus church of the Magdalene and in the Tournus hospital, where his grandfather Jean Perrier and his mother, Ymbelette, were patrons. On his deathbed, Aymé obviously prefers to be remembered for his maternal rather than his paternal lineage because of the former's elevated status. The bequests in his will are consistent with the other evidence of Aymé's social aspirations. By the time he died in 1513, he was an *eschevin* (alderman) of the city of Chalon and *bastonnier* (leading lay patron) of the cathedral church of Saint Vincent.

Sometime in the second half of the fifteenth century, Aymé's father, Jacques, passed the *Miroir* manuscript on to his son, and inscribed in it we can read Aymé de Beaumont's quest to become a leading citizen in Chalon. We would not know he had owned the *Miroir* manuscript at all except for his daughter Loyse's notation of his death and the entry recording the ritual of the *pain benys* that marked him as a significant head of household. The act of supplying the bread for church services by households in the parish was a development of late medieval lay piety, as Eamon Duffey has shown for England.[20] Through such rituals, the laity appropriated some of the powers that had been vested in the clergy. But, more than that, the selection to be a household supplying the sacred bread marked one as a member of the bourgeois elites that held political power in late medieval towns. Aymé's innocuous entry at the conclusion of the conduct text is potent with implication for his social ascendance in Chalon. And the street, the rue de la Poulayerie, that Aymé identifies as his 1483 address is still visible in Chalon. It is only a block away from Saint Vincent's church, at the center of town. Later, it appears that Aymé moved to an even more proximate and socially prestigious location, since we know from records that his sons eventually inherit a house right on the Place Saint Vincent facing the church.[21]

At his death, the manuscript passed to his middle daughter Loyse, rather than to her older sister, the "well-loved" Philiberte (as their father

Aymé terms her in his last will and testament), whose impending birth had been recorded in the *Miroir* manuscript. Neither is it left to Aymé's two male heirs, his sons François and Claude. Instead, it is Loyse who expresses her filial piety in the manuscript she appropriates with her signatures and claims of ownership. However, the exact ownership and location of the manuscript for the next fifty years is obscure. Did Loyse keep it? If so, she did not continue adding family records. As we discover from Aymé's 1513 testament, Loyse and her younger sister Anne became wards of Pierre Grozelier, one of the executors of the will, who was the mayor of Beaune, a town twenty miles north of Chalon. The close relationship between Pierre and Aymé, these two urban magistrates, is indicated by Aymé's description of Pierre as *mon cousin* (a term indicating close affectionate ties though not, in this case, kinship), and also Aymé's arrangement that Loyse was to marry Pierre's son Jean—evidence of a marriage strategy among the bourgeoisie like that often attributed to the aristocracy. The marriage did not take place for another twelve years (c. 1525), but Loyse and Jean went on to have a large family, and Jean became mayor of Beaune in his turn.[22] Loyse's two brothers, Claude and François, were doing so well financially in Chalon by the 1520s, 1530s, and 1540s that they were able to begin to buy up the lands of impoverished noblemen and acquire their titles—becoming the *seigneurs* of Diconne and other fiefs in the region.[23] They could then live off the "rentes" as unchallenged noblemen. If Aymé had achieved substantial wealth and respectability by the time of his death (as we see from his will and testament), his sons and their descendents moved ever upscale through careful marriage alliances and the purchase of noble status.

The manuscript containing the *Miroir* then made its way into another family, the Thésuts of Chalon, rather than becoming a *livre de raison* for the next generation of Beaumonts or Grozeliers. It is interesting to note that two generations later, however, Loyse de Beaumont's grandson, Jean Grozelier, who was then *greffier* (secretary) for the salt tax depot in Beaune, obtained a high quality fifteenth-century Book of Hours that he began to use as a systematic Grozelier family *livre de raison* in 1583. Family birth, death, and marriage data were faithfully entered in the margins of almost every page for the next three hundred years by the head of household until 1898, when the Grozelier family name was extinguished. One hundred years later, the book is still owned by descendents of the Grozeliers and cherished as a family treasure. It testifies to the formation of a Grozelier family identity by the sixteenth century and its continuing strength through four more centuries.

The genealogy of the sixteenth-century owners of the manuscript—written in the eighteenth century—claims that the Thésuts had been titled from time immemorial, but the archives tell a different story.[24] It is a story of upward mobility by bourgeois elites, climaxing in their case with the earning of a rare letter of nobility from the king in the late sixteenth century by Louis, the brother of the last two women owners of the manuscript, Jacquette and Huguette de Thésut.[25] Their great-grandfather, Louis, was a merchant who had moved to Chalon from southern Burgundy in 1464.[26]

There is an interesting clue to the closeness of the Beaumont and Thésut families in a draft of a marriage contract from the year 1500 between Aymé de Beaumont and Philiberte de Thésut, the daughter of the merchant Louis de Thésut and sister of Aymé's good friend Jacques.[27] (Aymé and Jacques frequently witness each other's legal documents at the end of the century). One surmises that Aymé's wife, the mother of his five children, had died by then and a second marriage was being arranged between two bourgeois families. However, the contract is not signed, and I've found no other evidence in the archives that the marriage ever took place. Aymé's last will and testament mentions no wife. Along with the presence of Thésut signatures on many other documents of the Beaumonts and Grozeliers, the closeness implied by the marital arrangements does, however, suggest one reason why the *Miroir* manuscript ended up in the Thésut family for the rest of its known history. And, as in the Beaumont family, both fathers and daughters in the upwardly mobile bourgeoisie own the manuscript in the sixteenth century.

Aymé's friend Jacques de Thésut was an official at the *bailliage* of Chalon, a *maistre de comptes,* and sufficiently wealthy and well connected to acquire in 1511 a large piece of land called Charreconduite on the outskirts of Chalon from the nearby royal chateau of Germolles.[28] There he proceeded to build his family a small but handsome chateau, which still stands among the fields across the river from the modern city. Though it is now used as a (rat-infested) granary by tenant farmers who live in an adjacent building and bears pock marks from World War II bomb fragments, it is owned by a descendant of the Thésuts. It is recognizably an early sixteenth-century Burgundian chateau, scarcely changed since it was built. On the outside of the building and on the dining hall fireplace, you can still see carvings of the Thésut family coat of arms.

Jacques's son, Jacques II, and his children continued to use the chateau as their country home throughout the sixteenth century. As I discovered from looking at his signature on other documents, it is Jacques II's signature on folio 1 of the *Miroir* manuscript, and the attribution at the end of the manuscript "A Jacquette et Huguette de Thesut" is also in his handwriting. So it appears that Jacques de Thésut gave the manuscript to his two daughters, presumably at some point in the mid–sixteenth century before they were married to men of similar class and aspirations. Marriage contracts still exist for Jacquette in 1562 with Joseph de Vezon, who went on to a career at the Parlement in Dijon, and for Huguette in 1565 with Robert Mussard, who was also on the fast track to noble status as the archival records show.[29] I can easily imagine the sisters reading the *Miroir des bonnes femmes* in their chateau, Charreconduite, outside of Chalon around 1560. However, the later history of this manuscript is unknown. No more names are inscribed in it and further history of any individual owners is unknown, but I think we can see in the owner histories I have recounted the embedding of the text within a dynamic of social advancement and family identity formation between 1406 and the 1560s.

The males of all three interconnected families (the Beaumonts, the Grozeliers, and the Thésuts) belonged to town oligarchies, the bourgeois elites of Chalon, Beaune, and Dijon in the fifteenth and sixteenth centuries. In generation after generation, they served as town counselors and mayors. They became lawyers and moved into the civil bureaucracy of Burgundy, first in the *bailliages* (the tax-collecting governmental agencies) and then in the Parlement and Chambre de Comptes in Dijon. They accumulated substantial wealth in the form of town "rentes" and eventually country properties. George Huppert has made the case that social mobility in the late Middle Ages and the early modern period produced a crisis in the definitions of elites. In France, the old distinctions between the bourgeoisie and the *gentilshommes* (the hereditary nobility) were no longer clear. There was now an intervening and distinguishable group, an urban elite class whom Huppert identifies by the oxymoron *bourgeois gentilshommes*. This elite succeeded in "living nobly"—not having to work and being exempt from taxes—by acquiring the combination of law degrees, capital, and administrative power that we have seen in our three families. According to Huppert,

> This "social category, complex in its origins, but homogeneous in its way of life," these wealthy families, whose imposing townhouses were grouped in the center of the city, "led an existence which defined an elite." . . . these families had a clear feeling of their common interest, they thought of themselves as a community, they had a kind of class consciousness.[30]

Their genealogies, so far as I have been able to reconstruct them, show a high rate of intermarriage among the families in this emergent class (Huppert suggests 85 to 95 percent), not just within a single city but between major towns in the region—Dijon, Beaune, and Chalon—as we have seen.

The new configuration of elites is described most fully by Charles Loyseau, a French magistrate who published an anatomy of French society in 1610, the *Traite des ordres et simples dignitez* (Treatise on the orders and common ranks). He classes with the aristocracy of "an ancient line" a new nobility of rank that derives from high office, including legal and financial officials, doctors of learning, lawyers, and civil officials. This group is above the merchants, even the wealthy ones, who are called "worthy men" or "bourgeois of the towns."[31] This new elite continually aspired to the nobility, even though they might be scorned as mere *noblesse de robe* and taunted with the term "bourgeois."

The liminality of the new elite is revealed by the controversy surrounding their legislative status. According to Loyseau, the urban nobility sit with the Third Estate in the Estates General; however, that assignment raised frequent challenges. The brother of Jacquette and Huguette, Louis de Thésut, had been granted letters of nobility by the King in 1586, marking the Thésut family's century-long rise up from the merchant class to noble rank. Nevertheless, when his brother François was elected to the chamber of deputies of the Parlement in Dijon in 1595 by the Third Estate, the ambiguous social rank of the family—located somewhere between the usual Third Estate members and the traditional hereditary nobility—provoked acrimonious debate that had to be resolved by the intervention of the King's representative.[32] This debate illustrates the instability of the new social class emerging as the *noblesse de robe,* which aspired to the status and lifestyle of the old nobility while actually defining itself by a new set of values.

"La Bonne Renomée"

One value of particular interest to this new class is emphasized in women's conduct literature—that is, the woman's honor. The *Miroir des bonnes femmes* is a textual site that articulates the importance of female honor, not just for women, but in the symbolic economy of early bourgeois culture as a whole. In their search for status, the urban elites turned to a rhetoric of gentility and codes of courtesy that were designed to demonstrate fitness for high rank. This late medieval social discourse appropriates the rhetoric of earlier aristocratic literature, but with one significant difference: whereas aristocratic family honor rested upon its male members, for the bourgeoisie it was female honor that reflected most crucially upon her family's social standing.[33] I would argue that books shaping female conduct to earn "bonne renomée" (a good name or reputation) address not just the individual woman but also her family's social aspirations, and, indeed, in the *Miroir des bonnes femmes* an overwhelming concern is with female behaviors that can cause a woman and her family to gain or lose their reputation.

While most analyses of this phenomenon have stressed the importance of female virginity to honor, the *Miroir* 's concept of good reputation is far wider. The ideal of *renom* is articulated as being untouched by malicious gossip: "de tant bonne renomee que onques une parolle n'en fut dite en mal. Ce est trop bonne chose que de avoir bonne renomee" (f. 129v). The metaphor of a scent that permeates the country describes a good female reputation: "Quant elle est plainne de bonne ouvres et de bonnes vertuz et de bonne mours que la flaiveur de la bonne renomee de li va par tout le pais" (f. 129v). Central to this definition of female honor is conduct, broadly construed as virtue, good works, and proper behavior.

The *Miroir* itself consists of exempla of thirty-six bad women of the Bible and thirty good women, combined with nonbiblical exempla and moralizations in the voice of the Franciscan preacher. The biblical women depicted in the *Miroir* model behaviors that will build or destroy one's public, secular reputation. The precariousness of maintaining a good reputation and the danger of losing it, even inadvertently, are illustrated through many vivid examples. Among the women identified as bad is the beautiful married woman Bathsheba, who unwisely chose to bathe in the open where King David could see her. The King lusted after her and arranged that her husband should be killed in battle, acts the narrator blames on Bathsheba, who should have performed her ablutions in private (f. 98v–99). Staying sheltered in the home away from predatory males is the most often recommended way of maintaining one's good name in the *Miroir.* Even brothers are not above suspicion, as the example of Tamar shows, leading to the conclusion that the only males a careful woman should be alone with are her husband and her father (f. 99).

On the positive side, the *Miroir* praises the Virgin Mary specifically for remaining alone and cloistered because young women should not leave home except to carry out necessary tasks, for the merchant does not show the merchandise he wants to sell: "Ci preigne exemple toutes jeunes femmez en quelque estat que elle soit de soi tenir close. Li mercheans ne moustre mie la merchendise que il ne vuelt vendre. Tout ansi preudefemme quant elle est juene comme nostre dame se doit tousjours tenir a l'ostel se besoing ne la mainne selon l'enseignment saint pol" (f. 134). Mature women are also counseled to be very careful whom they take into their household, even with the best of intentions, since there are so many bad men around. The *Miroir* first describes Martha as praiseworthy for harboring our lord: "Ci puent dames exemple prendre de tenir hospitalite et de herbergier povrez gens ceulx meismes qui portent la parolle dieu" (f. 137v). Then it paradoxically reverses direction to offer cautionary exempla of various women such as Lucrece and Dido and an unnamed "preudefemme" who took in what seemed like respectable men and suffered harm as a result. It concludes, "Hostel a preudefemme n'est mie lieus a mauvez hommez" (f. 137v).

Although most of its examples come from the Bible and with reference to the moral virtues, the *Miroir* 's message is ultimately and often explicitly one of proper social behaviors and maintaining a good reputation with regard to status obligations. For example, the Virgin is praised for her courtesy when she visits Elizabeth during the latter's pregnancy; the *Miroir* says this is appropriate behavior toward a kinswoman: "Apres loe l'escripture sa courtoisie quant elle visita sainte elysabeth qui estoit ensinte pour lui veoir et pour lui servir. Dont elle dit que ce est trop grant chose de la mere dieu qui l'estoit venue veoir. Ja prenez exemple de aidier de visiter de compaignier vous povres parens ou parentes ou vos vosines et aux siens humbles et cortois" (f. 135). Whereas religious texts might use the visit of the Virgin to her cousin as the opportunity to celebrate the mystery of the Incarnation, including Elizabeth's saying of the "Magnificat," the *Miroir* emphasizes Mary's secular good manners. It concludes this exemplum with the comment that the more a lady rises in honor, the more she should show good manners.

This predominantly secular interpretation of the biblical exempla is picked up in the conduct book written by Geoffroy de la Tour Landry for his daughters in the mid–fourteenth century, which drew largely on our *Miroir* for its examples, as John Grigsby demonstrated in an important article.[34] Exempla and moralizations from the *Miroir* also made their way into English when Caxton translated Geoffroy's conduct book in 1484. In Caxton's introduction to the translation, he acknowledges the centrality and reinforces the significance of the social honor a woman earns by her good conduct. Caxton's translation of Geoffroy's prologue then says that "the good maners and good dedes of good ladyes and wymmen / and of theyr lyves" will be recounted "soo that for theyr vertues and bountees they ben honoured / And that after theyr dethe ben renommed and preysed . . . for to take of them good ensample and contenaunce." He adds that he shows the vices of evil women leading to their being "Blamed / shamed / and dyffamed."[35]

While lip service is paid to the proper behaviors owed to God in the first eight chapters of Geoffroy's conduct book, the other 136 chapters focus chiefly on how to earn "the love and the grace of theyr neyghbours, and of the world"—as Caxton's translation puts it. The "savacion of theyr sowles" receives much less attention than "thenoure of theyr body erthely" in the economy of Caxton and his source texts. Achieving "bonne renomee" for the woman is the leitmotif of the *Miroir* and its descendants, a goal that I would link not just with sexuality—as it often has been—but also with the social constructions of family honor in aspirants to higher class status.

It cannot be accidental that Christine de Pizan, in her conduct book addressed to all ranks of women in society from princesses to prostitutes, identifies this social class—in her words "women of importance in cities: those who are married to clerks, to the counsellors of kings or princes, or to guardians of justice and other officials"—as women especially concerned with four aspects of worldly prudence: love and fidelity to their husbands, management of the household, grooming and clothing, and avoidance of blame and dishonor.[36] She writes: "Women wishing to protect themselves from blame should avoid bad or dishonest company."[37] Christine cautions and especially advises against the women of this class going to garden parties or on pilgrimages:

> Nor should a young woman go trotting about town, as is the custom—on Monday to St. Avoye; on Tuesday, to who knows where; on Friday to St. Catherine, and elsewhere on the other days. Even if some do it, there is no need for it. Of course, we do not wish to prevent anyone from doing good works. But considering a woman's youth and exuberance, plus men's desire to seduce women as well as the fact that words so often are spoken so readily and so rashly, the surest thing for the soul's profit and the body's honor is to avoid the habit of trotting here and there. . . . For all these and similar reasons, a wise woman who loves honor and wishes to avoid censure should exercise great caution.[38]

This is not to say that the spiritual and social aims of conduct literature are regarded as incompatible. Far from it. In discussing wifely obedience, for example, the *Miroir des bonnes femmes* notes in the same breath that this virtue pleases God and the world: "Certes il fait bon faire sanz desdit le voloir son seigneur quar ce est une chouse qui merveilleusement plait a dieu et au monde" (f. 103). The *Miroir* also recounts the example of a "saige dame" who carries around two images—one of Christ and the other of her husband—which function to protect her from sin and villany: "Nous trouvons en i autre livret escript qui raconte d'une saige dame qui portat tous jours avec soi en deux chassetz comme d'un mireoir l'ymaige ihesu crist et la semblance de son seigneur espous, et la raison estoit si comme celle disoit. Pour ce que la remembrance de son creatour que elle tant amoit la gardest de pechie et le recort de son signeur que elle tant amoit et cremoit la contre gardait de vilonie faire" (f. 126). The parallel construction of the statement in effect produces an equivalence between committing a sin and behaving in a lower-class manner.

One of the successful strategies of the conduct genre is to reduce good manners and good morals to essentially the same thing. As Caxton writes, "For there is no gretter vertue for to cause yow to have the grace of god / and the love of alle people than for to be humble and curtoyse.... Curtoyse is the fyrst waye and the entre of alle frendship and of alle worldly love."[39] In this view, the social graces ease your path to heaven as well as your way in this life. The rhetoric of courtesy virtually erases the distinction between the two worlds, between the "grace of god" and the "love of alle people." Learning virtue and learning courteous manners are presented as the same process in conduct literature, and the popularity of didactic works on the vices and virtues in this period may owe something to this equation between morality and social acceptability.

Just as in these conduct books the language of religious virtue has been transmuted into a message about social advancement, so the language of aristocratic male prowess (of chivalry) is appropriated for female honor. The Caxton translation of Geoffroy de la Tour Landry's book makes an analogy between the good woman's behaviors, which earn her a good reputation, and the knight's trials and battles:

> And as he hath suffred payne and travail ynough / he is put and enhaunced in to grete honour / And grete yefts ben thenne gyven to hym / and grete wonder and merveylle it is of the grete worship and grete renommee that men beren unto hym. Lyke wyse it is of the good lady and good woman / which in every place is renommed in honoure and worship.[40]

The worthy woman's social prestige in an essentially bourgeois ideology is equivalent to the honor of a knight in the aristocratic status system.

I have been arguing that this manuscript is a site where gender, class, and family identities intersect. What we can discover about the owners of the Dijon manuscript containing the *Miroir des bonnes femmes* supports a view that a majority of late medieval conduct books were acquired by bourgeois readers as guides to upward mobility. The Beaumont and Thésut families—as well as the families with whom they formed marital alliances—were members of an urban elite class busy ameliorating its social position through accumulations of social capital—wealth, education, and civil status. I think we must go beyond a purely instrumentalist analysis, however, to suggest that the conduct of women—and particularly the obsession with women's honor and reputation to be found in the *Miroir* and its descendants—signal the formation of a specifically bourgeois ideology in which the female is inscribed as the site of family identity. In this, the emergent bourgeois ideology of the early modern period differs from an aristocratic ideology where masculine conduct and honor are symbolically central. Not only does the upwardly mobile family use conduct literature as guides to gentility, but the rhetoric of female honor leading to "bonne renomee" represents a significant shift in the gendering of social discourse. Whereas for the traditional aristocracy the conduct of males was addressed through a literature of "mirrors for princes," the new urban elites make the female the ideological locus of social prestige upon which the whole family builds its new status. The inclusion of a conduct book addressed to women within a manuscript owned by males and females in several of these related families is thus not surprising.

To read the *Miroir des bonnes femmes* as relating only to women, therefore, would be to misunderstand its role in the formation of new ideologies during the fourteenth through the sixteenth centuries. The conjunction of female-based rhetoric, familial identities, and the promise of social advancement through proper conduct marks the first stage of a distinctive bourgeois ideology that will be fully articulated and culturally dominant by the late eighteenth and nineteenth centuries. Despite the assumption, perhaps, on the part of conduct book owners that they are justifying a claim to "noble" rank, it is in bourgeois culture that female honor is made the symbolic basis of a family's social reputation. As they cultivated that reputation and fostered a process of social advancement, fathers as well as their daughters therefore had a vital interest in owning conduct texts addressed to women.

NOTES

Versions of this essay were given at the University of Iowa, Bates College, and the Centre Georges Chevrier pour l'Histoire de la Bourgogne in Dijon, France. I would like to acknowledge assistance in this research from Mme Martine Chauncy, Bibliothèque Municipale of Dijon; Mme Eliane Lochot, conservateur of the Dijon city archives; Professor Michel Petitjean, Université de Bourgogne; Professor Véronique Plesch of Colby College; and M. Henri Huet.

1. Michel de Certeau, *The Practice of Everyday Life*, trans. Steven Rendall (Berkeley: University of California Press, 1984), xiii.

2. Claire Sponsler, "Medieval Ethnography: Fieldwork in the Medieval Past," *Assays* 7 (1992): 1–30.

3. The three manuscripts are Ms. fr. 32 in the University of Pennsylvania library, Ms. 2156 in the Bibliothèque de l'Arsenal in Paris, and Ms. fr. 213 in the Bibliothèque Municipale of Dijon.

4. Geneviève Hasenohr, "L'essor des bibliothèques privées aux XIVe et XVe siècles," in *Histoire des bibliothèques françaises,* vol. 1, *Les bibliothèques médiévales du VIe siècle à 1530,* ed. André Vernet (Paris: Editions du Cercle de la Librairie, 1989), 214–63.

5. "Miroir des bonnes femmes," *Romania* 82 (1961): 462.

6. François Rabelais, *The Histories of Gargantua and Pantagruel,* trans. J. M. Cohen (Harmondsworth, England: Penguin, 1981), 368.

7. Gerald Bruns, "The Originality of Texts in Manuscript Culture," *Comparative Literature* 32 (1980): 113–29.

8. Kate Harris, "Patrons, Buyers, and Owners: The Evidence for Ownership and the Role of Book Owners in Book Production and the Book Trade," in *Book Production and Publishing in Britain, 1375–1475,* ed. Jeremy Griffiths and Derek Pearsall (Cambridge: Cambridge University Press, 1989), 177.

9. Seth Lehrer has summarized much of this scholarship in *Chaucer and His Readers: Imagining the Author in Late-Medieval England* (Princeton, N.J.: Princeton University Press, 1993), 88–89. Lehrer goes on to argue that this "advisory literature" is also indebted to Chaucerian language in the *Canterbury Tales,* and that the annotations on the Helmingham manuscript suggest that it was made for "general family use" since there are both adult and children's annotations on it (93).

10. Claire Sponsler, *Drama and Resistance: Bodies, Goods, and Theatricality in Late Medieval England* (Minneapolis: University of Minnesota Press, 1997), 55.

11. Felicity Riddy, "Mother Knows Best: Reading Social Change in a Courtesy Text," *Speculum* 71 (January 1996): 69.

12. Ibid., 68.

13. Gérard Genette, *Palimpsestes: La littérature au second degré* (Paris: Editions du Seuil, 1982), 10.

14. L'an mil CCCC.IIII.XX et troys, le dymanche appres la sainct martin XVIe jour du moys de novembre moy demeurant en ma mayson en la rue de la pouleylerie je fis le pain benys et en ce temps marguerite de la perriere, ma femme estoyt enceincte de unge fille qui a nom Philiberte son deusyesme enfant qui naquit le ——— jour du moys de avrys.

15. Feu mon pere ayme de beaulmont que dieu absoille trespassa le jeudy jour du feste st morys XXVI du moys de septembre en l'an mil V c. treize. Dieu par sa saincte grace et misericorde luy veuille parddoner ses pechez et luy octroys en son paradys.

16. Geneviève Hasenohr notes that the book was not an object like others, but functioned as a "dépositaire du souvenir du disparu dont, au cours de colloques intimes, il a suscité et recueilli les réflexions, les larmes ou les joies. Tout particulièrement lorsqu'il s'agit d'un livre d'heures, d'un psautier ou d'un bréviaire, pour lesquels se manifeste, dans les testaments, un attachement réel. . . . Aux yeux de l'entourage familial, le bréviaire ou le livre d'Heures est pour ainsi dire le mémorial de celui dont il fut le confident journalier. . . . Dans les grandes familles, il devient le symbole tangible et inaliénable de la lignée" (229–30). There are numerous examples of Books of Hours used as *livres de raison* by early modern families in Burgundian libraries.

17. Documents in which Jacques de Beaumont is named as presiding lieutenant of the Chalon *bailli* may be found in the Chalon town archives at the Bibliothèque municipale. Bundle AA14 contains numerous documents from 1408 through 1446; bundle FF76 also contains numerous documents from 1444 through 1446 produced under his authority. See also Côte d'Or archives in Dijon, B3686 (f.53v), where he is named as recipient of ten francs and two solz in connection with holding his office, and see the Saône-et-Loire archives in Macon, where documents E1256 and E760 mention Jacques's position at the *bailliage* of Chalon.

18. Saône-et-Loire archives, E1095. According to Thierry Dutour, the word "sage" connoted expertise, especially as acquired through the study of law; *Une société de l'honneur: Les notables et leur monde à Dijon à la fin du Moyen Age* (Paris: Honoré Champion, 1998), 403. Similarly, "honorable homme" was used for owners of a law degree, according to Monique Sommé, *Isabelle de Portugal, Duchesse de Bourgogne: Une femme au pouvoir au XVe siècle* (Paris: Presses Universitaires du Septentrion, 1998), 153.

19. Saône-et-Loire archives, E1315.

20. Eamon Duffey, *The Stripping of the Altars* (New Haven, Conn.: Yale University Press, 1992), 124–27, on the holy bread or "holy loaf." For a discussion of the custom in France, see Virginia Reinburg, "Liturgy and the Laity in Late Medieval and Reformation France," *Sixteenth Century Journal* 23 (1992): 526–46, especially 531–32 and 541–42.

21. Raoul Violot, *Histoire des maisons de Chalon,* tome 1 (Paris: Librairie Guénégaud, 1969), 266.

22. Jean was mayor of Beaune in 1522–1523 and again in 1542–1543 according to J. Delissey, *Les maires de Beaune jusqu'en 1789* (Beaune: Imprimerie Beaunoise, 1937), 45–46. However, his father Pierre was mayor from 1504 until his death in 1515, longer than any other mayor in the fourteenth through the sixteenth centuries (40).

23. See, for example, the 1545 document describing their holdings at Diconne in Côte d'Or archives B10621.

24. For a summary of the genealogy of the multibranched Thésut family, see M. M. Martin and G. Jeanton, "Mémoire historique et généalogique de la famille de Thésut en Bourgogne (D'après le manuscrit original annoté par les éditeurs)" in *Mémoires de la Société d'histoire et d'archéologie de Chalon-sur-Saône,* 2e série, tome 4 (1911): 11–238.

25. For Louis's official letter of nobility, see Côte d'Or archives B74 (f. 65v).

26. See Saône-et-Loire archives E1324 (f.52) for a description of Louis as "marchant habitant de Chalon." Some nineteenth-century historians who accepted the family's fake aristocratic credentials had a difficult time explaining why the fifteenth-century Louis was called a merchant or why his sixteenth-century descendent had to apply for letters of nobility from the king.

27. Saône-et-Loire archives 3E5037.

28. See Côte d'Or achives B10595 for purchase of land and B1088 for documents concerning Charreconduite throughout the sixteenth century.

29. For the sisters' marriage contracts, see Saône-et-Loire archives E1304 and E1116.

30. George Huppert, *Les Bourgeois Gentilshommes: An Essay on the Definition of Elites in Renaissance France* (Chicago: University of Chicago Press, 1977), 21. Huppert is quoting from Henri Drouot, *Mayenne et la Bourgogne,* 2 vols. (Paris: A. Picard, 1937).

31. Roland Mousnier, *Social Hierarchies 1450 to the Present,* trans. Peter Evans, ed. Margaret Clark (New York: Schoeken Books, 1973), 67, 68. For the complete French treatise, see Charles Loyseau, *Cinq livres du droit des offices, suivis des seigneuries et de celui des ordres* (Paris, 1610).

32. The original letters and supporting materials are in Côte d'Or archives B72, B74, B107, and B457. The case has been commented on by Jules d'Arbaumont in his study of letters of nobility sent by the king and registered in the Chambre de Comptes at Dijon, "Les anoblis de Bourgogne," *Revue Nobiliaire* (1866): 1–19. D'Arbaumont points out that registration was not just a formality; the Chambre de Comptes examined the letters, chose a commissioner to conduct an inquiry into the birth, conduct, and lifestyle of the petitioner, called witnesses, and listened to those opposed to the ennoblement (4). Although relatively few (about twenty) letters of nobility had been given out prior to 1584, the wars of religion prompted their use to reward loyalists like Louis de Thésut. For general background on the fluidity of noble status at this time and the giving of letters of nobility, see Arlette Jouanna, *La France du XVIe siècle, 1483–1598* (Paris: Presses Universitaires de France, 1996), especially 58–69 and 84–88.

33. For an anthropological argument about the Mediterranean region's cultural connection between family honor and female virtue, see Jane Schneider, "Of Vigilance and Virgins: Honor, Shame, and Access to Resources in Mediterranean Societies," *Ethnology* 10 (1971): 1–24. In *Pursuing Honor while Avoiding Sin: The Monte Delle Doti of Florence* (Milano: Dott. A. Giuffre Editore, 1978), Julius Kirschner shows the centrality of female behavior to the family's honor in late medieval Florence: "A worthy woman, in the words of the merchant banker Paolo Sassetti, 'fecce onore a casa nostra, sempre.' The *casa* was feminine, filled and perpetuated by men, and, like a woman, vigilantly protected against defilement and shame. On a metonymic level, the *casa* was a woman and the woman a *casa,* both receptacles of male honor. For a nubile woman to be honorable meant, in the eyes of the merchant Giovanni di Pagolo Morelli, that she be 'bene nata,' that she be legitimate, descended from a socially esteemed family, and that she, her mother, and even maternal grandmother have an honorable reputation" (6–7). He adds, "as for dishonor, Florentine memoirs are punctuated by anathematic references to women of ill-repute *(male fama),* leading an evil life *(male vita),* who brought shame and dishonor to the family *(verghogna e disonore a tutta la casa)*."

34. John Grigsby, "A New Source for the *Livre du Chevalier de la Tour Landry,*" *Romania* 84 (1963): 171–208.

35. *The Book of the Knight of the Tower,* trans. William Caxton, ed. M. Y. Offord, EETS, SS 2 (London: Oxford University Press, 1971), 12.

36. Christine de Pizan, *A Medieval Woman's Mirror of Honor: The Treasury of the City of Ladies,* trans. Charity Cannon Willard, ed. Madeleine Pelner Cosman (New York: Bard Hall Press/Persea Books, 1989), 185, 186.

37. Ibid., 192.

38. Ibid., 192–93.

39. *The Book of the Knight of the Tower,* 23–24.

40. Ibid., 151.

5

Fathers to Think Back Through

The Middle High German Mother-Daughter and Father-Son Advice Poems Known as *Die Winsbeckin* and *Der Winsbecke*

Ann Marie Rasmussen

Alle Poesie soll belehrend sein, aber unmerklich; sie soll den Menschen aufmerksam machen, wovon sich zu belehren wert wäre; er muß die Lehre selbst daraus ziehen wie aus dem Leben.

Johann Wolfgang von Goethe, *Über das Lehrgedicht*[1]

For we think back through our mothers if we are women.

Virginia Woolf, *A Room of One's Own*

When thinking about medieval conduct literature as a genre, perhaps the first issue a scholar ponders is whether there is any medieval German secular text that does not explore in some fashion the question of proper conduct that leads to good repute in this world or to salvation in the next. All medieval literature can seem at heart a moral-didactic enterprise; whence, from what place, arises a separate genre of conduct literature? Yet when modern scholars reflect on medieval conduct literature as a thematically defined genre, they are often revisiting a clearly profiled medieval topos—sage advice imparted by a mature and knowledgeable narrator to a young person (or to all youth). Such didactic literature enjoyed a secure place across the medieval literary tradition. Most works of German language advice literature have come down to us in multiple manuscripts, and advice on right conduct could take on just about any formal guise. There are, for example, epic-length rhymed advice texts such as Thomasin von Zerclaere's *Der Wälsche Gast* (1215–1216)[2] and Hugo von Trimberg's *Der Renner* (1290–1300); the genre of *Spruchdichtung* (didactic and eulogistic verse) includes Freidank's *Bescheidenheit* (c. 1230); lyric poetry includes advice poems such as *Der Winsbecke* and *Die Winsbeckin* (first half, thirteenth century). Among short rhymed-couplet texts we find several versions of *Der Deutsche Cato,* the popular medieval German translation of the *Disticha Catonis.* Advice and conduct literature were omnipresent in medieval literature and enjoyed a long and vital life.

Though grounded in careful attention to historical evidence, the genre of medieval German conduct literature (*Lehrdichtung*) is also a category constructed largely by nineteenth-century scholarship, reflecting the assumptions and biases of previous—and present—learning, and producing the answers and the questions that communities of scholars past and present have deemed useful and legitimate. Both then and now, the category of medieval German conduct literature is culturally and historically shaped, the product of modes of thought and acquired habits of inquiry that change over time. The category itself does cultural work and is the product of cultural ways of knowing, no less so now than in the Middle Ages. Hence the title of this essay, rewriting Virginia Woolf's moving assertion (which in 1929 was as much a call to action as a statement of belief), in order to remind us that since the early nineteenth century scholars of medieval literature have constructed through their editorial and interpretive practices the paternal authority—the fathers—it wished to think back through.[3]

Not surprisingly, Goethe's legacy cast a long shadow over scholarship on medieval German literature. Two useful surveys of medieval German *Lehrdichtung* from the 1970s, which continue to serve as standard reference works for the field, rely on traditional literary discourse of poetics and genre theory, which were classically formulated by Goethe, to frame their work. Sowinski (1971) relies primarily on genre theory. His study, which includes useful chapters on conduct literature in the classical tradition, is framed in terms of Goethe's definition of conduct literature as "a creation halfway between literature and rhetoric" [ein Mittelgeschöpf zwischen Poesie und Rhetorik] (*Über das Lehrgedicht,* 1827). Boesch's survey (1977) proceeds from a similar set of poetological concerns to briefly explore the fluidity of medieval genre boundaries when viewed from the perspective of conduct literature, a fluidity that arises, he argues, because there is no such thing as "disinterested 'belles lettres'" [zweckentbundene "schöne Literatur"] in the Middle Ages (9). In both surveys, the continuity with nineteenth-century traditions is striking. Since the 1980s new approaches have been attempted: alongside traditional scholarly definitions, Bennewitz (1988) sets the contrastive alterity of four significant medieval conduct texts; Bumke's virtually exhaustive survey is largely descriptive and nonevaluatory (1990). Scholars have also begun systematically inquiring into the cultural processes and ideological strategies through which dominant frameworks and categories of literary study, such as categories of genre, were created and legitimized.[4]

This essay analyzes some of the intellectual assumptions and ideological investments bound up in the process of creating and maintaining the category of conduct literature by focusing on a single set of thirteenth-century conduct texts and the scholarship about them. The texts are a father-son text known among scholars as *Der Winsbecke* and a mother-daughter text known among scholars as *Die Winsbeckin* (collectively, the *Winsbecke* poems).[5] These didactic poems offer promising ground for our questions. They enjoy a four-hundred-year postmedieval reception history, excerpts having been first published in 1609 in an influential anthology of Latin and medieval German texts, *Paraeneticorum veterum,* compiled by the early modern legal historian and diplomat Melchior Goldast (1578–1635) (Zimmermann 1980). Second, the philological and editorial choices made by nineteenth-century *Winsbecke* scholars formatively shaped later scholarship on the poems. Agreeing with the precept that "editing is not simply prior to interpretation, it is consubstantial with it" (Hult 1991, 127), this essay examines some of what Lee Patterson in his book *Negotiating the Past* has called the "enabling assumptions" (1987, 113) guiding the editorial choices made by scholars as they fixed, that is to say, stabilized, the manuscript versions of the *Winsbecke* poems into the published editions upon which virtually all subsequent interpretive work has been based. In particular, the essay examines the "enabling" notions of authenticity, authorship, and paternal authority that shaped scholarship on the poems from 1845 to 1985.[6] The trope of a father instructing his son furnished a productive framework for the overwhelmingly male professional caste of nineteenth- and twentieth-century scholars to "think back through," I will argue, as they constructed notions of conduct literature that privileged a version of paternal, secular authority and that rested at times on a nostalgic belief that didactic literature was imbued with an authentic connection to lived medieval experience. In tracing out a small section of intellectual history, this essay suggests, for the *Winsbecke* poems, a bipartite answer to Patterson's question: "While any usable past must be based upon enabling assumptions of some kind, do these assumptions in fact prescribe the use to which the past will be put?" (1987, 113). A preliminary answer to this question suggests that evaluatory conceptual frameworks based upon hierarchies of gender were at work in the scholarly creation of the *Winsbecke* poems, and that those hierarchies have continued to inform scholarship into the present day. In its last section, this essay looks beyond past scholarship and explores ways in which the *Winsbecke* poems themselves suggest new venues for scholarly interpretation. For it is equally true, as the rhetorical nature of Patterson's question implies, that prescriptive or inherited assumptions need not predetermine how we read the past.

Even to name and to describe the texts in question, *Der Winsbecke* (The Knight from Winsbecke) and *Die Winsbeckin* (The Lady from Winsbecke), engages the philological and textual choices made by earlier scholars; there is no point of entry that does not implicate interpretive processes. The names customarily used to designate these texts derive from the *Codex Manesse* (Heidelberg, Universitätsbibliothek, cg 848, compiled c. 1320–1325 in Zurich), a magnificent illuminated collection of medieval lyric and gnomic poetry ordered by the category of authorship. Like most of the one hundred thirty-seven authors represented in the codex, the texts of *Der Winsbecke* and *Die Winsbeckin* are accompanied by full-page illuminations. See Figure 5.1. Above the image of father and son has been written "Der Winsbeke"; above the facing text, in a later medieval hand, "vo(n) Winsbach"; above the mother-daughter text, "Diu Winsbekin." No other manuscript or fragment containing these poems uses

Figure 5.1. *Der Winsbecke*. Heidelberg, Universitätsbibliothek, cpg fol. 213r.

these names, but the male version is attested to in the epic didactic poem, *Der Renner,* which might predate the *Codex Manesse* by a few years: "Greed, gaming, and whoring, fickleness and bad German have possessed so many lords that they have completely forgotten the songs once sung by the noble lords von Botenloube and von Morungen. Von Limburc and von Windesbecke, von Nîfen, Wildonie and von Brûnecke, Master Walther von der Vogelweide—I pity those who would forget them" (lines 1179–88).[7] The custom of using *Die Winsbeckin* and *Der Winsbecke* to identify these poems began with the first printed version from 1609, which was based on the *Codex Manesse.* As we shall see, the assumption that at least one of these names, *Der Winsbecke,* named a male author (an interpretation that can be supported by the name in *Der Renner* and by the compilation principle at work in the *Codex Manesse*) became a foundational "fact" for the notions of authenticity subsequently constructed around these two poems.

The poems known to scholars as *Die Winsbeckin* and *Der Winsbecke* are preserved in a small number of manuscripts and manuscript fragments, of which the three oldest manuscripts are also the most complete: The *Codex Manesse* (Heidelberg, Universitätsbibliothek, cpg 848) from c. 1320–1325; Berlin, Staatsbibliotheik zu Berlin Preußischer Kulturbesitz, mgf 474, from 1323 (formerly Tübingen mgf 474); and the *Weingartner Liederhandschrift* (Stuttgart, Württembergische Landesbibliothek, cod. HB XIII.1) from c. 1290–1310.[8] These three manuscript witnesses preserve the father-son advice poem and immediately following it the mother-daughter advice poem, both using the same stanzaic form. In *Der Winsbecke,* the father, in a monologue, earnestly advises his son on rules for virtuous, god-fearing worldly conduct (stanzas 1–56 in the standard edition), the son responds with an energetic rejection of his father's worldliness (stanzas 57–61, 64), and the father closes with prayer-like praise for the spiritual retreat from the world he and his son are undertaking (stanzas 62–63, 65–80). The stanzaic order matches relatively well across the three chief manuscript witnesses, though the length of the poem in them varies: *Der Winsbecke* is either sixty-seven stanzas long (*Weingartner Liederhandschrift*), seventy-five stanzas long (*Codex Manesse*), or seventy-eight stanzas long (Berlin, Staatsbibliothek zu Berlin Preußischer Kulturbesitz, mgf 474). These three manuscripts preserve *Der Winsbecke* as a single unified poem that includes the father's worldly teachings, the son's intervention, and the father's embrace of a spiritual life.

In contrast, the first scholarly edition of the poem from 1845 breaks up the codicologically unified poem into two sections: *The Old Poem,* deemed the original poem, which consists of the father's monologue (stanzas 1–56), and *The Continuations,* deemed the work of one or two later anonymous writers, in which the father's advice, motivated by the son's intervention, takes a spiritual turn (stanzas 57–80). This essay attends closely to this construction of the text, which has been maintained in subsequent editions (second edition in 1888, second edition revised in 1928, third edition in 1962), and to the ways in which it has shaped subsequent scholarship.

Die Winsbeckin's mother and daughter engage in a give-and-take dialogue about the perils, attractions, and attributes of *Minne* (love), with the mother speaking in total slightly more stanzas than the daughter. The *Weingartner Liederhandschrift* contains thirty-seven stanzas, the *Codex Manesse* thirty-nine stanzas, and Berlin mgf 474, thirty-nine stanzas. Following the same editorial principle, the standard edition includes all stanzas deemed authentic to create a poem longer than any manuscript version, in this case, one containing forty-five stanzas. Although *Die Winsbeckin* has been published continuously together with *Der Winsbecke, Die Winsbeckin* has stood in *Der Winsbecke*'s shadow and received little scholarly attention, being judged an aesthetically inferior text. See Figure 5.2.

The entwined editorial and interpretive history of the *Winsbecke* poems begins in the seventeenth century. The *Winsbecke* poems were first published in 1604 by Melchior Goldast (Zimmermann 1980). Following the title in the *Codex Manesse,* Goldast named "Der Winsbecke" as a medieval poet and proceeded to invent a life for him based on the poems' content. He asserted that the poems had been written by one Knight Winsbecke, who had served at the courts of Frederick Barbarossa and his son, Henry VI, together with his wife, Lady Winsbecke, who had governed the ladies of the royal household. Moriz Haupt, who in 1845 produced the first edition of the *Winsbecke* poems, rightly dismissed Goldast's view in this matter as a "dreamt-up assertion" [erträumte[r] behauptung] (1845, x).[9] Goldast's publication inaugurated a period of sustained learned interest in medieval German literature, which had been largely forgotten since the Reformation. In his 1986 article, Wolfgang Harms chronicles periodic discussions of the *Winsbecke* poems, references to the figures of Knight and Lady Winsbecke, and reprintings of the poems in the seventeenth and eighteenth centuries. Harms notes that during the seventeenth century the *Winsbecke* poems were elevated to the status of a major work of German literature—exemplars of a newly emerging German national identity—because of the linguistic and moral

Figure 5.2. *Die Winsbeckin.* Heidelberg, Universitätsbibliothek, cpg fol. 217.

purity that early modern writers held to be intrinsic to the "antique" language in which the *Winsbecke* poems were written. The poems' celebration of secular values also drew strong praise from some anti-Catholic writers during the confessional struggles that marked early modern Germany. During this period, the assumption that a Knight Winsbecke was both the author and the first-person narrator of the poem was widely believed, but it was challenged by the Swiss enlightenment thinker Johann Jakob Bodmer (1698–1783), who believed that the *Winsbecke* poems had been composed by Wolfram von Eschenbach (1729, 7).[10] Bodmer judged *Die Winsbeckin* to be a model chivalric poem and repeatedly singled it out for praise (Harms 1986, 48–49), and Harms's evidence suggests that early modern writers generally held *Die Winsbeckin* in high regard. This judgment was to change with the creation of a standard edition in 1845.

Harms's survey makes clear that before Haupt's edition of 1845 there was some debate around the problems of authorship and authenticity in *Der Winsbecke*. Though it was widely held to be and often celebrated as an autobiographical text offering a view into the honorable ethos of a real, medieval mind, Bodmer, a well-regarded thinker, dissented from this view. As late as 1838, in his massive anthology and literary history of medieval German poetry, Friedrich Heinrich von der Hagen (1780–1856) agreed in large part with Bodmer's assessments (311–14). The *Winsbecke* poems "had been placed in the mouths of these figures [i.e., Lord and Lady Winsbecke], even if they once lived" (1838, 311). Von der Hagen also found that the poem's ending—that is to say, the son's intervention and the father's embrace of a spiritual way of life—was in the spirit of "old chivalry" [des alten Ritterthums] (313).

In 1845 Moriz Haupt (1808–1874) published the first edition of the *Winsbecke* poems based on Lachmann's principles of textual criticism.[11] In his introduction Haupt rehearsed the codicological and prosopographical evidence for the name Winsbecke, and dismissed as speculation (as we saw above) the "biographical" details concocted by Goldast and others. Yet, Haupt also vehemently rejected the hypothesis that "Der Winsbecke" and "Die Winsbeckin" might be "invented persons" [erdichtete personen] (ix) or "historical figures into whose mouths the poet placed these ethical memories" (ix). Haupt concluded that "Der Winsbecke" was a poetic pseudonym ("Dichtername") (x) for a knight from Bavaria or perhaps Franconia [Für einen baierischen oder vielleicht fränkischen ritter werden wir also den Winsbeken halten dürfen] (xii). Haupt's judgment on the question of authorship became a commonplace of scholarship. The debate on these questions had, as we shall see, ended for the next one hundred and forty years.

Haupt had concluded that the name, Winsbecke, was a fiction, but that the untraceable author, like the narrator, was authentically a knight. This enabling assumption struck middle ground between Goldast's imaginary reconstruction of a life from what seemed to him a named, autobiographical text, and Bodmer/von der Hagen's suggestion of complete fictionality. It had far-reaching consequences for Haupt's goal of reconstructing the original text because it established the social and political profile of the author that was to guide Haupt's editorial choices for *Der Winsbecke.* The problem for Haupt was that the intervention of the son and the father's subsequent embrace of a spiritual life (stanzas 57–80 in the standard edition) seemed to make implausible the conclusion that a knight was the original author, yet his three best manuscripts all contained the, to him, implausible strophes. Haupt chose a twofold solution. He remained true to the manuscripts by publishing all the strophes in his edition, and he remained true to his goal of establishing a text that reconstructed what he believed to be the original by dividing the poem into two parts with different titles.[12] Thus were born *The Old Poem* [Das alte Gedicht], which contains the first fifty-six stanzas in which the father advises about good conduct in the temporal world, followed by *The Continuations* [Die Fortsetzungen], stanzas 57 through 80, in which the son intervenes and the father subsequently advocates a religious life. *The Old Poem,* Haupt argued, had been authored by a knight; *The Continuations,* by a cleric.

Haupt followed his predecessors by publishing full texts of the poems as they appeared in the manuscript transmission, but his edition introduced a hierarchical rupture to the *Der Winsbecke* based on notions of authentic authorship. Haupt drew on stylistic and thematic evidence to uphold his assessment that *Der Winsbecke,* as his best manuscripts presented it to him, was in fact a composite work written by different authors at different times. His summary judgment of *The Continuations* was wholly negative: "I can see in them only a pious but foolish appendix" [ich kann in ihnen nur einen frommen aber albernen anhang erblicken] (viii). It is the relationship of the later stanzas to the father's opening verses that particularly vexes him.

> *The Continuations* do not amplify the wisdom of the father's advice nor do they give the father's advice a new spin or refute it.

> Rather they suddenly destroy the previous fifty-six strophes, which are coherent in and of themselves. I see in this the work of a cleric or a clerically minded man who wishes to outbid the elder's courtly teachings with the son's pious warning. (1845, viii–ix)[13]

For Haupt, the plausibility of his notion of thirteenth-century knighthood is at stake: it was simply unbelievable that this poet, shown to be a "reasonable" [verständiger] (ix) knight by the first part of the poem, would embrace so quickly a pious outlook that, to Haupt, destroyed his first teachings about living virtuously in the world. Therefore, "Der Winsbecke" or "The Knight from Winsbecke" could be the author of *The Old Poem* only. Haupt's introduction suggested that while he did not posit the absolute identity of "The Knight from Winsbecke" and the narrator of *The Old Poem,* the narrator's beliefs mirrored the author's beliefs closely. *The Old Poem* was deemed original and, therefore, authentic, because of the coherence of the worldly ethos expressed by the father, while the son's reply and the father's elaboration of the value of a retreat from worldly life (*The Continuations*) appeared contradictory and implausible and were judged to be an accretion to the original poem that attempted to compete with and revise it.

Haupt, who had been elected to Carl Lachmann's professorship upon the latter's death in 1853, belonged to the second generation of German philologists. They saw it as their mission to preserve the legacy of the founding fathers, Lachmann and the brothers Jacob and Wilhelm Grimm, by professionalizing and institutionalizing the study of Germanic philology. In this context, Haupt's rejection of von der Hagen's argument that *Der Winsbecke* is fiction and his editorial intervention creating a single, aristocratic, paternal voice represents a larger ideological struggle to distance the field of Germanic philology from its romantic roots.

Until 1985, when Hans-Joachim Behr published an article arguing vigorously against the traditional division of *Der Winsbecke* into two separately authored and discontinuous parts, Haupt's assessment of the evidence and his division of the poem was a fixture of scholarship. Albert Leitzmann's second edition of the poem (in 1888) kept the division into *The Old Poem* and *The Continuations.*[14] Leitzmann's introduction (which was largely reprinted in his 1928 revision of the second edition) deals at length with the problems of authorship and authenticity, positing three separate authors for *Der Winsbecke,* corresponding to three narrative shifts (1888, 8; 1928, xxi). He agrees with Haupt's division of the poem, arguing for it with a rhetorical question: "What purpose would have been served by the entire, far-ranging education in chivalrous morals if the poet's goal had been to devalue and negate it?" (1888, 8; 1928, xxi).[15] Yet questions of authorship and authenticity remain at the heart of Leitzmann's interpretation. Probably the most interesting point in the introduction comes after Leitzmann's disagreement with Haupt over which of the several "von Windesbach" from the documentary record might be the poet (1888, 10; 1928, xxii–xxiii). Haupt did not explicitly argue that the poet and the narrator were one, but Leitzmann does so. For him, the autobiographical content of *The Old Poem* is manifest. "I argue that the father in the poem is to be identified with the poet, and I believe that treating these precepts as instructions to a son does not owe its existence merely to old, traditional techniques, but to the fact that the poet really did have a son to whom he directed this poem or who was in his thoughts as he worked on the poem" (1888, 10–11; 1928, xxiii).[16] To support this conviction, Leitzmann appealed to what was, for him, the emotional immediacy of *The Old Poem:* "This assumption is made plausible by the expressions of feeling that arise anew again and again in diverse variations" (1888, 11; 1928, xxiii–xxiv).[17] Because such a judgment could not, as Leitzmann well recognized, be substantiated through the surviving evidence, he invited the reader to similarly overcome the gap in the historical record by turning instead to the "higher truth" of a spontaneous, sympathetic response. "Therefore I must appeal to the impression made by the work and to the reader's unbiased judgment" (1888, 11n. 1; 1928, xxivn. 1).[18] I will return to this point later.

In much scholarship of the nineteenth and twentieth centuries, *Der Winsbecke* meant *The Old Poem* only, which was usually discussed as if it were a freestanding text. References, if any, to *The Continuations* and *Die Winsbeckin* were dismissive. The presumed unity of author, message, and narrator in *The Old Poem* was maintained for decades in the face of conflicting evidence from the manuscript material and from within the textual complex itself. The belief in the reality of the author was so firm that "Der Winsbecke" was given a biographical entry, written by Leitzmann, in the first edition of the compendious biographical encyclopedia, the *Allgemeine deutsche Biographie,* a valuable scholarly resource begun in the late nineteenth century (1898). In the most influential literary history of the nineteenth century, Georg Gottfried Gervinus praises the moral and ethical ideals he finds embodied in *The Old Poem; The Continuations* and *Die Winsbeckin* are not mentioned (1853, 426–28).[19] Gervinus does not appear to distinguish between author and narrator, and such positions were repeated well into the post–World War II era. As late as 1969 Alfred Mundhenk could write: "I see no reason to doubt that a settled and aged knight really is speaking here, a knight who has been forced against his temperament and his will to lead a withdrawn life, but in whom the ethos of his estate lives on unbroken" (270).[20]

Influential literary histories from the twentieth century distanced themselves from the assumption that author and narrator in *The Old Poem* were identical without, however, directly challenging it. Gustav Ehrismann's literary history did not address the question of the identity of author and narrator, but summarized the arguments in favor of viewing the poem as the work of more than one poet. Since evidence is lacking, such arguments must be made not on the basis of style but on the basis of psychology: "It is vulgar when the youth suggests to his father that he, once so agile, has now become old and weary" [Es ist geschmacklos, wenn der Junge dem Vater Vorstellungen macht, daß der einst so Behende nun alt und müde geworden ist] (1934, 312–14, here 313).[21] Helmut de Boor's postwar literary history (1953, 408–9) concurred with Ehrismann's assessment, noting that the father's lament in *The Continuations* "is a slap in the face of the elevated ethics of *The Old Poem*" (409). De Boor viewed the presumed identity of author and narrator as a kind of fantasy modern readers should be allowed to indulge: "It is a pretty and not forbidden notion that the poet truly wrote his little work for his own son"(408).[22] Finally, Ingo Reiffenstein's third edition of the *Winsbecke* poems in 1962 presents the complex manuscript evidence in a manner that makes transparent the many differences between the edition and the manuscript transmission. However, it retains Haupt's by now canonical divisions without explanation, since the introduction does not touch, in any form, on the evidence, the debates, or the historiography regarding authorship and authenticity in the *Winsbecke* poems. The edition seems to reserve judgment without challenging received opinion.[23]

Since the 1980s scholars have moved away from the autobiographical view of the poem. Behr's article (1985) has been mentioned.[24] Ursula Schulze upholds the authenticity of "Der Winsbecke" as the author's name without claiming authenticity: "Der Winsbecke (perhaps a lord from Windesbach in Eastern Franconia), [is] an author represented in the Manesse manuscript with a text and an image" (1988, 476).[25] Winfried Frey implies that the rhetorical structure and techniques employed in *The Old Poem* suggest a clerical author (1984). Very recently Joachim Bumke has cast doubts on the entire claim: "Whether Winsbeke is really the name of a poet, whether the poet was named after the small Franconian city of Windsbach or perhaps a member of the noble family von Windesbach—all of this is entirely uncertain" (1990, 333).[26]

And what about *Die Winsbeckin?* Scholarly opinion from the nineteenth century to the present regarding *Die Winsbeckin* has been relatively uniform. When discussed at all, it was quickly dismissed as an inferior work. It is not mentioned by Gervinus. In Haupt's opinion, *Die Winsbeckin* "is much weaker, chattier, poorer in its thoughts" [ist viel schwächer, redseliger, ärmer an gedanken] (Haupt 1845, xiii); according to Leitzmann, *Die Winsbeckin* represents an "imitation" [nachahmung] of *Der Winsbecke* and suffers from "poverty of thought" [gedankenarmut] and "repetitiveness" [wiederholung] (Leitzmann 1888, 7; 1928, xx). De Boor characterizes *Die Winsbeckin* as "superficial and flat, directed more towards formal training than towards the development of character" (1953, 409).[27] Only recently has critical interest in *Die Winsbeckin* awakened. In 1986 Trude Ehlert's pioneering article argued that the female characters in the poem are drawn from a patriarchal perspective that viewed women exclusively in terms of their instrumental function as an object of male desire. This argument focuses on the mother's conformity to patriarchal expectations. My recent work on the poem argues that the daughter's voice bears witness to the contradictions and resistances that pressed upon patriarchal discourse about women (1997, 138).

But one might well ask: given the postulated identity of male author and male narrator in *The Old Poem,* why could a woman not have authored the female-voiced verses, *Die Winsbeckin?* Why does the paradigm of a coherent and "reasonable" [verständiger] author/narrator apply to *The Old Poem* but not to *Die Winsbeckin?* In their introductions, Haupt and Leitzmann do not even entertain the idea of female authorship for this female-voiced text. Was such a notion deemed too improbable or too scurrilous for words? According to Harms, early modern writers did not deem female authorship an impossible proposition.

Christoph Gryphius's play from 1690 includes characters from around the year 1200, among them Knight Winsbecke, who obligingly recites two verses from *Die Winsbeckin,* which he says were written by his learned wife, whose absence he excuses by remarking: "My wife knows full well the demands of honor and virtue, and she is now busy at home instructing our children and composing poems full of advice" (Harms 1986, 52).[28] In fact, our knowledge of secular medieval German literature, for which no women writers are named until the fifteenth century, makes female authorship unlikely. From Haupt and Leitzmann to the present, the scholarly consensus has been that the name "Die Winsbeckin" was an editorial or scribal attribution that was created to reflect the sex of the female speaker and to make apparent the poem's thematic and formal parallels to *Der Winsbecke.* As Ursula Schulze succinctly put it: "An anonymous author composed a female counterpart to the father-son-instruction" [Zu der Vater-Sohn-Belehrung hat ein unbekannter Autor ein weibliches Pendant verfaßt] (Schulze 1988, 478).

The vital question is not "Was *Die Winsbeckin* (or for that matter *Der Winsbecke*) written by a woman" but rather "If *Die Winsbeckin's* title came from a compiler, if its author was anonymous, and its female narrator a fiction, why could the same not be true of *Der Winsbecke?*" For if one stops thinking of *Die Winsbeckin's* circumstances of origin and transmission as the exception and instead thinks of them as the rule, then its evidence powerfully confronts the notions of authorship and authenticity undergirding scholarly evaluations of *The Old Poem.* To put it another way: viewed from the perspective of *Die Winsbeckin,* the unitary category of an authentic narrator-author imbued with a powerful, lived connection to an ideal of right conduct falls apart.

Although *Der Winsbecke* and *Die Winsbeckin* have been excerpted, reproduced, edited, and debated together since 1609, professional philologists from the nineteenth century onward apparently overlooked the challenge posed by *Die Winsbeckin* to their notions of the origins of *Der Winsbecke* and the notions of an authentic and authenticating unity of name, author, and voice it so powerfully underwrote. Side by side, *The Old Poem* was held to represent a felicitous historical voice, *The Continuations* a dubious, clerically inspired, invented attack, and *Die Winsbeckin* a muddled, obscure, derivative fiction. In *The Old Poem* a historically authenticated, knightly voice was held to speak truths about medieval chivalry; the other texts are merely belated and second-rate medieval embellishments on its themes.

The collapsing of the categories of author and narrator in *Der Winsbecke* and the claims for its privileged proximity to medieval reality can be maintained only by severing and discounting parts integral to the codicological material, *The Continuations* and *Die Winsbeckin*. Why, in the face of such incontrovertible codicological evidence and in the absence of convincing corroborating evidence for the attribution in the *Codex Manesse,* have these notions taken such a long time to die? In creating *The Old Poem,* Haupt underwrote an idealized and idealizing construction of the ethics of medieval noblemen, more specifically, of aristocratic medieval fathers, in short, of medieval patriarchy. By viewing *The Old Poem* as nonfictional speech, Leitzmann and others could interpret the moral standards promulgated in it as evidence for aristocratic ethics in action rather than as a representation of the fashioning of aristocratic values that may not even have been created by an aristocrat.

Yet it is a particular reading of the father figure in *Der Winsbecke* that inspired these nineteenth- and twentieth-century scholars, or, more specifically, it is the trope of the father instructing his son in how to live a virtuous life in the secular world. The evidence from the preceding section makes clear that for these scholars the father's authority in the first part of the poem is invested with unique importance. They construct paternal authority as a feature of the text that has produced a psychologically realistic and coherent portrayal of medieval aristocratic fatherhood, one that is deemed valuable aesthetically and morally for both the past and the present, and, most significantly, one that can function as a criterion for judging all the *Winsbecke* poems editorially and evaluating them interpretively. On these grounds the son's intervention and the poem's new direction is judged to be implausible or vulgar or destructive or insubordinate, embodying the wrong attitude toward paternal, secular authority, which apparently instead should have been affirmed in a spirit of respect and deference.

The primacy of *The Old Poem* in the complex of *Winsbecke* poems and the nineteenth-century creation of *The Old Poem* as a separate and unique text flow directly from this ethos of paternal authority, which may well have resonated strongly with patriarchal norms of domesticity and male honor in the emerging bourgeois and professional classes of nineteenth-century Germany. Scholars since Gervinus and Haupt read the figure of the father as the mouthpiece for an idealized notion of benevolent, paternal rule that upheld the social order by creating and maintaining an orderly household. This point is well illustrated by a passage from Gervinus's scholarly portrait of the father in *The Old Poem* from 1853, which is cited as authoritative in Leitzmann's second edition (1888, 11; 1928, xxiv). The example from Gervinus also provides a further example of the strongly affective quality that reoccurs in scholarship on *The Old Poem*.

> The honorable old man speaks, one who has closed the books on his life and now turns all his delight and hope towards his son to whom he—with heartfelt intimacy, with noble humility—now entrusts the safekeeping of his household's honor after it has been in his own custody, holding before his son the experiences and the model of his own life and with no care except that his heir not fare poorly on earth or in heaven, his sole wish that his name and the honor of his name be preserved in his son. (1853, 426)[29]

For Gervinus, the father figure in *The Old Poem* is a wise and virtuous man. He describes the father with earnest, heartfelt reverence, in tones of deferential sentimentality not uncommon in earlier scholarship on *The Old Poem*. As discussed previously, Leitzmann's introductions note that he was similarly moved by *The Old Poem* and the ideal of paternal love he found embodied in it. For this modern reader, *The Old Poem* seems sententious and arid, characterized by a dearth of emotion rather than by a plenitude of it; Leitzmann, Mundhenk, and others found in *The Old Poem* an authentic and personal emotional immediacy, and Leitzmann at least constructed in his introduction a sympathetic and responsive reader who found this sentimental connection equally accessible and compelling. *The Old Poem* was a felicitous text for producing and legitimizing shared fantasies of the benevolent patriarchal father. The respectful, almost devout tone of most scholarship on *The Old Poem* (which rehearses the entire poem's sober tone), coupled with the muted indignation directed toward *The Continuations*, prompts speculation: perhaps scholarship spoke so reverentially about *The Old Poem* and invested it with such pathos because it could mirror idealized and socially legitimated male self-fashionings as benevolent patriarchs; or perhaps it did so because the values of *The Old Poem* placed medievalists in the position of good sons diligently following "Father" Winsbecke's teachings, "safeguarding the household honor" and "preserving the good name" of the new field of philological studies.

To restate the obvious: the professional and political world in which scholars such as Gervinus, Haupt, and Leitzmann acted was overwhelmingly male. Their scholarship on the *Winsbecke* poems can also be viewed as an attempt to construct a particular kind of continuity between generations of male scholars.[30] Continuity between father and son in the world is the father's theme in *The Old Poem* (and indeed, though overlooked by these scholars, continuity between father and son is reestablished at the end of *Der Winsbecke,* when the father joins his son in affirming the superior worth of the spiritual life). Lack of continuity is the reoccurring theme in the scholarly justifications for severing *The Old Poem* from *The Continuations,* for the kind of continuity offered by *Der Winsbecke* does not uphold the secular paternal authority they seek to validate. That continuity can be found rather in their own scholarship, which establishes a normative mode of philological research that is respectful and deferential toward what it constructs as legitimate authority past and present.

The enabling assumption that *The Old Poem* articulates both the lived experience of medieval noblemen (and especially that of the author) and the exemplary values of medieval, aristocratic patriarchy created continuity between past and present—the present found its norms and conventions mirrored and affirmed by the past. Philology, in the guise of the editions by Haupt and others, did ideological work; it realized a fantasy of benevolent paternal rule and honorable male domesticity coinciding with and bolstering one another in the objective, textual form of *The Old Poem.*[31] Problems were seen as discontinuities and were literally excluded, as *The Continuations,* from the text or, in the case of *Die Winsbeckin,* discounted. It is perhaps not surprising that the trope of the mother-daughter instructional dialogue did not resonate in this world, that the humor of *Die Winsbeckin* was overlooked, was unreadable. For the irreverant *Die Winsbeckin* might contest the solemnity of *Der Wins-*

becke, a solemnity endorsed by scholars as a measure of the positive value of medieval didactic literature.

The field of medieval studies has moved far away from positions based on the assumption that there is a simple and transparent relationship between medieval literature and the world in which and for which it was produced. Yet the legacies of older scholarly practices live on. I continue, for the sake of preserving continuity and intelligibility in intellectual debates across time, to refer to the poems discussed here as *Der Winsbecke* and *Die Winsbeckin.* In the field of medieval German studies, some works are still only available in nineteenth-century editions, for example, the late thirteenth-century epic poet Der Pleier or the fourteenth-century author Suchenwirt. Even new and reliable editions such as the third edition of the *Winsbecke* poems are built on the foundations of the indispensible and formidable philological labor of scholars such as Haupt and Leitzmann and—more irksome for us—on those same scholars' belief in the existence of singular and unique, authorially sanctioned works and their ultimate retrievability and reconstructability.[32] As simple notions of medieval authorship are jettisoned and as the search continues for methodological frameworks that can usefully articulate the irreducible complexity and equivocality of medieval textual evidence and medieval literary traditions, it seems useful to ask what else might have been overlooked in the construction of a category of didactic literature. What hints can a text such as *Die Winsbeckin* provide us in this matter? Are there other enabling assumptions it might profitably challenge?

New directions for further research are suggested by the work of Sarah Westphal, who uses the methods of codicology to deploy new interpretive strategies that analyze the compilation practices of medieval manuscripts as bearing witness to the act of interpretion in the medieval reception process (1993). We might profitably reexamine the manuscript contexts within which these texts are transmitted, for while the *Codex Manesse* and the *Weingartner Liederhandschrift* (both large and diverse collections of courtly poetry) seem a logical setting for the *Winsbecke* poems, some of the other text assemblages seem unusual. In Berlin mgf 474, for example, the *Winsbecke* poems are preceded by the heroic epic, the *Nibelungenlied.* In other manuscripts and manuscript fragments, only selected stanzas, and often very few, appear. The manuscript transmission of this text is diverse, raising interesting questions about the roles played by didactic literature in the medieval tradition.

Westphal argues strongly for abandoning the modern critical lens that views the single text as a "literary monad . . . a self-sufficient unit of literary meaning"; she demonstrates in her book, which treats late medieval rhymed couplet texts, that "the most ubiquitous feature of couplet text codicology . . . is the dyad, or pointed juxtaposition of two couplet poems" (1993, 12). Does the textual dyad sometimes feature in compilation practices for other genres as well? We might test this hypothesis on the *Winsbecke* poems, for though *Die Winsbeckin* and *Der Winsbecke* are not rhymed couplet texts, they are transmitted as a textual dyad in the three chief manuscript witnesses. Some other manuscripts appear to contain only *Der Winsbecke,* but the entire manuscript tradition, which contains a number of fragmentary remains, bears reexamination in light of this question. To what extent, then, are the two texts linked together in the medieval reception process? How might we explain the decoupling of *Die Winsbeckin* and *Der Winsbecke* in the fifteenth-century *Kolmarer Liederhandschrift* (Munich, Bayerische Staatsbibliothek, cgm 4997)? If we view such fragmenting of textual groupings as another medieval reception practice that would reward further study, we might also wish to reconsider the two unique stanzas that open *Die Winsbeckin* in Berlin mgf 474, which are written from a collective female perspective: "We women wish, if it could be . . ." [wir frauwen wolten, moht ez sin].

It may also prove profitable to take the notion of the textual dyad, the productive linkage of contrasting texts, and move beyond its use in understanding the medieval reception of its literary heritage to using it as a heuristic device for discussing other points of productive, contrastive linkage between texts. The most salient feature of the *Winsbecke* poems that springs to mind in this regard is the formal difference between the two: *Der Winsbecke* is a monologue, while *Die Winsbeckin* is a dialogue. This fact has often been remarked upon in previous scholarship but never analyzed. Yet these differing communicative strategies are surely worth exploring for they suggest that as a textual dyad, *Die Winsbeckin* and *Der Winsbecke* set notions of right conduct and authority into contrastive play with one another.

With the exception of the son's six stanzas (out of eighty), *Der Winsbecke* is a monologue spoken by the father. It is interesting that earlier scholars were blind to a crucial point about the rhetorical representation of the father's authority in *Der Winsbecke*. Although the poem's message changes because of the son's intervention, that new message is proclaimed by the father. The son's brief rebuke and decisive intervention do not undermine paternal control; the father immediately affirms and elaborates the son's conviction of the superiority of the spiritual life. In other words, the son's beliefs are legitimated by means of the paternal voice. The structure of the poem as a monologue is challenged, but ultimately sustained. Because the father's voice dominates the poem, a structural link between authority and monologue is maintained as a communicative strategy: the authoritative voice is authoritative because it can and does hold forth without interruption. The best medieval analogy for this rhetorical pattern is the sermon, a fact often noticed in *Winsbecke* scholarship. Like much medieval German advice literature, *Der Winsbecke* represents binding, authoritative instruction through a univocal, male-voiced recitation of received truths. The *Winsbecke* parody upholds this structural pattern as well, for it imitates the authoritative paternal voice, which, however, systematically inverts all the moral teachings in *Der Winsbecke*.

Die Winsbeckin employs an entirely different communicative strategy: dialogue. In numerical terms, the mother's voice is slightly dominant: based on the standard edition, she speaks twenty-five stanzas versus twenty stanzas for the daughter. Nevertheless, the mother and daughter speak and respond to one another, each representing a different point of view on courtly love. Their voices, though distinct from one another, are completely intertwined.

I have argued elsewhere that the use of dialogue in *Die Winsbeckin* contributes significantly to the ways in which maternal authority is constructed differently from paternal authority in the *Winsbecke* poems, being represented as more fragile, contradictory, and self-divided (Rasmussen 1997, 152–59). What is significant for this essay is that the dialogue structure of *Die Winsbeckin* makes it closely resemble debate or dispute literature.[33] The rhetorical form of the dispute has deep roots in the structures of the medieval university and in medieval clerical culture. It found written expression not just in the "sic et non" of learned medieval treatises composed in Latin, but also in a wide variety of vernacular texts. Through the use of dialogue (which also brings to mind the question-and-answer format of master-student texts such as *Lucidarius*), *Die Winsbeckin* suggests the didactic model of an evolving, instructional dialogue that emerges in response to a different perspective on the truth rather than an ethos of authority that is premised on a monovocal recitation of received truths. The daughter is neither a passive recipient of her mother's teachings, nor is her role limited to making a single, decisive interruption. Instead, the daughter asks questions, suggests topics, redirects the conversation, challenges her mother, and expresses respect and love, as well as indignation, anger, and fear. The poem's wit and humor grow out of these exchanges, and the daughter's changing emotions provide the mother with opportunities to expand on and clarify her teachings.

Like debate literature, *Die Winsbeckin* can deflect the reader's attention from the product—an ultimate, authoritative meaning—to the rhetorical processes through which shared meaning is created. It can leave open the ultimate or decisive meaning of a text, though this would be an unusual move in a medieval text. *Die Winsbeckin* moves in this direction. Though the poem closes with three rules of courtly love set forth authoritatively by the mother, the daughter's hesitations and objections are never fully answered but rather are set aside "in favor of a mother-daughter alliance based on aristocratic solidarity" (Rasmussen 1997, 159). Further, in comparison with monovocal advice literature, debate poems can better enact or dramatize qualities of mind (mental agility, obstinancy, cognitive flexibility, curiosity, rigidity), a potential activated in *Die Winsbeckin* in order to characterize the speakers more fully.

The transmission of *Die Winsbeckin* and *Der Winsbecke* as a textual dyad in the earliest manuscripts suggests the manuscripts set these two genre-based horizons of conduct literature, monovocal advice literature and debate literature, in productive debate with one another. Viewing them in this light can open up new configurations of interpretation: what if the mother talks to the son, the daughter to the father? The late medieval parody can be seen as another voice in this debate. Further, the contrastive play of the communicative strategies in the *Winsbecke* poems could suggest ways of opening up and complicating representations of gender and authority in conduct literature as a whole, offering a promising venue for further research. And what might it mean for scholarship to look at conduct literature as being fundamentally about debate and not a monologue of received truths? What might be made visible if we were to shift the focus of scholarly thinking from the ethical meanings represented in conduct literature to the processes of creating meaning that it harnesses and represents? Such a paradigm might counteract the tendency toward the overdetermination of paternal authority in scholarship devoted to conduct literature that has been traced out in this essay. Perhaps scholarship on medieval German literature could at last put the paternal authority of *Der Winsbecke* back in the text, where it belongs.

NOTES

1. All belles lettres should instruct, but obliquely, drawing attention to that which is worth learning. The moral of the story one must deduce for oneself, just as in life.

2. *Der Wälsche Gast,* which survives in over a dozen richly illuminated manuscripts, is currently being studied by scholars interested in the interplay of visual, oral, and literary rhetorics (Wenzel 1995). A translation into English is planned.

3. See also Sheila Delany's article (1987), which explores the ambiguities that arise when scholars use the trope of thinking back through mothers in unquestioning, ahistorical ways to construct a history of great foremothers.

4. The preceding paragraphs do not argue that Germanists have neglected the history of their discipline, but rather note how long nineteenth-century categories of thought and methods of inquiry have been influential in the study of German literature. A milestone for the writing of the history of medieval German studies is Hermann Paul's book-length essay on the history of Germanic philology, published in 1901, which surveys German, Dutch, and Scandinavian scholarship in the field of Germanic philology (understood broadly as the study of medieval Germanic languages and literatures) from the sixteenth century to his own times.

Jeffrey Peck's interesting article on nineteenth-century German nationalism and medieval studies is an unreliable source of information on the formation of the field of Germanistik (1996). For an English language overview see Regina Bendix, *In Search of Authenticity,* especially chapters 1 and 2 (1997, 27–67). Ursula Peters (1984) provides a brief, cogent, historical overview of trends in medieval scholarship. Jürgen Fohrmann's work attends in detail to the intellectual history of *Germanistik* (1989; Fohrmann and Vosskamp 1994). On Carl Lachmann, see Weigel (1989). On the editorial methods devised by the brothers Grimm and Lachmann, see Lutz-Hensel (1975). For a provocative study of the origins of the study of German (and Germanic) languages and literatures see Ulrich Wyss's *Die wilde Philologie: Jacob Grimm und der Historismus* (1979).

5. The standard edition is Leitzmann (1962). This edition contains two late medieval manuscript fragments (one fourteenth century, one possibly early fifteenth century) that preserve portions of a *Winsbecke* parody, in which the father instructs the son in such vices as drinking, gaming, and lying. See Wernfried Hofmeister (1991).

6. Again see Bendix's comparative monograph on the origins of folklore studies in America and Germany, which provides an excellent discussion of the historical and cultural notions of authenticity at work in folklore studies and medieval studies (1997).

7. Gîtikeit, luoder und unkiusche, / Muotwille und unzimlich getiusche / Habent manige herren alsô besezzen, / Daz si der wîse gar hânt vergezzen / In der hie vor edel herren sungen: / Von Botenloube und von Môrungen. / Von Limburc und von Windesbecke, / Von Nîfen, Wildonie und von Brûnecke, / Her Walther von der Vogelweide: / Swer des vergêze der tête mir leide.

8. Berlin mgf 474 titles *Der Winsbecke* "This book is called valuable counsel" [Ditze buch heizzet der wertlich rat] and *Die Winsbeckin* "Here a mother counsels her daughter" [Hie ratet ein muter irre tohter]. The *Weingartner Liederhandschrift* leaves both poems untitled. Later manuscripts use various titles. Two fifteenth-century manuscripts attribute the poem to thirteenth-century poets. The *Kolmarer Liederhandschrift* (Munich, Bayerische Staatsbibliothek., cgm 4997) attributes the melody to "The virtuous Scribe" [In der grüßwyse dez tugenthafften schrybers]. This poet is represented in the *Codex Manesse* (but not with our texts), and he also appears as a fictional character in *Der Sängerkrieg auf dem Wartburg* [The war of the poets at Castle Wartburg], an anonymous work probably written in the middle of the thirteenth century. Rome, Bibl. Apost. Vaticana, Rossiano 708, attributes the stanzas it records to the famous poet known as Frauenlob (Heinrich von Meißen, c. 1250–1318): "This is Frauenlob's poem on teaching children common sense and wisdom" [Dit ist frawenlabis gedichte wie man synne und wisheit leren sal dy kynder]. Frauenlob also appears in the *Codex Manesse,* but not with the *Winsbecke* poems.

9. The hypothesis that the author of *Der Winsbecke* was one Knight Winsbecke was reasonable enough, considering that authorship is the principal category of organization in the Codex Manesse and that the manuscript also makes an attempt to order the authors hierarchically, beginning with emperors and kings. However, Goldast also collapsed the categories of author and narrator, holding that Knight Winsbecke was also the father who spoke in the poem.

10. While this view has long since been discarded, *Der Winsbecke* and *Die Winsbeckin* contain allusions and references to Wolfram's works, which is quite common in thirteenth-century German literature (Leitzmann 1889).

11. One of the first two professors of medieval German literature in German-speaking lands, Friedrich Heinrich von der Hagen (1780–1856) began lecturing on Germanic philology in Berlin in 1810. An enthusiast and popularizer who published prodigiously, von der Hagen fell professionally afoul of Jacob and Wilhelm Grimm and Carl Lachmann because his research, and in particular his methods of text editing, lacked a coherent methodology and thus were deemed unsystematic and unscholarly (see Weimar 1989, 224–45). Von der Hagen eschewed the kind of critical text editing that Lachmann and the brothers Grimm were devising (on which see Lutz-Hensel, 1975). His many publications of medieval German texts sometimes resembled what we call diplomatic transcriptions (with editorial interventions such as rearranging the order of texts for a pleasing effect), sometimes "gentle" modernizations that produced a kind of hybrid text between original and translation. Needless to say, such approaches pleased none of his more methodologically conscious colleagues. On von der Hagen, see the standard reference work, *Allgemeine deutsche Biographie,* as well as Grunewald (1988).

Moriz Haupt (1808–1874) was a prolific scholar who founded the most prestigious scholarly journal of medieval German studies, *Zeitschrift für deutsches Altertum,* and produced, among other works, *Minnesangs Frühling*, the first scholarly edition of German courtly love poetry. He, too, took a dim view of von der Hagen's scholarship.

12. This division is not without a late medieval precedent. A single, fifteenth-century compilation manuscript, the *Kolmarer Liederhandschrift* (Munich, Bayerische Staatsbibliothek, cgm 4997) splits *Der Winsbecke* into two parts separated by about eighty folios. The second poem begins, as Haupt's edition does, with stanzas 57–64, the stanzas spoken by the son. It then repeats a number of the father's stanzas from the first part of the poem. Eight stanzas from *Die Winsbeckin* precede the second *Winsbecke* poem by three folios.

13. [S]ie steigern nicht etwa die lebensweisheit der väterlichen lehren oder geben ihnen andere wendung oder widerlegen sie, sondern sie machen plötzlich die vorhergehenden sechsundfünfzig in sich abgeschlossenen strophen vollkommen zu nichte. ich sehe hier einen geistlichen oder geistlich gesinnten mann, der die ritterlichen lehren des alten durch des sohnes fromme ermahnung überbieten will.

14. Behr refutes arguments for splitting *Der Winsbecke* into *The Old Poem* and *The Continuations* based on stylistic criteria and codicological evidence; he does not ask why older scholarship embraced Haupt's division. Leitzmann's 1888 version revisited questions of grammar and word forms in the text based on a comparative analysis of the manuscripts, of which a few more fragments had been found since 1845.

The second and third editions include the previously unpublished fragments of another father-son didactic poem from the *Codex Manesse, Tyrol und Fridebrant*. These names refer to "King Tyrol from Scotland and his son" (the title from the *Codex Manesse*), characters from a now lost epic poem. Nineteenth-century scholarship had no difficulty recognizing the fictive nature of this "author."

Leitzmann maintains the overall structure of Haupt's edition, including the number of strophes, but he uses Berlin mgf 474 as his chief manuscript (a choice followed in the third edition as well), and so there are many changes in the text itself.

15. Denn was hätte die ganze weitläufige unterweisung in ritterlicher moral für einen zweck, wenn das ziel des dichters gewesen wäre, sie hinterher zu entwerten und zu negieren?

16. Ich halte dafür, dass wir den vater im gedicht mit dem dichter zu identifizieren haben, und glaube, dass auch die behandlung der lehre als unterweisung eines sohnes nicht bloss altüberkommener technik ihr dasein verdankt, sondern dass der dichter tatsächlich einen sohn hatte, an den er das gedicht richtete oder an den er bei ausarbeitung des werkes besonders dachte.

17. Diese annahme wird mir wahrscheinlich durch den immer von neuem und in mannigfachen variationen hervorquellenden unmittelbaren ausdruck des gefühls.

18. [I]ch muss daher an den eindruck des werkes und an das unbefangene urteil des lesers appellieren.

19. The same is true for the third edition of Wilhelm Scherer's history of German literature, which was only available to me in an English translation. Scherer uses *Der Winsbecke* to introduce a discussion of the "moral character of German chivalry" (Scherer 1899, 212–13). Leitzmann points out that *Der Winsbecke* was often used in secondary school teaching, names four such editions from 1887, 1889, 1900, and 1902 (1928, xxvi; I have not been able to locate them), and notes the formative effect medieval conduct literature

had on him: "I learned middle high German from Winsbecke, Thomasin, and Freidank [Winsbecke is named as an author, not a title; my note] and I made them so much my own that I knew long passages by heart, which continues to be an advantage to me even today" [An Winsbecke, Thomasin und Freidank habe ich eigentlich mittelhochdeutsch gelernt und sie mir so zu eigen gemacht, dass ich sie auf weite strecken hin auswendig wusste, was mir noch heute von vorteil ist] (vi).

20. Ich sehen keinen Grund zu zweifeln, dass hier wirklich ein sesshaft und alt gewordener Ritter spricht, der wider Temperament und Willen genötigt ist, ein zurückgezogenes Lebens (sic) zu führen, in dem aber das Ethos seines Standes noch ungebrochen lebt.

21. Ehrismann notes the similarity in the rhetorical structure of the complete *Der Winsbecke* as it appears in the manuscripts with the "reprobatio" in Andreas Cappellanus, *The Art of Courtly Love* (313, n. 1).

22. Die schlägt der hochgemuten Ethik des alten Gedichtes ins Gesicht. Es ist eine hübsche und nicht unerlaubte Vorstellung, daß der Dichter sein kleines Werk wirklich für seinen eigenen Sohn verfaßt hat.

23. Boesch follows the tradition of viewing *The Old Poem* and *The Continuations* as individual poems. He treats *Die Winsbeckin* separately (1977, 43–48, 107–8). *The Old Poem* is discussed over four pages; *Die Winsbeckin* in two sentences. Sowinski's book, a very brief introductory survey, describes the texts in one paragraph (1971, 81). See also Wolfgang Heinemann's essay on *Lehrdichtung* in the monumental East German history of German literature (1990).

24. There has been dissent from Behr's conclusion that *Der Winsbecke* is one long poem. Hofmeister argues that there are enough formal criteria to justify the "self-sufficiency" of *The Continuations:* "even if we were to presume that there is only one poet, we would still have to speak of two acts of composition" [daher hätten wir selbst im Falle einer Verfasseridentität weiterhin von zwei Dichtungsakten und damit von einer weitgehenden Eigenständigkeit der "Winsbecke-Fortsetzung" auszugehen] (1991, 1n. 5).

25. Der Winsbecke, ein in der Manessischen Handschrift mit Text und Bild vertretener Autor (vielleicht ein Herr von Windesbach in Ostfranken).

26. Ob Winsbeke ein wirklicher Dichtername ist, ob der Dichter nach dem fränkischen Städtchen Windsbach hieß oder gar ein Mitglied der adligen Familie von Windesbach war, ist alles ganz unsicher.

27. [Ä]ußerlicher, flacher, mehr auf formale Erziehung als auf Charakterbildung gerichtet.

28. Mein Weib weiß schon was Ehr und Tugend erfordert und wird sich unterdessen zu Hause mit Unterweisung unserer Kinder und Aufsetzung lehrreicher Gedichte unterhalten.

29. Es redet der ehrwürdige Alte, der die Rechnung seines Lebens abgeschlossen hat, dessen ganze Freude und Hoffnung hinfort auf den Sohn gerichtet ist, dem er, nachdem er selbst mit Ehren seines Hauses gewaltet, die Pflege desselben vertraut, mit herzlicher Innigkeit, mit edler Bescheidenheit ihm die Erfahrungen und das Beispiel seines eignen Lebens vorhaltend, und ohne fürder eine andere Sorge zu haben, als daß es seinem Erben auf Erden und im Himmel nicht missegehe, ohne einen anderen Wunsch, als daß sein Name und seines Names Ehre auch im Sohne erhalten werde.

30. The opening chapter of Wyss's book probes sensitively the dilemmas of continuity, veneration, and rejection as they inform Wilhelm Scherer's writings on his teacher, Jacob Grimm (1979, 1–22).

31. For a forceful analysis of similar trends in the scholarship on Walther von der Vogelweide, particularly scholarly constructions of the demure maiden as a feature of his poetry, see Bennewitz (1989). Clare Lees and Gillian Overing analyze the operation of similar concepts in Anglo-Saxon studies (1994).

32. For introductions to current scholarship's challenges to such positions, see Patterson (1987) and Bumke (1996).

33. Ingrid Kasten has written an excellent survey of medieval German debate poetry (1973).

BIBLIOGRAPHY

Behr, Hans-Joachim. 1985. "'Der werden lop' und 'gotes hulde': Überlegungen zur konzeptionellen Einheit des Winsbecke." *Leuvense Bijdragen* 74: 377–94.

Bendix, Regina. 1997. *In Search of Authenticity: The Formation of Folklore Studies.* Madison: University of Wisconsin Press.

Bennewitz, Ingrid. 1988. "Moraldidaktische Literatur." In *Deutsche Literatur: Eine Sozialgeschichte.* Vol. 1, *Aus der Mündlichkeit in die Schriftlichkeit: Höfische und andere Literatur 750–1320,* ed. Ursula Liebertz-Grün, 333–43. Reinbek bei Hamburg: Rowohlt.

———. 1989. "'Vrouwe/maget': Überlegungen zur Interpretation der sogenannten Mädchenlieder im Kontext von Walthers Minnesang-Konzeption." In *Walther von der Vogelweide: Beiträge zu Leben und Werk,* ed. Hans-Dieter Mück, 237–52. Kulturwissenschaftliche Bibliothek, vol. 1. Stuttgart: Stöffler & Schütz.

Bodmer, Johann Jakob. 1759. *Sammlung von minnesingern aus dem schwäbischen zeitpuncte.* Zurich.

Boesch, Bruno. 1977. *Lehrhafte Literatur: Lehre in Dichtung und Lehrdichtung im deutschen Mittelalter.* Grundlagen der Germanistik, vol. 21. Berlin: Erich Schmidt.

Bumke, Joachim. 1990. *Deutsche Literatur im Mittelalter.* Ed. Joachim Bumke, Thomas Cramer, and Dieter Kartschoke. Vol. 2, *Geschichte der deutschen Literatur im hohen Mittelalter.* Munich: Deutscher Taschenbuch Verlag.

———. 1996. *Die vier Fassungen der "Nibelungenklage": Untersuchungen zur Überlieferungsgeschichte und Textkritik der höfischen Epik im 13. Jahrhundert.* Berlin: de Gruyter.

de Boor, Helmut. 1953. *Die höfische Literatur: Vorbereitung, Blüte, Ausklang, 1170–1250.* Vol. 2 of *Geschichte der deutschen Literatur von den Anfängen bis zur Gegenwart,* ed. Helmut de Boor and Richard Newald. Munich: Beck.

Delany, Sheila. 1987. "Mothers to Think Back Through: Who Are They? The Ambiguous Example of Christine de Pizan." In *Medieval Texts and Contemporary Readers,* ed. Laurie A. Finke and Martin B. Shichtman, 177–97. Ithaca: Cornell University Press.

Ehlert, Trude. 1986. "Die Frau als Arznei: Das Bild der Frau in hochmittelalterlicher deutscher Lehrdichtung." *Zeitschrift für deutsche Philologie* 105: 42–62.

Ehrismann, Gustav, ed. 1908. *Hugo von Trimberg, Der Renner.* Bibliothek des litterarischen Vereins in Stuttgart. Tubingen, Germany: Litterarischer Verein.

———. 1934. *Geschichte der deutschen Literatur bis zum Ausgang des Mittelalters.* Vol. 2, part 2B, *Die mittelhochdeutsche Literatur.* Munich: Beck.

Fohrmann, Jürgen. 1989. *Das Projekt der deutschen Literaturgeschichte: Entstehung und Scheitern einer nationalen Poesiegeschichtsschreibung zwischen Humanismus und Deutschem Kaiserreich.* Stuttgart: Metzler.

Fohrmann, Jürgen, and Wilhelm Vosskamp, eds. 1994. *Wissenschaftsgeschichte der Germanistik im 19. Jahrhundert.* Stuttgart: Metzler.

Frey, Winfried. 1984. "'Die rede ich in dîn herze grabe': Zur Vermittlung von Herrenethik im 'Winsbecke.'" In *Philologische Untersuchungen.* Gewidmet Elfriede Stutz zum 65. Geburtstag, ed. Alfred Ebenbauer, 176–95. Philologica Germanica, vol. 7. Vienna: Wilhelm Braumüller.

Gervinus, Georg Gottfried. 1853. *Geschichte der deutschen Dichtung.* Vierte gänzlich umgearbeitete Ausgabe. Original title of work *Geschichte der poetischen National-Literatur der Deutschen.* Original work published 1835–1842. Leipzig: Wilhelm Engelmann.

Grunewald, Eckhard. 1988. *Friedrich Heinrich von der Hagen 1780–1856: Ein Beitrag zur Frühgeschichte der Germanistik.* Berlin: de Gruyter.

Hagen, Friedrich Heinrich von der. 1838. *Minnesinger: Deutsche Liederdichter des zwölften, dreizehnten, und vierzehnten Jahrhunderts.* Vol. 4, *Geschichte der Dichter und ihrer Werke.* Leipzig: Joh. Ambr. Barth.

Harms, Wolfgang. 1986. "Des Winsbeckes Genius: Zur Einschätzung didaktischer Poesie des deutschen Mittelalters im 17. und 18. Jahrhundert." In *Mittelalter-Rezeption: Ein Symposion,* ed. Peter Wapnewski, 46–59. Germanistische Symposien Berichtsbände, vol. 6. Stuttgart: Metzler.

Haupt, Moriz. 1845. *Der Winsbeke und die Winsbekin.* Leipzig: Weidmann.

Heinemann, Wolfgang. 1990. "Frühe Gesellschaftskritik und soziale Verhaltenssteuerung in der weltlich-didaktischen Literatur." In *Mitte des 12. bis Mitte des 13. Jahrhunderts.* Vol. 2 of *Geschichte der deutschen Literatur von den Anfängen bis zur Gegenwart,* ed. Kurt Böttcher and Günther Albrecht. Berlin: Volk und Wissen, 645–80.

Hofmeister, Wernfried. 1991. "Literarische Provokation im Mittelalter am Beispiel der 'Winsbecke-Parodie.'" *Sprachkunst* 22, no. 1: 1–24.

Hult, David F. 1991. "Reading It Right: The Ideology of Text Editing." In *The New Medievalism,* ed. Marina S. Brownlee, Kevin Brownlee, and Stephen G. Nichols, 113–30. Baltimore: Johns Hopkins University Press. Reprinted from *Romanic Review* 79 (1988): 74–88.

Kasten, Ingrid. 1973. "Studien zur Thematik und Form des mittelhochdeutschen Streitgedichtes." Dissertation, University of Hamburg.

Lees, Clare A., and Gillian R. Overing. 1994. "Birthing Bishops and Fathering Poets: Bede, Hild, and the Relations of Cultural Production." *Exemplaria* 6, no. 1: 35–65.

Leitzmann, Albert. 1889. "Der Winsbeke und Wolfram." *Beiträge zur Geschichte der deutschen Sprache und Literatur* 14: 149–52.

———. 1898. "Winsbecke und Winsbeckin." In *Allgemeine deutsche Biographie,* 43: 461–62. Leipzig: Duncker & Humblot.

———, ed. 1888. *König Tirol, Winsbeke und Winsbekin.* 2d ed. Altdeutsche textbibliothek, vol. 9. Halle, Germany: Niemeyer.

———. 1928. *Tirol und Fridebrant, Winsbecke, Winsbeckin.* Zweite, verbesserte, und erweiterte Auflage. In *Kleinere mittelhochdeutsche lehrgedichte.* Altdeutsche textbibliothek, vol. 9. Halle, Germany: Niemeyer.

———. 1962. *Winsbeckische Gedichte nebst Tirol und Fridebrant.* Rev. Ingo Reiffenstein. 3d ed. Altdeutsche Textbibliothek, vol. 9. Tubingen, Germany: Niemeyer.

Lutz-Hensel, Magdalene. 1975. *Prinzipien der ersten textkritischen Editionen mittelhochdeutscher Dichtung: Brüder Grimm, Benecke, Lachmann: Eine methodenkritische Analyse.* Philologische Studien und Quellen, vol. 77. Berlin: Erich Schmidt Verlag.

Mundhenk, Alfred. 1969. "Der Winsbecke oder die Erziehung des Ritters." In *Interpretationen mittelhochdeutscher Lyrik,* ed. Günther Jungbluth, 269–86. Bad Homburg, Berlin, and Zurich: Verlag Gehlen.

Patterson, Lee. 1987. *Negotiating the Past: The Historical Understanding of Medieval Literature.* Madison: University of Wisconsin Press.

Paul, Hermann. 1901. "Geschichte der germanischen Philologie." In *Grundriss der germanischen Philologie,* 2d ed., 1: 9–158. Strassburg: Trübner.

Peck, Jeffrey M. 1996. "In the Beginning Was the Word": Germany and the Origins of German Studies." In *Medievalism and the Modernist Temper,* ed. R. Howard Bloch and Stephen G. Nichols, 127–47. Baltimore: Johns Hopkins Press.

Peters, Ursula. 1984. "Geschichte der Interpretation." In *Epische Stoffe des Mittelalters,* ed. Volker Mertens and Ulrich Müller, 475–90. Stuttgart: Kröner.

Rasmussen, Ann Marie. 1993. "Bist du begehrt, so bist du wert: Magische und höfische Mitgift für die Töchter." In *Mütter-Töchter-Frauen: Weiblichkeitsbilder in der Literatur,* ed. Helga Kraft and Elke Liebs, 7–35. Stuttgart: Metzler.

———. 1997. "'If Men Desire You, Then You Are Worthy:' The Didactic Mother-Daughter Poem *Die Winsbeckin.*" Chapter 5 in *Mothers and Daughters in Medieval German Literature,* 136–59. Syracuse, N.Y.: Syracuse University Press.

Scherer, Wilhelm. 1899. *A History of German Literature.* Vol. 1. Trans. Mrs. F. C. Conybeare. Ed. F. Max Müller. 3d ed. New York: Charles Schribner's Sons.

Sowinski, Bernhard. 1971. *Lehrhafte Dichtung des Mittelalters.* Sammlung Metzler, vol. 103. Stuttgart: Metzler.

Weigel, Harald. 1989. *"Nur was du nie gesehen wird ewig dauern": Carl Lachmann und die Entstehung der wissenschaftlichen Edition.* Freiburg: Verlag Rombach.

Weimar, Klaus. 1989. *Geschichte der deutschen Literaturwissenschaft bis zum Ende des 19. Jahrhunderts.* Munich: Fink.

Wenzel, Horst. 1995. *Hören und Sehen, Schrift und Bild: Kultur und Gedächtnis im Mittelalter.* Munich: C. H. Beck.

Westphal, Sarah. 1993. *Textual Poetics of German Manuscripts 1300–1500.* Columbia, S.C.: Camden House.

Wyss, Ulrich. 1979. *Die wilde Philologie: Jacob Grimm und der Historismus.* Munich: Beck.

Zimmermann, Manfred, ed. 1980. *Melchior Goldast von Haiminsfeld: Paraeneticorum veterum pars I* (1604). Litterae, vol. 64. Goppingen, Germany: Kümmerle.

6

Gendered Theories of Education in Fifteenth-Century Conduct Books

Anna Dronzek

Education has always served as a means of socialization, a way to train children in the conduct their society considers acceptable. In fifteenth-century England, education was not limited to mastery of the seven liberal arts, nor was it restricted to the classroom; equally important was children's instruction in proper conduct. Many of the Latin texts used in the classroom, such as the *Distichs of Cato*, were designed to foster not only language skills, but social skills.[1] The classroom, however, was only one of a number of arenas in which children were educated, and one to which not all children had access.[2] For many children, home was the only place where anyone taught them anything. Education was an expensive process. Reading and writing not only required costly materials, but also removed children from the work force or, at the least, from housework that might free their parents to work for wages outside the home.[3] Formal classroom education was thus restricted to the upper classes of society, but these classes did not always take advantage of the opportunity. The nobility, for instance, could afford to send their children to school, but they also brought tutors into their households to teach their children reading, writing, dancing, singing, hunting, and other physical skills.[4] Merchants' children might go to school to learn at least the skills required in their trades, but often an apprenticeship took the place of formal schooling. Moreover, people in occupations requiring less formal training had little incentive to send their children to school.[5] Gender also affected a child's access to formal education. Although precise statistics are difficult to obtain, the majority of children who attended school were boys.[6] Girls of any class, like lower-class boys, were likely to receive their only education at home.

Little information remains about the medieval version of home schooling, but one exception is conduct books, texts that outline how children were supposed to behave. Given that conduct was such an important aspect of children's education, these texts offer historians a valuable glimpse into medieval attitudes toward education. Moreover, both texts addressed specifically to boys and texts addressed specifically to girls survive, providing a rare opportunity to examine ways in which medieval education was gendered. It is the latter issue that this essay will address. Comparing texts outlining proper conduct for boys with those doing the same for girls shows that medieval authors expected boys and girls to learn in different contexts, to absorb information in different ways, to require different uses of physical correction as an educational tool, and to possess honor grounded in different principles. Throughout, the scientific/medical view of women as more rooted than men in the physical world, as creatures of the flesh rather than the spirit, informs authors' views on women's education and conduct.

The focus on the views held by the authors of conduct books sets this essay somewhat apart from the others in this collection. The goal of this essay is to examine theory, not practice; it does not address how successful the authors of conduct literature were in imposing this educational model upon their readers or their readers' responses. Understanding the ideals informing didactic works such as conduct literature, however, remains a crucial foundation for evaluating medieval people's responses to such works. In de Certeau's terms, as discussed in the introduction to this volume, understanding the "tactics" that individual people used to deal with the dominant "strategies" requires knowing what those strategies were. Previous scholarship has too often dismissed conduct literature as a subject not worthy of study for these strategies to be completely understood.

At this point some discussion of the texts under consideration in this essay is probably necessary. In the introduction to this volume, the editors make a useful distinction between courtesy texts, which usually deal with court etiquette, and conduct literature, a broader and more inclusive term. The term "courtesy" presents some problems when applied to all varieties of conduct literature. In fifteenth-century England, "courteisie" and its variants held a wide variety of potential meanings. The term could take on both strongly courtly and strongly religious overtones.[7] The texts analyzed in this essay, however, are neither overwhelmingly courtly nor overwhelmingly devout. As is discussed further below, their origins are obscure, but they suggest a more urban, middle-class, secular context than the term "courtesy" implies. Moreover, in discussing courtesy literature, some modern scholars have also felt the need to distinguish between "courtesy" books—that is, books that deal with moral qualities—and "etiquette" manuals—books that focus on behavior.[8] While it is possible to make a distinction between texts that deal primarily with an individual's internal qualities and those that prescribe an individual's external behavior, in this instance the morality/behavior dichotomy is not particularly useful because it is not one medieval people themselves would have recognized. In a society such as medieval Europe, in which external qualities were believed to reflect internal qualities, people would no doubt consider a person's behavior toward others as an indicator of that person's morality or goodness, thus erasing the modern distinction between courtesy and etiquette. Therefore, although a number of these texts do label themselves "courtesy books," the term conduct literature is more encompassing and neutral.

Despite the broadening of the scope of inquiry that the term "conduct" implies (and to which many of the essays in this volume testify), for the purposes of this essay it has been necessary to narrow the definition of conduct literature in order to create a discrete group of comparable texts. The works considered here discuss exclusively secular daily life. They have no goal other than to teach their readers proper behavior for a range of social situations. This definition excludes a number of texts that have much to offer for the more general study of conduct literature. For instance, John Russell's *Boke of Nurture,* a guide for servants in noble households that includes a large section on carving at the table, and the *Boke of St. Albans,* a guide to hunting, hawking, and heraldry, both fall outside the group of texts chosen for this essay due to the specialized nature of the subjects they discuss.[9] Both works share similarities with the group under discussion here, but the specialist's information they provide—particularly the long lists of technical vocabulary included in both—sets them apart from general guides to life and renders them relevant to the daily existence of only a small number of people. This essay considers the following works, all of which circulated in manuscript form in fifteenth-century England: for girls, "The Good Wife Taught Her Daughter," "The Good Wyfe Wold a Pylgremage," and *The Book of the Knight of the Tower*; and for boys, "The Babees Book," "Lerne or Be Lewde," "The ABC of Aristotle," "Urbanitatis," "The Lytylle Childrenes Lytil Boke," "The Young Children's Book," "Stans puer ad mensam," "How the Wise Man Taught His Son," "The Boke of Curtasye," and "Symon's Lesson of Wysedome for All Maner Chyldryn."[10]

These books share a view of education as the transmission of ideals of proper behavior rather than any formal intellectual program. They are texts not of the classroom, but of the household, for the household provides the setting in which proper behavior takes place. They cover a wide range of subjects, but their primary focus is behavior in society—interactions between human beings. The writings chosen for consideration here are secular and vernacular, as they would have been accessible to the largest number of people. Even the still significant segment of the English society unable to read any language at all would have understood the vernacular when they heard it, unlike Latin.[11] The majority of this literature only appears in English in the fifteenth century; only one of the conduct books considered in this essay dates from before 1400.[12] By the end of the fifteenth and the beginning of the sixteenth centuries, conduct books were no longer written but printed, creating the potential for new and wider audiences. Therefore, this essay considers only manuscript versions and stops at around the end of the fifteenth century.

The precise audience and readership for these conduct books are difficult to determine.[13] The books themselves provide only vague clues. The texts for boys often appear to describe conduct in the context of aristocratic households, outlining behavior such as waiting on the lord at his meals and acting politely in a large group of people of different social ranks, the kind of group commonly encountered in a noble hall.[14] Conversely, the households described in both "The Good Wife Taught Her Daughter" and "The Good Wyfe Wold a Pylgremage" appear more modest.[15] This apparent contrast, however, does not necessarily prove that the texts for different genders were written for different social classes as well. One of the factors leading to the popularity of conduct books in the late Middle Ages was the increase in social mobility that followed the labor shortages of the Black Death. Thus while the texts for boys can be read as set in an aristocratic context, they may have in fact found an audience in the wealthy urban middle class, who looked to suit behavior to newfound economic or social status. Members of the nobility, after all, would hardly need a book to spell out appropriate behavior for their social status, surrounded as they were by suitable role models in everyday life.[16] Whether the authors of conduct books wrote for the nobility, only to be read by the middle class as well, or whether they wrote the boys' texts as if for aristocratic children, with the intention of attracting the upwardly mobile middle class, is unclear. This suggests, however, that authors did not necessarily expect the male and female audiences for conduct books to be of different classes, but that they expected the boys to venture into the world and interact with the widely varied groups of people who could be found in noble circles, while girls were to stay home and negotiate the more homogeneous social arena of their own households.

The third text written for women, *The Book of the Knight of the Tower,* further highlights the difficulty in identifying readership for these texts. *The Book of the Knight of the Tower* was written in the late fourteenth century by the minor Angevin nobleman Geoffroy de la Tour Landry. It might be reasonable to expect, therefore, that the original readership for this book was the lower nobility of France. By the fifteenth century, however, *The Book of the Knight of the Tower* appeared in English translation in two forms—an anonymous translation, surviving in only one mid-fifteenth-century manuscript, and a second translation undertaken independently of the first, carried out and printed by William Caxton in 1484.[17] Clearly, the appeal that this work held for its original audience could not be the same appeal that led to the English translations a century later, especially as there is little evidence that the English translations were aimed for or read by the presumed aristocratic audience of the original text.[18]

In fact, manuscript evidence suggests that the conduct books under consideration here were more likely to belong to and be read by the urban elite than by any aristocratic audience. Felicity Riddy has explored in great detail how "The Good Wife Taught Her Daughter" functioned in an urban setting, to help create what she calls a "bourgeois ethos."[19] What has been less commonly noted is that "The Good Wife Taught Her Daughter" often appears in manuscripts with "How a Wise Man Taught His Son" or other conduct texts for boys, suggesting that the two poems shared a readership.[20] Other texts written for boys appear in manuscripts known to be connected to wealthy urbanites, such as the Plymouth cloth merchant Walter Pollard, the merchant Richard Calle, the grocer Richard Hill, and, finally, William Gregory, who became Lord Mayor of London in 1451.[21]

The importance of readership for this essay lies in the fact that until now little scholarship has compared the texts for boys with those for girls to determine how ideals were gendered masculine and feminine. Rather, an assumption that the conduct books for boys were aimed at an aristocratic audience, while those for girls were written for a more middle-class audience, prevented scholars from examining the two kinds of texts in the same light.[22] Understanding that the texts considered here shared a reading audience allows such a comparison and highlights the differences in the way authors viewed men and women, particularly the two genders' capacity for learning.

The pedagogical theories underlying the conduct books appear first of all in the way the texts are structured. The texts written for boys and the two Good Wife poems written for girls are rhymed poems of modest length, usually divided into stanzas of some kind.[23] The Good Wife poems, however, end each stanza with a two-line aphorism that restates the point of the preceding lines, dividing up the text much more distinctly and regularly than the boys' texts do. Many of these couplets are familiar as common proverbs. For instance, in "The Good Wife Taught Her Daughter," one stanza reads, "And yif thi nede be grette, and thi tyme streite, / Goe thiselfe therto, and make an housewifis breyde. / All thei schall do the better that thou bi hem standes. / the werke is the soner done that hath many handes," and concludes, "Many handys make light werke, / My leue childe."[24] "The Good Wyfe Wold a Pylgremage" uses similar aphorisms to mark the change from one stanza to another, including, "Witt an O and a I, my tall thou atende: / Syldon mossyth the ston that oftyn ys tornnyd and wende."[25] The authors of these texts seem to have believed that female readers needed help gleaning the moral lessons and included regular, catchy summaries to drum the main points into their brains. Male readers apparently needed no such help, as this structure appears only in the texts written for girls.[26]

The use of these maxims in the girls' poems also may have functioned as aural cues, signaling to a listener that one "lesson" had finished and a new one was beginning. The repetition of the phrase "my dear child" (or "my leue child") after almost every stanza in "The Good Wife Taught Her Daughter" clearly marks the shift to a new subject.[27] Similarly, the author of "The Good Wyfe Wold a Pylgremage" uses the phrase "Witt a O and a I" to introduce the proverb that follows each stanza, in the same way a recurring refrain or chorus functions in a song. Although modern editors traditionally break the poem up into rhyming lines, two of the manuscripts of "The Good Wife Taught Her Daughter" present the poem as a block of unbroken prose, without the visual cues modern readers would expect for dividing the poem. In one of these manuscripts, however, the proverbs are written in red ink, emphasizing the purpose they would have played in organizing the text.[28] While the red ink may have served as visual cue to a reader, it may also have suggested to someone reading the text aloud that these were lines that deserved extra weight, in the same way signs in musical texts signaled where the singers should take their breaths. In any case, the structure of the two Good Wife poems suggests that their authors may have expected the poem to be read aloud, rather than to oneself.[29] The song-like structure of these poems may also have served as a mnemonic device, in that rhymes and regular meters allowed a listener to memorize material more easily than unbroken chunks of prose.

Although the boys' texts were also written in verse, they present a different reading experience from the girls' texts. Some boys' poems, such as "The Lytylle Childrenes Lytil Boke" and "The Young Children's Book" are not broken up into stanzas at all, but present undifferentiated lists of duties and manners.[30] Others, such as "The Babees Book," are organized in stanzas that neither announce themselves with any repeating phrases nor follow any distinctive change in rhythm or meter; unlike the Good Wife poems, the rhythm and meter remain the same throughout. There are no obvious changes that would be striking to a listener as opposed to a reader. And while some boys' conduct books such as "The ABC of Aristotle" are organized around the alphabet, which would serve as an aid to memorization, such a device is less aural than the "refrains" of the girls' conduct books, relying more on visual cues and the boy's ability to recall knowledge already learned in the classroom. The vertical orientation of the alphabet, running down the left hand of the page at the beginning of each line, is similarly geared to a reader, not a listener. In short, authors appear to have expected boys to read their texts, perhaps as they would study in a schoolroom, but anticipated that girls would listen to another person read the texts to them.

Moving from the format of the texts to their content reveals another striking pedagogical difference between the boys' and girls' conduct books. As authors assumed that boys and girls would be exposed to these texts in two different ways (i.e., visually and aurally), they also presumed that boys and girls would process information in two different ways. The literature for girls uses a more experiential format than the literature for boys. Authors invariably present lessons for girls through the device of a parent advising her or his daughters, a narrative device that is an exception in the boys' literature.[31] Mustanoja, editor of the Good Wife poems, has a simple solution for this dichotomy; at this time, the practice of sending children at about age fourteen to be educated in households other than their own was common among the nobility and gentry. The theory was that parents would be too indulgent with their own children to have the discipline to teach them effectively.[32] Mustanoja argues that because boys were educated in households other than their own, they were likely to learn appropriate behavior not from their parents but from the residents of the other household, and the poems simply reflect this phenomenon.[33] This solution would be perfectly satisfactory, except for two factors: first, as discussed above, the conduct books for boys were not primarily aristocratic texts, and, more pertinently, girls as well as boys were sent to other households for their education.[34] Why do the texts written for them ignore this fact? Clearly actual educational practices are less important here than authors' beliefs about how boys and girls learned. What explains this contrast between the boys' and girls' conduct literature?

One answer can be found in the medieval view of the physical differences between men and women. According to a number of medieval medical theories, women were physically inferior to men. Many of these theories were heavily influenced by the writings of the Greeks and Romans.[35] Aristotle, for instance, held that women were born through an imperfection, when there was insufficient heat for the male seed and the female matter to combine to create man, the more perfect being. Hippocratic theory believed that women were cooler and moister than men, which doomed women according to the Aristotelian idea that the greater amount of heat led to perfection. By no means did all writers accept the Aristotelian idea of women as imperfect, but in Thomas

Aquinas's synthesis of many previous writers he, too, affirmed women's physical inferiority, although he argued that as women were created by God as part of God's plan, they could not be imperfect.[36] According to these theories, this physical inferiority contributed directly to intellectual inferiority. Philo, who wrote in the late first century B.C., made a clear distinction between the female, who was associated with the corporeal and sense perception, and the male, who was associated with incorporeal rational thought.[37] This belief persisted in various forms throughout the Middle Ages.[38] Men's physical superiority made them capable of greater understanding than women, lifting them to a more rational plane and enabling them to absorb and comprehend abstract thought. Women, in contrast, were creatures of the flesh. Anchored in the corporeal world, their physical inferiority rendered them incapable of understanding abstract thought.

This understanding of men's and women's intellectual differences explains the different forms of the boys' and girls' literature. Authors believed that boys could absorb information told to them in abstract absolutes. Consequently, for boys they wrote lists of duties, devoid of examples or illustration. Some of their poems even refer to the heavenly nature of courtesy and allegorical intellectual figures such as Facetia.[39] The tone remains in the erudite world of the rational and learned.

Authors believed, on the other hand, that girls needed knowledge tied to the physical, to the world of the body that was at the very center of their nature. The Good Wife poems accomplish this by presenting their prescriptions through the physical figure of the mother. One implication of a mother teaching her daughter is that the mother is passing on knowledge gained through her own life experience. This model of life experience presents moral lessons in a far more tangible way than authors use in most of the boys' literature. The Knight accomplishes the same purpose by using examples of ideal women to illustrate each aspect of the good behavior he wants his daughters to learn. Although the life experiences thus described do not come from a parent, nor are they the Knight's own, his lessons are drawn from women's life experiences (if fictional).[40] The text in which the Knight outlines abstract moral precepts is invariably short in comparison to the examples that follow. In fact, of the 144 chapters in the book, only thirteen present absolute statements about women's behavior without incorporating some kind of an example.[41] When, for instance, the Knight discusses charity in chapter

LXXXVIII, he does not simply tell his daughters that they should act charitably; he sets before them the examples of how Rahab of Jericho, St. Anastatia, and St. Aragon Queen of France all prospered through their charitable deeds.[42] By providing examples for his daughters, the Knight gives them something tangible, something that appeals to the physical senses that govern them. The situations he portrays are often quite vivid, such as the story of a knight who came to a king's daughter at night with dalliance on his mind. However, because the girl had prayed for the dead before she retired, when the knight approached he "thought he sawe a thousand ded bodies about her in shetis; And he was so sore afraied and aferde, that he ranne awaie."[43]

In other instances, the Knight provides physical, tangible symbols of the abstract concepts he is discussing. In one tale, a woman dreams of a silver plate with black spots that she is commanded to scour clean. Her priest explains to her (and consequently the Knight's daughters) that the silver plate is the soul, and the black spots are sins; she must strive to remove all traces of sin from her soul if she wishes to be saved.[44] The plate serves as a something tangible that women, with their physical natures, can comprehend, leading them to understand the concept of sin's impact upon the soul more easily than abstract discussion. Moreover, a silver plate is not simply a random object, but a common household good. The plate's ability to register the state of the woman's soul also recalls other objects, common in folklore, such as shirts, handkerchiefs, and garlands that possess a similar capability, which may have also been familiar to the Knight's audience.[45]

Another pedagogical theory apparent in conduct books for both men and women advocated physical chastisement as an effective educational tool. Corporal punishment has a long history as part of medieval pedagogy, doubtless because of the important place it also held in ancient education and the use that medieval educators made of many ancient writers.[46] Pierre Riché has demonstrated that physical chastisement was considered a standard part of secular education in the early Middle Ages, inspired by biblical texts and supported by the belief that young children were not yet capable of understanding the reasoning behind moral correction. The monastic approach to education was more moderate, as St. Benedict and a number of his followers argued for "mildness in correction" of children under fifteen.[47] The fact that St. Benedict felt it necessary to specify such mildness, however, suggests the prevalence of corporal punishment in educating even quite young children. Monastic and secular educators agreed that as children entered adolescence (approximately age fifteen) their physical urges awoke, and despite their greater capacity for understanding moral correction, these children required greater discipline in order to tame their renegade bodies.[48] Art portrayed the schoolroom as a place where children were beaten, and in his study of the iconography of grammar, Ayers Bagley has found many representations of the discipline as a woman wielding such unpleasant instruments as scourges, whips, and files.[49] Despite changes in educational practice throughout the Middle Ages, such attitudes had changed little by the fifteenth century, when Edward IV's household ordinances called for the young men serving in his household to be beaten in privacy. They earned the privilege of privacy due to their social rank, but there was no suggestion that they should be exempt from the beating itself.[50]

The medieval word "chastien" (and its variations) meant "to correct or improve (someone's) behavior; ... rear a child properly; ... learn proper conduct from another."[51] Modern definitions of the verb "to chastise" and its noun form "chastisement" make explicit the physical nature of such correction that doubtless would have been understood in the Middle Ages, given the medieval assumption that corporal punishment helped children to learn. Chastisement, implying both education and the infliction of suffering for the purpose of education, appears frequently in conduct books for men and women; yet here, too, gender played an important role in the differing expectations authors brought to women's and men's texts.

At first glance, the conduct books appear to share St. Benedict's preference for "mildness in correction." Their tone is notably pleasant throughout. The authors of the boys' texts refer to the reader as "dere childe" or "dere sone," "swete children," and "yonge Babees, whome bloode Royalle / Withe grace, Feture, and hyhe habylite / Hathe enourmed," who enjoy "soverayne beaute."[52] The Good Wife poems, slightly less demonstrative, address their advice to "der doghttor" and, constantly, to "my dear [or leue] child."[53] These examples come, however, when the writer directly addresses the ostensible child reader. When authors stop speaking *to* children and start speaking *about* children, the usual references to the rod as a teaching tool appear. In "Stans puer ad mensam" (Lydgate), for example, the author generally addresses boys directly. In the second-to-last two stanzas, however, he begins describing children's quarrels to a nonchild reader (a parent or other authority figure?), and advises that "To theyr [children's] playntes gyve no credence; / A Rodde refourmythe al theyr insolence; / In theyr corage no Rancour dothe abyde; / Who sparithe the yerd, al vertu set aside."[54]

The Good Wife poems include similar precepts. In "The Good Wife Taught Her Daughter," the mother advises the girl that if she loves her children, when they do wrong she should not curse them but "take a smerte rodde and bete hem all by rowe."[55] *The Book of the Knight of the Tower,* however, uses physical chastisement as an educational tool in a different way. Images of violence serve indirectly to reinforce the explicit moral lessons of the text. The Knight does not threaten his daughters with physical chastisement if they act inappropriately, but the illustrative tales he provides usually contain some act of violence, legitimated through its chastising function but graphic nonetheless, that befalls a woman following her bad behavior. When a king's daughter does not pray for the dead, the ultimate consequence of this act (or in this case, failure to act) is her death when her father casts her into a river.[56] When a woman dares to berate her husband in front of others, he knocks her to the ground, kicks her in the face, and breaks her nose.[57] A woman who holds immoral parties in her wardrobe ultimately loses an eye at her husband's hand.[58] In each case violence to the women occurs upon their mistakes, in the same way that a schoolboy's mistake would incur violence upon him. If the question is "How should a good woman behave?" the incorrect answer (such as berating her husband) leads to immediate physical chastisement, either in the form of death or permanent physical disfigurement. This, in turn, inscribes the correct answer—the recognition of the error of her ways—directly upon the fictional woman's body, where the book's audience can read it. This physical correction invariably comes from a husband or a father—authority figures to whom a woman owes obedience and from whom she should learn. The reader of the Knight's book does not suffer chastisement directly, nor does the Knight suggest that she should. Nonetheless, the images of violence serve as an important pedagogical technique, indirectly conforming to the theory that physical correction led a student to learn better, and allowing women to read lessons verified through corporal punishment that they themselves do not have to undergo. This, too, can be linked to the experiential model underlying women's conduct books; as women learn best through physical experience, so threats of chastisement are less useful than are explicit descriptions of the effects of chastisement upon a woman's body.

The indirect physical correction in *The Book of the Knight of the Tower* finds no parallels in the texts aimed at boys, but some echoes in the other texts directed at girls. The closest the two Good Wife poems come to this removed chastisement is in "The Good Wyfe Wold a Pylgremage." When the Good Wife warns her daughter against hanging her girdle too low or showing her white legs and tight-fitting hose because it will "make men have delytt," the caution resonates with implications of male violence.[59] Men are not the only offenders, however, as women who show their legs and hose are bluntly compared to a meatseller, the poem declaring, "The bocher schewyth feyr his flesche, for he wold sell hit full blythe."[60] While this conjures up the unpleasant image of dead animals and perhaps suggests that similar violence will occur to the daughter, it speaks literally not of male violence, but of the mercenary unpleasantness of women who set out to capture a man.[61]

Physical chastisement was not the only result of misbehavior that authors of conduct books described; they also foretold dire consequences to the reader's honor or reputation. While both boys' and girls' texts proclaimed that failure to act appropriately would tarnish an individual's honor, understandings of honor were gendered and varied between men and women. Consistent with their view of women as corporeal creatures, mired in the material world, authors constructed a woman's reputation or honor as a function of her sexual behavior, whether or not her actual transgression was sexual in nature. Men's honor, however, was a function of social standing and rank in the eyes of other men. While inappropriate bodily behavior could certainly disgrace a man, the sexual element so prevalent in the girls' books is absent entirely from those for boys.

In *The Book of the Knight of the Tower,* the Knight describes women losing their reputation or honor due to sexual impropriety. Remarkably few cases result from straightforward sexual misbehavior on the woman's part, however. More frequently the Knight demonstrates how simply the hint of impropriety, even when the woman in fact did nothing wrong, can ruin a woman's reputation. For instance, the Knight recounts one tale in which a woman's brother-in-law discovered her sitting alone at a feast with a knight who was not her husband. Such behavior opened the woman to the suggestion of improper behavior and was enough to ruin her reputation. The lesson that the Knight is trying to impart, however, is not so simple. On one level, he is simply warning women to guard their honor at all times and all ways. On another level, his story is consistent with the experiential model of learning described above: the damage to the woman's reputation has very tangible consequences. In this instance, although the Knight states that "in good trouthe y trow there was no thing done but good" between the woman and the knight, her husband finds the experience has so shattered his trust in his wife that he can no longer love her, "and so there was neuer pees betwene hem, but euer glomying, louring, and chiding, and all her householde yede to not for this cause."[62] Apart from the emotional misery of such a marriage, given that the household was the locus of the family economy during this period, the fact that "all her householde yede to not for this cause," suggests that poverty and economic hardship resulted from the woman's shattered reputation. Moreover, given the inequality of women's official access to political power at this time, bad relations with her husband might restrict a woman's political influence as well. Therefore, damage to a woman's reputation resulted in material consequences that allow the story to work as part of the experiential model of learning best suited to women.

The Knight takes the connections between a woman's honor and her body further, however. Rather than suggesting that the only sins a woman could commit were sexual, in many of the tales a woman's sexual misbehavior is often only a symptom of her true, nonsexual sin. In the episode described above, the woman's true crime was not putting herself in a compromising position with another man (although this was bad enough), but going to jousts and feasts without her husband and so displeasing him. Only because she persists in this unwifely behavior does she find herself alone in the corner with a knight where her behavior can be misconstrued. Similarly, when the elder daughter of the emperor of Constantinople becomes pregnant, and her father casts her into a river to drown, her sin is not that she dallied with a knight (although this behavior is hardly to be recommended), but that she did not pray for the dead before going to sleep.[63] In contrast, both the emperor of Constantinople's younger daughter and the gentlewoman whose story immediately follows that of the emperor's daughter took the time and effort to pray for the souls of the dead. When the potential arises for improper sexual conduct to lead them to shame and dishonor, the dead come to their rescue; both the knight who has arranged a tryst with the emperor's daughter and the lord who pursues the gentlewoman against her will find the objects of their desire surrounded by thousands of dead people and run away in fear.[64] Therefore, although a woman's original transgression may not have been sexual, damage to a woman's honor or reputation—damage that might ultimately extend to her physical person—nonetheless takes place only through the catalyst of inappropriate sexual behavior. Conversely, exemplary moral behavior can protect a woman from sexual threats that might otherwise ruin her.

Moreover, female reputation or honor is closely tied to a woman's domestic relationships. On the one hand, it is her relationship with her father or husband that suffers from a woman's sexual impropriety. On the other hand, should a woman behave well, her reward is often presented in terms of her domestic relationships: many virtuous women find their fathers making them advantageous marriages.[65] In reinforcing his moral lessons this way, the Knight locates women's honor firmly in the realm of the domestic, physical, and sexual. This portrayal both fits with the medieval understanding of women as more corporeal creatures than men and also renders the Knight's stories consistent with an experiential model of learning rooted in the physical.

Although to a lesser degree than *The Book of the Knight of the Tower,* the Good Wife poems also physicalize women's honor by locating it in the realm of sexual behavior. In both poems, the potential for slander—or rumors questioning a woman's virtue—arises in the context of the daughter's actions toward a man; both, for instance, warn against sitting with a man for "ther synne may be wroght."[66] Another example is the verse previously cited from "The Good Wyfe Wold a Pylgremage" about women who show their legs and white hose to catch a man.[67] Unlike *The Book of the Knight of the Tower,* however, the Good Wife poems do not describe the physical consequences to loss of reputation upon which the Knight dwells. The Good Wife poems place greater weight on the importance of maintaining one's reputation than on the consequences of losing it: "A slaunder that is reised is euell to fell, My leue child."[68]

The complex relationship between corporal chastisement, education, and honor seen in the conduct books for girls finds little parallel in the texts for boys. Although, as we have seen, conduct books for boys advocate beating as a means of reinforcing a boy's education, they do not emphasize their moral lessons through concrete examples of that physical correction. This doubtless results from using an experiential model of learning to educate girls but not boys. Authors could hardly emphasize information presented in abstract absolutes by using examples of violence in the text, when their whole model for boys' learning dictated that they not use examples. In fact, authors rarely spell out the consequences for boys' misbehavior, and never describe the consequences as physical.

The result is a different model not only of male learning but of male honor. Male honor is removed from the domestic, sexual realm of girls' honor. Rather, it functions as a measure of social standing in the public world of other men. In the boys' texts, ironically, many of the transgressions outlined are in fact minutely physical: talking while another man is speaking, scratching oneself at the dinner table, spitting, breaking wind, and the like.[69] Despite this, men's honor, unlike women's, is not located in the physical arena, partly because there is almost no mention of sexual behavior in any of the men's texts, and partly because his transgressions have no bodily or sexual consequences such as those found in the girls' texts.[70]

Instead, improper behavior will lower a boy's social standing in the eyes of his audience (usually men). The author of "Stans puer ad mensam" declares of the child who will not learn courtesy, "no man off hym reiosynge will haue, / Yn what lond of crysdome at he commys Inne, / Bot oft-tymes rebukyd, and be callyd knaue, / Ne neuer is Abull worschippe to wynne."[71] The medieval terms "rebukyd" and "knaue" both carry strong connotations of shame. "Rebuken" means "to reprimand, reprove, reproach," but also "to scorn (something), despise," and a "rebuke" is an insult, shame, rebuff, or disparagement, as well as reproof or reprimand.[72] "Knaue" had many meanings that rendered it a potent insult in this context, including commoner, peasant, laborer, wastrel, good-for-nothing, rogue, and villain. The offense in the term doubtless also came from its primary meaning of male infant, boy, lad, or young man; the implications of youth and low class conflated very effectively to impugn a man's social status. The repetition throughout the texts of the threat that a man who misbehaves will be thought a knave or a churl makes explicit the impact a man's inappropriate behavior will have on his position in the social hierarchy.[73] In contrast, the "Babees Book" notes that good behavior will earn a man the name of "gentylnesse and good governaunce," and "Symon's Lesson of Wysedome for Chyldryn" declares that "by fayre manerys men may thee a-vaunce."[74] Men's honor is not tied to their behavior regarding the opposite sex but is determined solely by their behavior toward or in front of other men. And while the consequences for a man's loss in standing may in fact have been just as disastrous as the consequences of a woman's fall from grace, the high physical stakes involved in the loss of a girl's reputation are not spelled out in the conduct books for boys.

Comparing conduct books for boys and girls, then, shows that medieval ideas about gender dictated authors' understanding of how to educate children. Boys and girls needed to be presented with information in two different ways—for boys, visually, and for girls, aurally—and had different capacities for absorbing that information. Boys could handle abstract rational concepts, while girls learned more effectively from information presented in a tangible, physical way, through the use of examples or the experiential model of a parent imparting life wisdom. The parental advice format may also have been a result of the expectation that girls would listen to texts rather than read them; authors may have felt the device would personalize the experience and lend parental authority to whoever read the texts to the girls.[75] Conduct books also reveal the different way authors viewed physical correction as a pedagogical tool, as a consequence illuminating contemporary gendered notions of honor. Girls, with their corporeal, irrational natures and their physical inferiority, required threats of chastisement to reinforce moral lessons. While boys might receive corporal punishment if they behaved badly, examples of violence were not necessary to ensure obedience. Female honor was similarly tied to the body, inextricably linked to sexual conduct and the realm of the private and domestic. Male honor was determined not by the body's sexual conduct, but by the perception of a boy's bodily behavior, such as eating and speaking, by the people (probably men) of higher social rank. Even the consequences for women's loss of honor took on concrete physical form, while those for men did not.

Historians have long recognized that authors in the Middle Ages used the intellectual construct of a dichotomy between the flesh and the spirit to understand gender differences.[76] In conduct books, some of the ways that individuals applied this intellectual construct emerge. Identifying women with the bodily side of the equation led authors to use different methods to present material to girls than to boys. The result might be described as a self-fulfilling prophecy: an education that identified women as creatures of the corporeal world may also have been an education that provided women with few tools for thinking of themselves in any other way. While the texts add nothing to our statistical knowledge of girls' education, their authors' understanding of how boys and girls learned suggests that formal, schoolroom education was seen largely as a male province. In addition, although men's books suggested to parents that they should not hesitate to chastise their children physically, there are few, if any, examples of this actually presented. The violent images of chastisement common in the girls' texts are absent from the men's books. While men's misbehavior may in the end result in consequences as painful—whether physically or socially—as those for women's misbehavior, it is striking that the conduct books detail physical pain for one gender only. Here, too, the association of women with the body had an important influence on educational thought. How medieval readers received these ideas is unclear, but as conduct was an important part of education, so too was education doubtless an important part of conduct.

NOTES

1. Jonathan Nicholls, *The Matter of Courtesy: Medieval Courtesy Books and the Gawain-Poet* (Suffolk, England: D. S. Brewer, 1985), 65–67; Nicholas Orme, *From Childhood to Chivalry: The Education of the English Kings and Aristocracy, 1066–1530* (London and New York: Methuen, 1984), 133–41.

2. Determining precisely how many children had access to formal education in fifteenth-century England (excluding university schooling) remains difficult, but clearly many had only limited opportunities. Jo Ann Hoeppner Moran argues in *The Growth of English Schooling, 1340–1548: Learning, Literacy, and Laicization in Pre-Reformation York Diocese* (Princeton: Princeton University Press, 1985) that educational opportunities increased steadily throughout the course of the fifteenth century, but she also states that by the end of the first quarter of the sixteenth century, roughly 12 to 13 percent of the population of York diocese was receiving formal schooling, suggesting that the percentage of children receiving schooling in the fifteenth century was even smaller. For similar conclusions, see Nicholas Orme, *English Schools in the Middle Ages* (London: Methuen, 1970). For a useful synthesis of the debates on medieval schooling, see Moran's first chapter.

3. A common form of late medieval charity was to leave money in one's will for the education of poor children in the community. The extent to which such bequests were carried out, however, has not been fully explored.

4. Orme, *From Childhood to Chivalry*. Not all noble families with children employed tutors; many sent their adolescent children to another noble household for their education. See Orme, *From Childhood to Chivalry*, 55–60, and Gerald McCracken, "The Exchange

of Children in Tudor England: An Anthropological Phenomenon in Historical Context," *Journal of Family History* 8, no. 4 (1983): 303–13. McCracken argues that people tended to send their children to a household slightly higher in rank than their own, and that this practice was not restricted to noble households (307).

5. Sylvia Thrupp, in her classic study *The Merchant Class of Medieval London* (Ann Arbor: University of Michigan Press, 1948; reprint, 1989), 157–60, discusses the education of apprentices in skilled trades such as goldsmithing and points out that literacy rates were lower in lower-class occupations. She also argues, however, that while an apprenticeship might require education, this education might be rather minimal.

6. Paul Grendler has found that in sixteenth-century Venice, for instance, fewer than 1 percent of girls of school age attended school, many doubtless receiving education at home. See "The Organization of Primary and Secondary Education in the Italian Renaissance," *Church History* 71, no. 2 (April 1985): 204–5. While in England there are certainly references to girls in elementary schools, their presence remains exceptional. See Moran, *The Growth of English Schooling*, 69–70. Orme, *From Childhood to Chivalry*, 79, points out that the schooling of noble girls took place almost entirely in the home.

7. W. O. Evans, "'Cortaysye' in Middle English," *Mediaeval Studies* 29 (1967): 143–57. See also *The Middle English Dictionary*, ed. Hans Kurath, Sherman M. Kuhn, and John Reidy (Ann Arbor: University of Michigan Press, 1952), s.v. "courteisie."

8. See Nicholls, *The Matter of Courtesy*, 7–8, for the range of meanings "courtesy" could acquire, and 12, for the distinction between "courtesy" and "etiquette." Despite the problems he points out, Nicholls uses the term "courtesy," as his whole discussion of "courtesy" books is designed to illuminate the concept of courtesy in Sir Gawain and the Green Knight.

9. Frederick J. Furnivall, ed., *The Babees Book*, Early English Text Society O.S. 32 (London: N. Trübner and Co., 1868; reprint, Millwood, N.J.: Kraus Reprint, 1990), 117–228; Dame Juliana Berners, *The Boke of St. Albans* (London: Elliot Stock, 1881).

10. For "The Good Wife Taught Her Daughter" and "The Good Wyfe Wold a Pylgremage," see Tauno Mustanoja, ed., *The Good Wife Taught Her Daughter*, Annales Academiae Scientiarum Fennicae, BLXI, 2 (Helsinki: Suomalaisen Kirjallisuuden Seuran, 1948); see his introduction for manuscript information and earlier printed editions (Mustanoja prints a third poem addressed to women, "The Thewis of Gud Women," which is not considered here because it is written in Scots and therefore derives from a different context than the English poems). See also Geoffroy de La Tour Landry, *The Book of the Knight of La Tour-Landry*, ed. Thomas Wright, rev. ed., Early English Text Society O.S. 33 (London: Kegan Paul, Trench, Trübner & Co., 1906; reprint, New York: Greenwood Press, 1969), cited as *The Book of the Knight of la Tour-Landry*. In the body of the essay I refer to this work as *The Book of the Knight of the Tower*, the more generally accepted English version of the title.

For "The Babees Book," "Lerne or Be Lewde," "The ABC of Aristotle," "Urbanitatis," "The Lytylle Childrenes Lytil Boke," "The Young Children's Book," "Stans puer ad mensam," "How the Wise Man Taught His Son," "The Boke of Curtasye," and "Symon's Lesson of Wysedome for All Maner Chyldryn," see Furnivall, *The Babees Book*, 1–9, 9–10, 11–12, 13–15, 16–24 (even-numbered pages), 17–25 (odd-numbered pages), 26–33, 48–52, 299–327, 399–402. Different manuscript versions of "How the Wise Man Taught His

Son," "Stans puer ad mensam," and "The ABC of Aristotle" are also printed in Frederick J. Furnivall, ed., *Queene Elizabethes Achademy*, Early English Text Society, Extra Series, 8 (London: N. Trübner & Co., 1869; reprint, Millwood, N.Y.: Kraus Reprint Co., 1973), 52–55, 56–64, 65–67. Furnivall gives manuscript information for many of these texts, but for a comprehensive summary, see Nicholls, *The Matter of Courtesy*, 191–95.

11. Medieval literacy is notoriously difficult to determine, partly because standards for measuring literacy differ. Thrupp, *The Merchant Class of Medieval London*, 158, suggests that approximately 40 percent of merchant-class men could read Latin, while 50 percent would have been able to read English. These percentages of course decline for those further down the social scale, with, for instance, general laborers and others of less-skilled trades showing lower percentages of literacy than merchants such as the mercers and drapers. Thrupp (161, 171) also argues that intelligent women of the merchant class would have learned how to read and write some English, although women were not admitted to grammar schools (which taught Latin, as opposed to elementary schools, which taught the vernacular), and may not have had as many opportunities for education as men. F. R. H. DuBoulay argues that 30 percent of the general population could read in the fifteenth century (*An Age of Ambition: English Society in the Late Middle Ages* [London: Nelson, 1970], cited in Moran, *The Growth of English Schooling*, 19–20). Michael Van Cleave Alexander (*The Growth of English Education, 1348–1648: A Social and Cultural History* [University Park, Penn.: Pennsylvania State University Press, 1990], 233) states (with little supporting evidence) that by the end of the sixteenth century, 25 to 30 percent of women could read, by far the most optimistic estimate of female literacy. In contrast, David Cressy (*Literacy and the Social Order: Reading and Writing in Tudor and Stuart England* [Cambridge: Cambridge University Press, 1980], 177) argues much more pessimistically for a 90 percent male and 99 percent female illiteracy rate at the beginning of the sixteenth century; his argument is based on evidence from signatures, however, and does not take into account the ability to read without being able to write, a skill taught separately from reading throughout the Middle Ages. For an extremely interesting analysis of the functional literacy that could be found even in the lower classes in late medieval England, see Steven Justice, *Writing and Rebellion: England in 1381* (Berkeley: University of California Press, 1994). Even the most optimistic estimates, however, suggest that the majority of English society in the fifteenth century relied on being read to, rather than reading themselves.

12. The exception is one version of "The Good Wife Taught Her Daughter," dated mid–fourteenth century; see the introduction to Mustanoja, *The Good Wife Taught Her Daughter*. Felicity Riddy ("Mother Knows Best: Reading Social Change in a Courtesy Text," *Speculum* 71, 1 [January 1996]: 66–86) presents a convincing analysis of manuscript changes over the course of the later fourteeenth and fifteenth centuries. *The Book of the Knight of the Tower* was originally written in the fourteenth century, but the English translation does not appear until approximately one hundred years later; see *The Book of the Knight of La Tour-Landry*, xiv–xvi.

13. Elizabeth L. Eisenstein discusses this briefly in *The Printing Press as an Agent of Change: Communications and Cultural Transformations in Early-Modern Europe*, Vol. 1 and 2 (Cambridge: Cambridge University Press, 1979), 64, 430–31.

14. "How the Wise Man Taught His Son" and "Symon's Lesson of Wysedome for All Maner Chyldryn" are exceptions to the aristocratic tone of the boys' texts, but are far outnumbered by the other texts. For a discussion of the late medieval English noble household and its makeup, see Kate Mertes, *The English Noble Household 1250–1600: Good Governance and Politic Rule* (Oxford: Basil Blackwell, 1988). In a conduct book exclusively for servants, John Russell, a former member of the Duke of Gloucester's household, devotes a great deal of space to outlining the different ranks of people a servant might encounter and explaining how to seat them properly, so that their place in the hall might reflect their place in society. See his *Boke of Nurture,* printed in Furnivall, *The Babees Book,* 117–228. Furnivall also prints a number of other texts concerned with ordering the mix of people one might find in one's household: see "The Boke of Keruynge," 261–88, and "The Ordre of Goyng and Sittynge," 381, in Furnivall, *The Babees Book,* and "A Book of Precedence," in Furnivall, *Queene Elizabethes Achademy,* 13–28.

15. Mustanoja, *The Good Wife Taught Her Daughter,* 79, and Nicholls, *The Matter of Courtesy,* 17, both comment on this.

16. Riddy makes a similar point in "Mother Knows Best," 82–85, arguing that women would read the Good Wife poems not to their own daughters, who could learn from their mothers directly, but to the young girls working as servants in their household, who would not have a mother's example before them. Eisenstein, *The Printing Press as an Agent of Change,* 430–31, points out that in fact the primary audience may have been parents. *The Book of the Knight of the Tower* presents a contrast in that it is clearly written for the nobility. Nonetheless, we cannot rule out the possibility that it, too, was read by a middle-class audience. As an import and a translation, it may easily have reached a different readership than the Knight originally intended.

17. The manuscript translation is the edition by Wright already cited; for Caxton's translation, see Geoffroy de la Tour Landry, *The Book of the Knight of the Tower,* ed. Margaret Offord, Early English Text Society, Supplementary Series, 2 (London: Oxford University Press, 1971).

18. For further discussion of this point, see my Ph.D. dissertation, "Manners, Models, and Morals: Gender and Conduct among the Middle Classes of Late Medieval England," University of Minnesota, 2001, chapter 3.

19. Riddy, "Mother Knows Best," 67.

20. "The Good Wife Taught Her Daughter" and "How the Wise Man Taught His Son" both appear in Cambridge, Trinity College R.3.19; Oxford, Bodley, Ashmole 61; and Lambeth Palace Library MS 853. See Nicholls, *The Matter of Courtesy,* appendix B; also Trinity College, *Manuscript Trinity R.3.19: A Facsimile* (Norman, Okla.: Pilgrim Books, 1987); Bodleian Library, *A Summary Catalogue of the Western Manuscripts in the Bodleian Library at Oxford* (Oxford: Clarendon Press, 1895–1953); Lambeth Palace Library, *A Descriptive Catalog of the Manuscripts in the Library of Lambeth Palace* (Cambridge: Cambridge University Press, 1930–1932).

21. Bodley Rawlinson MS D. 328, which contains Lydgate's "Stans puer ad mensam" and a number of Latin courtesy texts, was owned by Walter Pollard; Cambridge, University Library, MS Ee.4.35, containing "Lytylle Childrene," was owned at some point by Richard Calle; Oxford, Balliol College MS 354, containing "Lytylle Childrene," Caxton's "Courtesy Book," and Lydgate's "Stans puer ad mensam," was compiled and owned in the early sixteenth century by Richard Hill; and BL Egerton MS 1995, which also contained "Lytylle Childrene," was owned by William Gregory. See Nicholls, *The Matter of Courtesy,* 71.

22. Jonathan Nicholls does recognize the urban, middle-class readership of the boys' texts, but does not include the girls' texts in his definition of courtesy books, and thus removes the basis for comparison. Ibid., 156.

23. *The Book of the Knight of the Tower* is an exception to this pattern, as it is a prose work of much greater length, and consequently it does not figure very prominently in this portion of the essay. It is worth noting, however, that the Knight addresses the question of verse versus prose, writing "And thanne y made this boke. But y wolde not sett it in ryme, but in prose, forto abregge it, and that it might be beter and more pleinly to be understond" (*The Book of the Knight of La Tour-Landry*, 3). The editor of the French original, however, has demonstrated that the Knight in fact began his prologue in verse, and that the rhyme structure can still be traced. Ibid., xii.

24. Mustanoja, *The Good Wife Taught Her Daughter*, 167: 133–38. The *Boke of St. Albans*, which discusses the specialized arts of hawking, hunting, and heraldry, also uses the phrase "my dere child" to address its reader.

25. Mustanoja, *The Good Wife Taught Her Daughter*, 173: 11–12.

26. In *The Book of the Knight of the Tower*, the Knight's constant use of examples serves a purpose similar to that of the summary proverbs in the poems by reinforcing the main point with a memorable image; almost every chapter in the Knight's book contains the example of what happened to a specific woman when she did behave appropriately (reward) or did not (punishment). Again, this rhetorical strategy is lacking in the boys' texts.

27. The phrase "my dere child" is by no means exclusive to conduct literature for girls and appears in texts written for boys, including texts outside the scope of this discussion, such as the *Boke of St. Albans*; see below for a discussion of phrases such as "my dere child" and the tone that the conduct books take toward their ostensible child reader. Nor is the use of verse exclusive to girls' texts. The use in a verse work of such pointed repetition of a specific phrase, in the form of a refrain, however, is exclusive to the girls' texts.

28. Cambridge, Emmanuel College MS 106 (I.4.31) and London, Lambeth Palace Library MS 853 are written in prose; the former uses red for the proverbs. See Mustanoja, *The Good Wife Taught Her Daughter*, 94.

29. Again, *The Book of the Knight of the Tower* is clearly an exception to this pattern. The Knight himself explicitly states that he intends his daughters to read this book themselves; in the prologue and chapter 1, 3–4, and in chapter 90, 117–19, he discusses women's education and argues that daughters should be taught to read so that they may read books (such as his own) that provide examples for them to follow (although he states he wanted the book written in prose so it might be easier to understand). *The Book of the Knight of the Tower*'s deviation from the pattern of the other texts may be due to class differences, since the Knight wrote for a class of women who were more likely to receive a formal education.

30. Furnivall, *The Babees Book*, 16–25. See also in the same edition "Babees Book" and "Urbanitatis," 1–9, 13–15.

31. "How the Wise Man Taught His Son" is the only boys' text to use a parental-advice format.

32. Orme discusses this practice in *From Childhood to Chivalry*, 44–80. This practice of fostering, of course, had purposes other than education; McCracken, "The Exchange of

Children in Tudor England," describes how in a slightly later period such a practice served to bind a social class together and created obligations and alliances between different families. Patricia Fumerton, on the other hand, discusses child exchange as a process of "polishing" children in a purely decorative sense in *Cultural Aesthetics: Renaissance Literature and the Practice of Social Ornament* (Chicago: University of Chicago Press, 1991), 29–66.

33. Mustanoja, *The Good Wife Taught Her Daughter,* 78.

34. See Orme, *From Childhood to Chivalry,* 58–60. Much of Orme's evidence here is drawn from correspondence such as the Paston Letters, making it difficult to determine the extent of the practice, but clearly it was not unusual for girls to receive an education away from home.

35. Joan Cadden (*Meanings of Sex Difference in the Middle Ages: Medicine, Science, and Culture* [Cambridge: Cambridge University Press, 1993], 11) points out, however, that medieval use of ancient theories was complicated and far from a simple derivation.

36. This extremely cursory overview is drawn largely from Vern Bullough, "Medieval Medical and Scientific Views of Women," *Viator* 4 (1973): 485–501, and Ian Maclean, *The Renaissance View of Women: A Study in the Fortunes of Scholasticism and Medieval Science in European Intellectual Life* (Cambridge: Cambridge University Press, 1980), 28–46.

37. Vern Bullough, "Medieval Medical and Scientific Views of Women," 497.

38. Vern Bullough, Brenda Shelton, and Sarah Slavin (*The Subordinated Sex: A History of Attitudes toward Women,* rev. ed. [Athens: University of Georgia Press, 1988], 92) state that Philo enjoyed a great deal of influence on Christian thought, although they do not expand upon this. Thomas Aquinas wrote that women bore children so that men might be freed for intellectual pursuits, reinforcing the physical/intellectual dichotomy. See Bullough, "Medieval Medical and Scientific Views of Women," 500.

39. Furnivall, *The Babees Book,* 1: 8; 2–3: 50–56; 16: 3–6; 17: 5–8.

40. The Knight does draw somewhat upon his own life experience, however. He explains that he was inspired to write by the memories of how badly his fellows had behaved toward women in his youth and the personal knowledge of how young men could draw women into dangerous behavior that would cause scandal (*The Book of the Knight of La Tour-Landry,* 2).

41. Ibid., chapters I, II, V, XI, XXXVII, XXXVIII, CXVI, CXIX, CXXIV, CXXVI, CXXVII, CXXIX, CXXXII. Even these numbers are misleading, because from chapter CXXIV on, the Knight uses the device of his wife speaking to describe the way his daughters should act. While his narrative wife does not use the learned examples that the Knight includes, in a sense, by telling the story, her life serves as the example, as in the Good Wife poems.

42. Ibid., 111–14.

43. Ibid., 6.

44. Ibid., 11.

45. Stith Thompson, *Motif Index of Folk Literature: A Classification of Narrative Elements in Folktales, Ballads, Myths, Fables, Mediaeval Romances, Exempla, Fabliaux, Jest-Books, and Local Legends,* rev. and enl. ed. (Bloomington: Indiana University Press, 1955–1958), 3: 414.

46. H. I. Marrou (*A History of Education in Antiquity,* trans. George Lamb [Madison: University of Wisconsin Press, 1982], 22, 158, 272) traces the use of physical punishment in the ancient Near East, Hellenistic, and Roman cultures.

47. Pierre Riché, *Education and Culture in the Barbarian West,* trans. John J. Contreni, foreword by Richard E. Sullivan (Columbia: University of South Carolina Press, 1976), 454.

48. Ibid., 11, 448–49, 452, 454.

49. Ayers Bagley, "Grammar as Teacher: A Study in the Iconics of Education," *Studies in Medieval and Renaissance Teaching* 1 (1990): 19–20, 23–24, 31. Both Bagley and Orme (*From Childhood to Chivalry,* 34–35) suggest that noble children may have faced beatings less frequently than lower-class children, but if their rank protected them from egregious violence, the principle of violence in the education remained the same. In his collection of conduct literature, Furnivall includes a poem, ostensibly from the schoolboy's point of view, which vividly illustrates pedagogical beatings: in "The Birched School-Boy" (c. 1500), a boy is flogged for being late and dreams: "I wold my master were a watt / & my boke a wyld Catt, / & a brase of greyhowndis in his toppe: . . . I wold my master were an hare, / & all his bokis howndis were, / & I my self a Ioly hontere: / to blow my horn I wold not spare! / ffor if he were dede I wold not care" (Furnivall, *The Babees Book,* 404).

50. Orme, *From Childhood to Chivalry,* 32–35.

51. *The Middle English Dictionary,* s.v. "chastien."

52. Furnivall, *The Babees Book,* 26: 1; 27: 1; 2: 36; 1: 14–17, 19.

53. Mustanoja, *The Good Wife Taught Her Daughter,* 173: 2. The latter phrase occurs throughout every version of "The Good Wife Taught Her Daughter."

54. Furnivall, *The Babees Book,* 32: 88–91.

55. Mustanoja, *The Good Wife Taught Her Daughter,* 172: 188.

56. *The Book of the Knight of La Tour-Landry,* 6.

57. Ibid., 25.

58. Ibid., 9.

59. Mustanoja, *The Good Wife Taught Her Daughter,* 173: 26.

60. Ibid., 174: 30.

61. The comparison is all the more insulting in that butchering, a messy and smelly occupation (and doubtless particularly so in the Middle Ages), was considered far from respectable. Butchers and people with similarly unpleasant occupations, such as tanners, were segregated into one section of towns or cities, preferably one where no one of any account lived (such as Southwark in London, an area noted for its lowlife).

62. *The Book of the Knight of La Tour-Landry,* 35. "Yede" means "went," therefore "yede to not" means "came to nothing."

63. Ibid., 5–6.

64. Ibid., 5–7.

65. In one of many examples, the emperor of Constantinople's younger daughter ends up making a rich marriage to the king of Greece. Ibid., 6.

66. Mustanoja, *The Good Wife Taught Her Daughter,* 159: 23; 174: 38.

67. Ibid., 173: 26.

68. Ibid., 159: 24–25. See also 161: 36, "Gode name fele wynneth," and 161: 48, "Euell lak [blame], euell name."

69. Furnivall, *The Babees Book,* 4: 81, 92–93; 13: 19–20.

70. "How the Wise Man Taught His Son" does discuss how a man should treat his wife, but this is, again, a notable exception among the boys' books. "The Boke of Curtasye" briefly mentions that men should always speak honestly of women because all men are born of women, but any sexual connotation here is extremely vague. Ibid., 306–7: 259–66.

71. Furnivall, *Queene Elizabethes Achademy,* 57: 25–28. "The Lytylle Childrenes Lytil Boke," in Furnivall, *The Babees Book,* 18: 33–34, tells the reader at the table "Pyke not thyne Eris ne thy nostrellis; / If thou do, men wolle sey thou come of cherlis." "Cherlis" comes from *carl,* or lower class; Furnivall glosses the word as "poor, rude, and rough people." Conversely, good manners will lead men to say "That a gentylleman was heere." Furnivall, *Queene Elizabethes Achademy,* 271: 96. A major concern of many of these books is boys' appropriate behavior toward the lord of the hall; see "The Boke of Curtasye," "The Babees Book," and "Urbanitatis," in Furnivall, *The Babees Book.*

72. *The Middle English Dictionary,* s.v. "rebuken," "rebuke."

73. Furnivall, *The Babees Book,* 7: 176–77; 18: 33–34, 47–48; 25: 141–42.

74. Ibid., 8: 188; 401: 68.

75. Whoever read the texts aloud may not necessarily have been related to the girls listening to them. Riddy postulates that conduct books were read aloud by the lady of an urban merchant household, not necessarily to her daughters, who could learn from the example of her own behavior, but to the young women employed as her servants. Many such girls were immigrants, drawn to the nearest big city by employment opportunities, and would not have had their own mothers on hand to teach them proper behavior. See Riddy, "Mother Knows Best." Riddy's argument, as well as Sylvia Thrupp's assertion that intelligent women in London's merchant class probably managed to learn to read English, is supported by the choice of the mother to narrate the Good Wife poems; this choice suggests that the authors expected the person reading the books aloud probably to be a woman, as a man reading aloud in the voice of the Good Wife might be less convincing.

76. It is worth noting that a number of the household texts containing conduct books also contained various scientific, medical, and astrological texts purporting to explain human nature and behavior.

7

Constructing the Female Subject in Late Medieval Devotion

Robert L. A. Clark

Devotional manuals might appear at first glance an unlikely site for an investigation of medieval subjectivity. Written in a highly prescriptive mode, such texts seem to presuppose passive subjects who would have little choice but to submit to the models and programs of conduct that their authors, who were almost always male, sought to impose upon their readers. The type of subjectivity emerging from such an understanding would thus largely preclude agency or self-fashioning on the part of the consumers of these texts. Such an assumption would, however, be mistaken. In their efforts to understand how medieval texts construct subjectivity and how issues of conduct figure into this construction, students of medieval culture have an exceptionally rich field of investigation in devotional manuals, especially manuals destined for women. I propose in this essay to examine several manuals or guides produced for women. Using theoretical insights drawn from Michel de Certeau, Teresa de Lauretis, and others, I will argue for an interpretive model that allows us to appreciate how these texts, far from stifling agency, may in many cases have encouraged their readers actively to engage in the exploration and creation of subject positions that otherwise would not have been available to them. We shall see that devotional programs far exceed the prescription of devotional practice and that they typically seek to provide a totalizing model for their subjects' conduct. It is precisely this tendency to overreach their ostensible purpose that allows us to see how devotional programs required complex negotiations from their subjects through which the latter ultimately fashioned their conduct, not just before God but in the world.

Several of the texts under consideration here are among those included in a survey by Geneviève Hasenohr of fifteen devotional manuals written for lay women by their spiritual directors.[1] The texts studied by Hasenohr, from France, Italy, and Spain, and dating from the thirteenth to the early sixteenth century, present in great detail the ideal day of the female Christian. From these documents and others, such as preaching and confessors' manuals, one can learn a great deal about how the Church, or certain representative clerics and spiritual directors, sought to advise and counsel their charges. The picture that emerges is, on first sight, a bleak one. On the one hand, women were rarely classified according to their own socioprofessional status, as was increasingly the case for male Christians.[2] Women's place was most often determined first by their gender and then by the sole criterion of chastity according to the archaic and static triadic model of Christian society as consisting of virgins, the chaste, and married people. Following this model, women were classified as either virgins, widows (and other chaste women), or wives, and their relative spiritual merit determined as one hundredfold for virgins, sixty for widows, and thirty for married women.[3] On the other hand, the guides in Hasenohr's survey make it clear that women who wished to follow a devotional program were forced continually to negotiate between the expectations of such a program and the demands of their worldly position. Ideally, they needed to be women of both considerable means and leisure; in reality, social demands were a constant interference for those women who sought to follow a monastic, contemplative ideal while remaining in the world.

Texts like those studied by Hasenohr clearly provide valuable insights into the lives of female Christians. But if we wish to exploit them in order to determine how they seek to construct their female subjects, we are faced with a problem, for similar devotional programs were composed for men. On the basis of this similarity between certain programs conceived for men and women, one could conclude that gender is not an issue in medieval devotional practices and their construction of the subject. This would, however, be a serious error, an error that can only be corrected by viewing these texts and their subjects through the lens of gender theory. Before turning to the theorists of gender construction, I offer an example drawn from American public life of how gender expectations can result in radically different interpretations of similar actions committed by women and men.

In our society, there is a powerful injunction against crying in many public or professional situations. But this injunction, while applicable to both men and women, cannot be interpreted in the same way for both. Let us take two examples from the political realm. When presidential candidate Edmund Muskie appeared to cry before the news cameras in February of 1972, it effectively put an end to his hopes of winning his party's nomination. Crying was seen as a sign of weakness undesirable in a presidential candidate; Muskie was perceived by many as not being "man enough" for the job.[4] When Pat Schroeder cried while announcing her withdrawal from the presidential race in 1988, it was also seen as a weakness, but in her case she was being too much "like a woman."[5] Of course, such expectations are also largely dependent on context: if the context were religious and not political, tears could be read in a more positive light as a sign of contrition. (Television evangelist Jimmy Swaggart's tearful public confession that he had "sinned" comes to mind.) In short, the same injunction or the same actions may take on different meanings depending on context, and context will in turn play an important role in determining gender expectations. It is through such complex negotiations and interpretations and their deployment through discourse that the social construction of gender is effected.

In approaching the female subjects of medieval devotional manuals, we are of course limited to the texts' representation of them, and their presence, which is also an absence, is available to us only through language or discursive practice. It may seem to us that these textual subjects are thus situated at a tremendous remove, but we must remember that it is primarily, though not exclusively, through discursive practices that subjects become intelligible to *themselves* as subjects. Michel Foucault has made one of the stronger cases for the construction of the individual through discourse. In Foucault's view, it is in and through discursive practices that power is exercised, a power that "forces the individual back on himself and ties him to his own identity in a constraining way."[6] Feminist theorists of the subject, highly critical of Foucault for his lack of interest in gender, have proposed theoretical models in which gender is the pivotal but not absolutely determining principle in the construction of the female subject. In so doing, they have offered a more nuanced approach for interpreting the interplay between discourse and subjectivity. Teresa de Lauretis, for example, has stressed the extremely volatile and shifting identity of the gendered subject as the site where contradictory discursive and cultural practices come into play. The subject's identity is, in this view, "multiple, shifting, and often self-contradictory."[7] Furthermore, the subject is not simply the passive construction of language but will at times be at odds with language. She is subject in the sense of being subjectED to social constraint but also in the sense that, as a subject, she constructs herself through her participation in language and culture. De Lauretis's model is especially attractive in the way that it allows for a resistant and divided subject, one whose responses to interpellation include a range of possibilities. In their privileging of discourse, it may seem that Foucault and de Lauretis lose sight of material reality, but in fact both emphasize the body, or rather bodies, as the locus where material and discursive forces are joined and play themselves out. The work of Judith Butler is very helpful in understanding the connection between discursive and material practices. Discourse, as she puts it, "produces and regulates the *intelligibility* of the *materiality* of bodies."[8] That is, discursive practices must first produce or construct a representation of the material bodies that they would seek to control, and consequently, the opposition between discursive practice and material practice reveals itself to be only an *apparent* opposition. Indeed, discursive practice, from this perspective, *is* a material practice, and the effects of discursive practices on material bodies are "real" effects, what Butler terms the "violence of the letter."

If we accept, then, that it is through discursive practices that subjects are both constructed and constrained, it still remains for us to situate these practices with regard to the subjects in question and with regard to each other. For, to paraphrase Carroll Smith-Rosenberg, a particular discourse spoken by those not at the center of power will mean something quite different, socially and politically, from what it means when it is spoken by those at the center of power.[9] In the texts that I will be discussing, part of my task, and not an easy one at that, will be to locate the particular discourse in relation to the center or, more properly, centers of power. One must constantly ask if, in the case of any particular text, one is dealing with a hegemonic deployment of discourse in that text, one that emanates from a power center, or with a potentially subversive use of that discourse coming from outside.

Not all post-Foucauldian theorists, of course, accept the argument that cultural analysis is limited to discourse analysis. Michel de Certeau, in his *Practice of Everyday Life,* speaks of the "multifarious and silent 'reserve' of procedures [in which] we should look for 'consumer' practices."[10] These procedures, according to de Certeau, "lack the repetitive fixity of rites, customs or reflexes, [and are] kinds of knowledge which are no longer (or not yet) articulated in discourse."[11] In this connection, de Certeau's distinction between strategies and tactics is one which is particularly useful in dealing with the material at hand. That is, in a given devotional text, what we usually have is what de Certeau would term a strategy, issuing from a clearly defined position of power and seeking to impose certain sanctioned forms of conduct. But the complement of this strategic discourse is the tactics of the "consumer," the ways in which she uses the imposed models.[12] Although the tactics and unarticulated procedures of medieval consumers of devotional texts are of necessity a gray area in our historical knowledge, a careful reading of the prescriptive texts can, we shall see, shed some light on these practices.

Medieval devotional manuals are a privileged source of information about everyday life, for, as mentioned above, one of their primary concerns is the establishment of an equilibrium between the active and the contemplative life. In the case of women, the sphere, not to say battleground, in which these tensions are played out is, in most cases, the family, the home, and the body. Before turning to texts that are representative of these tensions, I would like briefly to examine one that is not typical of the genre in this regard. This short text, written for his sisters by Jean Gerson (1363–1429), can be used as a foil, a sort of control against which other, more problematic texts may be set.[13] Using the text in this way is justified with regard to both its author and its recipients. Gerson, chancellor of the University of Paris and one of the most important religious and political figures of his time, speaks from a position of indisputable authority, in social as well as familial terms, although in advising his sisters he takes care to defer to the authority of their father. As for his sisters, they were ideal recipients for their illustrious brother's solicitous advice in that, as unmarried women of means, they could in fact dispose of themselves according to his suggestions. Among the latter was Gerson's desire that they should join a community of chaste women that was neither a monastic order nor a beguinage. Perhaps it is for these reasons that his text is so flat and so little concerned with the minutiae of everyday existence: he knew that it would encounter no resistance. But let us listen to Gerson himself, who speaks what can only be termed a doubly patriarchal discourse, fusing as it does his own voice with that of his father. In this passage from *Sur l'excellence de la virginité* (1395–1398), Gerson states:

> Tandis que j'avoye ceste escripture et ceste matiere en mes mains, me sont venues lettres de par vostre pere et le mien lesquelles m'ont baillié telle et de si grande joye au cuer que dire ne le porroie; car en icelles estoient escriptez mot a mot ces parolles de vous: Par ma foy je ne sauroye mieulx escripre ne dire comme ellez se portent, la grace a Dieu. Premierement ellez aiment Dieu et doubtent péchié, et junent ung jour ou deux la sepmainne, et dient tous les jours leurs heures de Nostre Dame; et les ha Marion aprises puis que son mari fu mort; et ne sont effraez nez qu'ellez estoient de six ans; et n'apercoy point quellez se veuillent marier a nul estat, jusques atant qu'il plaira a nous et vous. C'est ce que nostre bon pere m'a escript de vous, mes suers.[14]
>
> [While I had this text and this matter in my hands, letters came to me from your father and mine which gave my heart joy so great that I could not say; for in them was written word for word these words concerning you: By my faith, I could not give a better account of how they are doing, thanks be to God. Firstly, they love God and fear sin, and fast one or two days a week, and say their hours of Our Lady every day; and Marion has learned them since her husband's death; and they are not frightened [by all this], any more than if they took six years. And I do not perceive that they wish to marry themselves to any estate, until such time as will be pleasing to you and me. This is what our good father wrote to me concerning you, my sisters.][15]

The sobriety of this passage is matched by that of the seven-point program that Gerson prescribes for his sisters, prescriptions that, given their disposition, must not have been hard for them to follow: they should dress and act without ostentation; say their hours regularly and attend as many masses as possible; live soberly, drinking only diluted wine and avoiding spicy foods; live in peace with each other; never speak to men they do not know unless it be in public in the presence of others, and even that as seldom as possible, and never go dancing; and, lastly, learn to read French (*romaunt*) so that they can read the letters and devotional books that Jean will send them. One could hardly be more straightforward. However, it should be noted that even a text as dry and succinct as this one participates in several different discourses (the spiritual, the moral, the familial, the medical). They are, however, so perfectly consonant and mutually reinforcing as to form, in effect, a single, patriarchal discourse. Consequently, the subject of this monologic text—subject in the sense of subject matter, but also in the sense of being subject to the constraints imposed—is given the illusion of participating in a single dynamic rather than in several potentially conflicting ones. The last of the seven points made by Gerson is of especial import: in learning to read the text, his sisters will at the same time be constructed by it. At least in theory, there will be a perfect fit between their devotional practices and their conduct in the broader world, and they will not be able to imagine themselves other than as constructed by the text.

The monologism of Gerson's text is not typical of most devotional guides written for women. These texts are more often characterized by an extreme dialogic tension between the active and the contemplative, a tension all the more pronounced for its being inscribed within the confines of the home. A fourteenth-century manuscript composed for a lady of the high nobility who was a widow at the time of its composition is fairly typical of the devotional guides produced by clerical or monastic spiritual advisers for women whose social and material existence allowed them the time and means to devote themselves to the independent pursuit of a more spiritual life, remaining in the world to do so as opposed to joining a monastic community.[16] This manuscript combines certain features of the Book of Hours with those of the devotional manual. Books of Hours, prayer books destined for use by the laity, either at home or in church, allowed their owners to recite the Hours of Our Lady and other prayers in a program of personal devotion modeled more or less freely on the chanting of the Hours of the canon as practiced by religious communities.[17] The Book of Hours is thus something of a paradox in that it reflects both the demand for a more personalized kind of devotion and the continuing prestige of the traditional, collective forms of devotion practiced within monastic communities. In the Book of Hours there is a tension, albeit a latent one, between the realities of personal practice and the spiritual ideal represented by monastic practice. As I have suggested, this tension is symptomatic in more ambitious devotional programs, such as manuscript 592, that were designed specifically for individual lay people, for the spiritual director had the difficult task of negotiating between the temporal and spiritual obligations of his charge. Thus, manuscript 592 begins as a typical Book of Hours, but this resemblance ends after the calendar (added to the volume in the fifteenth century) and the Hours of the Holy Spirit (which in a more standard format of the Book of Hours would follow the Hours of Our Lady). After the twenty-three folios containing the Hours of the Holy Spirit, the manuscript presents over 150 folios of prayers, the texts of which are often given in both Latin and French translation. The effort to personalize the cycle of devotions set forth in the manuscript is most evident in the *enseignements*, or instructions, that accompany the prayers, which are themselves not unique to the manuscript. The *enseignements*, on the other hand, were written specifically for the manuscript's *destinataire*, and they often instruct the lady as to the proper occasion for a particular prayer and occasionally indicate as well the mental or physical attitude to be adopted. They also bring into the open the latent tensions inherent in devotional programs devised for the laity.

The tone of these devotional exercises is set in the first *enseignement*, which states:

> Dame, quar Dex en ceste munde vous ha mise en grant estat, raisons est que vous de cuer et de corps vous humiliez devant soi. Ensinc le font li ange qui sunt ou reaume dou ciel, si com vit sains Jehanz en l'apocalipse qu'il s'ageloignoient devant Deu & metoient leur faces iusque a ses piez. Donc je conseilleroie que les premieres oeuvres que vous ferez devers matin que a l'oneur de deu vostre creatour, vostre seigneur & vostre juge, en l'yglise se il vous vient a point ou en vostre chambre se il vous vient mieuz agrei, vos ageloigniez humblement & devotement & vostre face metez jusque a la terre ou pres ensint com li dit saint font et dites les paroles qu'il dient & sont teles . . . (fol. 30 r-v).

> [My lady, since God has placed you in this world in high estate, it is right that you should in body and heart come before him in humility. The angels who are in the Kingdom of Heaven do so, as Saint John saw them in the Apocalypse, kneeling before God and placing their faces at his feet. So I would advise that the first actions that you do in the morning, in honor of God, your Creator, Lord, and Judge, *in church if it be convenient for you, or in your room if it be more to your pleasure,* be that you kneel in humility and devotion and touch your face to the ground, or nearly so, and, as the aforesaid saints do, say the words that they say, which are . . .] (Emphasis added)

A prayer in Latin follows with translation and commentary in French. The lady's day is to open, in fact, with a succession of six prayers, to be recited, as we have seen, in her room or in church.[18] The latter is the next step on her daily spiritual itinerary; she is to recite the following three prayers in the manuscript there during mass.[19] This first cycle closes with prayers to be read upon going to bed.[20] The sequence of prayers to be said at certain moments of the day is, however, only the beginning of the lady's devotional program, as is made clear by the following *enseignement:*

> Apres, quar Jhesucriz ha volu que vous soiez en l'estat de vouvetei, pour ce selonc la doctrine de Saint Poul, jour et nuit devez Deu prier en obsecrations. (fol. 44v)

> [Afterwards, since Jesus Christ has willed that you be in the state of widowhood, for this reason, according to the teaching of Saint Paul, day and night you must pray God in supplication.]

The following eight folios contain a series of eighteen prayers, each of which thanks Christ for one of his gifts to men, from his conception to the Last Judgment. The lady is to recite, or rather read to herself, these eighteen prayers daily ("plus de cuer que de bouche" is the instruction). There follow two long prayers for before and after communion, and then yet another series of prayers in the form of suffrages to the angels, apostles, and various saints that, according to the *enseignement,* the lady is to recite at her leisure. The same held, one may assume, for the numerous prayers contained in the more than one hundred folios in the rest of the manuscript, most of which have simple rubrics with no instructions.[21] With such a program, one may legitimately wonder what makes this lady's day any different from that of a member of a female monastic community. The answer is that there is in fact very little difference—only her presence in the world, from which, one is given to understand, she cannot withdraw due to her social responsibilities. (Mention is made of the people whom she must govern and of her children.) Her independent status, both in material and marital terms, makes it possible for her spiritual director to propose a devotional program marked by long daily periods of prayer and meditation. Her spiritual standing in the eyes of the Church could, in fact, be enhanced in only one respect: that is, if she had never married and had remained a virgin. Failing that, she will remain chaste, praying to Saint Cecilia to help her in protecting her chastity. Such an ideal program was, of course, far beyond what the vast majority of lay men and women could attain. Indeed, the special allowances noted above as to the proper place for the lady's devotions, while perhaps marking a certain deference on the part of the author, are an indication of the difficulties that even the high-born might encounter in observing a rigorous devotional program.

Other texts allow us to flesh out the sketchy details provided by manuscript 592. In addition, the tensions of which I have spoken as typifying this entire family of devotional texts are more readily apparent. Perhaps the single most important determining factor in these manuals is whether or not the woman is married. A young, unmarried girl or widow, as is the case for the user of manuscript 592, could follow a more rigorous devotional program, relatively closer to those followed by cloistered women. A married woman could not. Not only were there the practical concerns of running a household and caring for children, but there was also the even more important fact that she was not free to dispose of her person, which was the prerogative of her husband. This meant that anything approaching the contemplative life, which was the devotional ideal, was effectively closed to her. Even young girls and widows, though, might have fairly important social and familial responsibilities that could interfere with their devotional program. There were essentially two solutions to this problem, which was seen basically as the opposition between the active and the contemplative life. We shall see that, in any case, it fell to the women in question to juggle their various obligations and that, in so doing, they were actively engaged in constructing themselves as devotional subjects.

The first of the two available solutions involved a constant mental effort to override nondevotional activities by projecting spiritual significance onto them in a systematic way. Thus, in the *Petite instruction et manière de vivre pour une femme séculière,*[22] the author offers the following exhortation:

> [S'il vous semble] que vous estes fort empeschée de devotion pour vos petis enfans, je vous asseure que vous les pouez bien tourner a devotion et en faire vostre proffit spirituel.... Et puis apres occuppez-vous aux affaires de vostre maison et vostre antention soit pour l'amour de Dieu.... Et quant vous cousés ou filiez et allez et venez, eslevez souvent vostre cueur a Nostre Seigneur et luy priez que il vous doint grace de l'aymer de tout vostre cueur et qu'il vous vueille tousjours adresser a faire sa saincte voulenté.[23]
>
> [If it seems to you that your young children keep you greatly from devotion, I assure you that can turn them to devotion and from this derive your spiritual profit.... And then afterwards, turn your attention to the business of your house and let your intention be for the love of God.... And when you sew or spin and come and go, raise your heart often to our Lord and pray to him that he grant you the grace of loving him with all your heart and that he be willing ever to direct you to do his holy will.]

This redirection of one's mundane occupations is considerably more pronounced in the *Decor puellarum,* written expressly as a spiritual guide for young girls by the Venetian John the Carthusian, who died in 1483.[24] Typically, the beginning of the day is a precious moment to be used for prayer and contemplation before turning one's attention to domestic responsibilities. John instructs the young girl to begin her day as follows:

> Rise early and, upon waking, bless God and meditate on the mystery of the Trinity. When you get up, cross yourself three times in saying "Benedicamus Patrem et Filium..."; while dressing, raise your eyes and mind to Heaven in saying "Agimus tibi

> gratias . . ."; say your usual prayers and meditate on the attributes of the three divine persons; having dressed, coarsely but decently, and put on your shoes, wash your hands and face and comb your hair while praying, with your heart remaining in Heaven, meditating on the creation of the angels, the fall of the bad and the confirmation of the good angels. Immediately thereafter, turn your attention to the housework: wake up the servants, light the fire, sweep, start breakfast, dress the children, make the beds, do the laundry, take care of the chickens, etc., while meditating on the celestial hierarchies, the reasons for the damnation of Lucifer, the creation of the world in six days, etc.

The strain of maintaining this program must surely have reached its limits at the dinner table:

> When you sit down at table, meditate on the Nativity; say the *Benedicite* and make the sign of the cross on the table; while eating the first course, think of the Circumcision; while eating the second, of the Adoration of the Magi; and when you have had enough to eat, meditate on the Massacre of the Innocents and the Flight into Egypt.[25]

Clearly, such a program, even when it had become routine (if one can imagine such a thing), must have put tremendous demands on the mental reserves of the young girl or mother even as it sanctified her daily activities.

The other model, rather more reasonable in its demands, proposed that practical and spiritual preoccupations be addressed separately and that certain times of the day be set aside for devotion. The two solutions were by no means mutually exclusive, for virtually all the manuals designate certain moments of the day as being especially propitious for prayer, the early morning being one of these, as we have already seen. What is especially interesting is that the manuals very often designate a domestic space for these devotions: the girl's or woman's room. The room is a retreat from the world where she can retire, usually after supper, to read, meditate, and pray, away from distractions and prying eyes. And it is a space that, through these activities, becomes sanctified. Several manuals instruct the woman to maintain an altar in her room that she should decorate herself with holy images and with an altar cloth embroidered by her own hand.[26] A relatively early French manual from the late thirteenth or early fourteenth century instructs the woman to remain "in as much a state of reclusiveness as possible in your room, for it was in her room that the glorious Virgin was greeted and there conceived the Son of God."[27] Yet another, late fourteenth-century French manual specifically identifies the woman's conscience with the room, as follows:

> [T]u te retrairas en ta chambre assez tost et clorras ton huys aprez toy; et aussy dois tu faire espirituelement, c'est a dire que tu dois tez sens qui ont estez ocupez et espartis le jour en plusieurs lieus ez chosez mondainez retraire et rassembler avecquez toy, et clorre l'uys de ta conscience et toy mettre avec ton createur seulement; et ne dois parler jusquez a l'endemain, se ce n'est en grant necessité ou de grant prouffit.[28]

> [You shall retire into your room as soon as possible and you shall close the door behind you; and you must do so spiritually as well, that is, you must withdraw and gather your senses to you, which have been occupied and scattered during the day among worldly matters in various places, and you must close the door of your conscience and place yourself in the presence of your creator alone. And you must not speak until the next day, unless it be for great necessity or great profit.]

One could hardly hope for a clearer example in support of Georges Duby's statement in his introduction to the medieval volume of the *Histoire de la vie privée* that the creation of private, domestic space is concomitant with the tendency toward interiorization and introspection.[29] In any event, it seems clear that when the woman crosses the threshold of her room she has entered a liminal space or, more precisely, that her activities in this space are characterized by their liminality.[30]

The concept of liminality, which has been especially fruitful in the analysis of collective cultural performances such as ritual and theater, has seldom if ever been applied to private ritual of the sort to be found in devotional guides. I would like to suggest the heuristic value of the concept of liminality in the study of private devotion through a brief examination of the latter's liminal aspects. First of all, as we have seen, the devotional subject separates herself from the mundane space of her everyday activities and from her contacts with the larger community in which she lives. Through ritual images, objects, and gestures (kneeling, crossing herself, praying, in some cases self-flagellation), she projects herself into a liminal space-time that, as in Turner's formulation, is invested with tremendous spiritual and ludic potential.[31] More to the point, though, are the mimetic actions and role-playing that characterize certain prayers, for example the prayer to Mary Magdalene by Saint Anselm that is translated in manuscript 592. To illustrate this point, I quote briefly from this prayer:

> O tres piteus, mes bons sires Jhesucriz, le diex de mon cuer, par reverance de ta chiere amie Marie, je convertirai ma parole a toi et empresumant de ta gran debonerretei, je t'ouserai demander comment tu queris a li porquoi ele ploroit. Ne t'avoit ele pas vehu qui estoies ses cuers et la douce vie de s'ame si cruelment occirre et de si laide mort mort morir? Et tu li demandoies, "Pourquoi plores tu?" (fol. 81 r–v).
>
> [O most merciful, my good Lord Jesus Christ, God of my heart, out of reverence for your dear friend Mary, I will address my words to you and, presuming upon your great gentleness, I will dare to ask you why you asked her why she was crying. Hadn't she seen you, her heart and the sweet life of her soul, so cruelly killed and put to so odious a death? And yet you asked her, "Why are you crying?"]

The lady's identification with Mary Magdalene achieves two other effects of liminality: reflexivity and the forming of a bond of *communitas*.[32] For when the lady steps into the role of Mary Magdalene, as here, the purpose is to make her reflect on her own life as a sinner. (She designates herself as "pecheresse" throughout the prayer.) Although the bonds that are created are not those of *communitas* characteristic of collective ritual, they are nonetheless bonds that allow the praying subject to commune with the holy, as in the contemporary images known as *sacra conversazione*.

We have seen that devotional guides often go well beyond prescribing a program of devotions to be carried out or prayers to be recited. In order to fashion the devotional subject, appropriate physical attitudes and gestures are indicated; and, in some cases, propitious times, spaces, and objects may also be designated in what amounts to a veritable mise-en-scène of devotional conduct. Not surprisingly, such guides are often characterized by a proliferation of detail concerning everyday life; and in some texts, every corner of the subject's mind and body are invaded by the spiritual director's probing discourse. Such is the case in an anonymous text, composed after 1408, which is included among various treatises of Gerson in a manuscript in the Bibliothèque de l'Arsenal in Paris.[33] We thus return to the Gersonian enterprise with which we opened our discussion, that of providing spiritual guidance for the laity and of making the contemplative life attainable for them. But unlike the brief treatise Gerson composed for his sisters, the author of this treatise proposes an exhaustive program for the integration of mystical devotion into the subject's everyday life.[34] He assures his charge that neither *mariage* nor *mesnage* are obstacles to the attainment of spiritual perfection:

> Car vous voiez que en vostre vocacion de mariage vostre mary crie et fait noise, l'enfant se blesse et fait noise, la chamberiere ne fait pas bien sa besogne et ainsi des autres empeschements qui sont innombrables. Et pour ce, ma fille, vous qui serés gente columbe sans amer laquelle le grant Noë(l), c'est a dire Dieu la Trinité, a fait a son ymage et mise en terre pour apporter le bel rainsel d'olme qui signifie doulceur en la bouche de l'esperit, ne trouvez riens en terre ou le pié de vostre affection se puisse ficher ou arrester mais retornez a Noë(l), a l'arche de contemplative oroison. Car tant plus croissent les eaues de tribulacion, tant plus se doit eslever en hault l'arche d'oroison sur les montaignes d'orgueil et de tout autre peché.[35]

> [For you see that in your vocation of marriage, your husband shouts and carries on, your child hurts himself and carries on, the chambermaid doesn't do her job well, and so on with the other obstacles which are without number. And therefore, my daughter, you who will be the gentle dove without bitterness which the great Noah, that is, God the Trinity, made in his image and placed on earth to bring the beautiful elm twig which signifies sweetness in the mouth of the spirit, do not seek anything of this world where the root of your affection can take hold; but turn [your thoughts] again to Noah, to the ark of contemplative

prayer. For the higher the waters of tribulation rise, the higher the ark of prayer must be raised up above the mountains of pride and of all other sin.]

As in many such devotional guides, the harried wife is told to take refuge in her room where, late at night, she can freely deliver herself to her devotional exercises:

> Je croy, ma tres chere fille, que l'eure la plus prouffitable a vous et a nous seroit de mynuyt apres dormir, apres la digestion de la viande, quant les labours du monde sont separez et delaissez, et quant aussi les voisins ne nous verront point et que nulz ne nous regardera fors Dieu et qu'i[l] n'y aura personne qui puisse veoir noz gemissemens ne les lermes et souspirs venans du perfond du cuer, ne aussi les ameres clameurs, plainctes et complainctes entrerompuez par fors souspirs, les prostracions et agenoillemens d'umilité, les yeux moulliez, la face muante ou suante, maintenant rouge, maintenant pale, quant on ne voit aussi batre la coulpe souvant et par grant contricion, baisier la terre par grant et humble devocion, lever les yeulx au ciel et les mains par grant desir, souvent plaier et entrelasser les bras comme se l'en acoloit son amy par grant amour, estandre le corps sur terre ou tout sur piez comme en une croix par grant compassion: telle chose est bonne a faire ou temps et en lieu que nul fors Dieu ne voie ces choses et autres semblablez signes de doulce devocion, lesquelles choses sont moult requises a ceste gracieuse oroison et euvre. Non obstant que en toute heure et en tout temps on doit, comme dit est devant, estre prest et diligent de drecier tousjours et lever continuellement sa pensee a Dieu, toutesvoies l'especiale heure si est l'eure de mynuyt.[36]

> [I think, my very dear daughter, that the most profitable hour for you and us would be midnight, after sleeping, after the digestion of food, when the labors of the world have been separated and left behind and when also the neighbors will not see us, nor will anyone see us but God, nor will there be anyone who can see our moaning nor the tears and sighs coming from the depths of our heart, nor either our bitter cries, plaints, and la-

> ments interrupted by many humble sighs, prostrations, and kneelings, eyes moist, face changing and damp, now red, now pale; nor then can one see us often beat our breast in great contrition, kiss the ground in great and humble devotion, raise our eyes and hands to heaven in great desire, often bend and intertwine our arms as if embracing a lover with great love, stretch our body out on the ground or standing, as on a cross, in great compassion; such things are good to do at a time and place when no one but God may see these things and other similar signs of sweet devotion, which things are greatly required by this prayer and work of grace. Although at any hour and at any time one must, as we have said, be ready and diligent always to train and to raise one's thoughts to God, nevertheless the special hour is indeed the hour of midnight.]

The director concludes this curious passage by saying that since his charge has a husband, household, children, and family, she should set aside some time for meditation after supper, between seven and nine in the evening. If I have quoted this text at some length, it is because it makes explicit the battle that is being waged quite literally over the wife's body, in the first instance, and her soul. She is physically engaged in a battle between her devotional practices and her conjugal responsibilities, indeed, between her spiritual director and her husband. And it is the voyeuristic spiritual director, not the invisible husband, who is privy, through his text if not his person, to these moments of extreme physical and emotional passion, despite his reiterated assurances that none of her actions will be seen by anyone but God. This is not the strategic discourse of a Jean Gerson, radiating from a position of concentrated power, but more of a tactical, subversive discourse, coming from outside the home and seeking to sap the structures of everyday conjugal life. It is a challenge to the very real power that the husband has over his wife's person. As de Certeau says concerning tactics:

> The place of a tactic belongs to the other. . . . [A tactic] must vigilantly make use of the cracks that particular conjunctions open in the surveillance of the proprietary powers. It poaches in them. It creates surprises in them. . . . In short, a tactic is an art of the weak."[37]

In any case, in the wife's devotions there is another substitute for the occulted husband: Jesus himself. In this, our manual is not unlike other works of mystical spirituality, as in the passage when the lady is told that contemplation is always completed in an *amour vivant* with the Lord. This *supplément* occurs when the soul, as the text puts it, "throws her entire self into the arms of her gentle lover and leaves reason and understanding outside to muse at the door, and love puts the soul in a secret chamber, where she kisses and embraces her Lord, not like a lord to be feared but like a loyal and amorous spouse."[38]

The complete displacement of the husband by the divine lover and his entremetteur, the spiritual director, does not mean, however, that the lady has been freed from all worldly cares and concerns. On the contrary, the text works on several levels to integrate devotional practice and the more mundane matters of household, diet, and social responsibility. Diet is a major concern, and here the director takes a firm stand against the excessive fasting of certain people (referred to at one point as "les filles de ce pays"), a practice that he says results in melancholic and fantastic visions, debilitating physical problems, illness, and death.[39] He reminds his charge that there are cures for overeating but not for malnourishment, and he admonishes her to eat well, taking even more meat than one normally would, because of the physical and mental rigors of her contemplative program (fol. 112v). She is to sleep at least seven or eight hours a day, more if necessary (fol. 111v). In this way, she will avoid speaking impatiently or harshly to her servants (fol. 114). The lady's highborn position, far from being a hindrance, is in fact a great advantage because it allows her the leisure of following a demanding devotional program. The social specificity of the director's arguments is quite remarkable, in fact. If she thinks that she need not trouble herself with the rigors of a strict devotional program because those of small merit will be saved along with those of great worth, then she should go work in the fields and vineyards with the *petits!* She should realize that God has granted the labor of the socially humble to the church, nobles, and bourgeois, not so that they can be called *monsieur* or *mademoiselle* and wear fine clothes but so that they will have the instruction, intelligence, and strength to purge body and soul and turn themselves entirely to God (fol. 120).

Such a discourse must surely be read in terms of a resistance to the husband's control over the wife's body (although we can imagine that there was perhaps resistance as well to the rigors of the devotional program). Power, as Foucault would have it, would not be power without resistance. And with resistance comes agency. One may legitimately wonder if submission to the director's gaze, as represented in the passage quoted above, makes for a devotional subject so objectified (or self-objectified) as to nullify the possibility of agency. While this may seem to be the case on a textual level, if we look beyond the text, we can see how agency would come into play in the interface between text and practice, in the realization of the devotional "scene" itself and, especially, in the way in which such devotional practices were integrated into the subject's daily routine.[40] We can only imagine, of course, what tactical negotiations this female subject was required to make in balancing the rigors of her devotional program and the demands of her domestic arrangements. It is not an enviable posture. One may of course argue that no matter who wins, it is the woman who loses. The end result is the same: men's control over women's bodies. But this would discount the very real nature of the conflict engaged and the very real participation of the subject in negotiating between these conflicting demands. Through these negotiations—actions carried out on a day-to-day basis, opportunities seized on the run—the subject of this text is in a very real sense fashioning her own conduct—indeed, constructing herself and her world. She is that volatile and shifting gendered subject of whom de Lauretis speaks.

In this essay I have been able to suggest only some of the issues that one must address in a gender-informed analysis of late medieval lay devotion. In looking at even relatively simple texts like Gerson's, we have seen that it is necessary to contextualize the points of enunciation and reception of discourse. Likewise, specific practices like praying and fasting cannot be considered in isolation from other practices set forth in the text. Even the most straightforward devotional manual will not limit itself to what we call "devotional practices," and the relationships among various practices will be different in different texts. In some cases there will be consonance, in others dissonance. The overall effect of these texts is to naturalize all the practices they describe, to make any given set of practices indistinguishable from other ways of conducting oneself in the world. But in this apparently seamless web, no practice, devotional or otherwise, can be separated from the constraints of gender. I have argued that, through these practices, the devotional subject is empowering herself. It is, of course, a self-empowerment available only, in most cases, to those who already hold a position of privilege in society, but I hope to have shown that the source of this power lies not so much in the subject's social position as in the agency that she brings to bear in the practice of her everyday life. In the final analysis, the devotional behavior prescribed by the Church for both medieval men and women, but particularly for the latter, cannot be divorced from such ideological considerations as the containment of sexuality and the preservation of the social order. Nonetheless, it is against this rather negative backdrop that are projected those images of sacred play and human agency through which the closed space of a lady's chamber becomes an imaginary theater of devotion, a boundless ludic universe.

Notes

1. Genèvieve Hasenohr, "La vie quotidienne de la femme vue par l'Eglise: L'enseignement des 'journées chrétiennes' de la fin du Moyen-Age," *Frau und spätmittelalterlicher Alltag* (Internationaler Kongress, Krems an der Donau, 2. bis 5. Oktober 1984), Österreichische Akademie der Wissenschaften, Philosophisch-Historische Klasse, Sitzungsberichte 473, Veröffentlichungen des Instituts für mittelalterliche Realienkunde Österreichs 9 (Vienna: Verlag der Österreichischen Akademie der Wissenschaften, 1986), 19–101. Hasenohr's article joins to a detailed treatment of her topic a survey of primary texts with descriptions and partial transcriptions of them. I have relied on Hasenohr in those cases where I have not been able to consult original texts.

2. Ibid., 23; cf. Maria Corti, "Models and Antimodels in Medieval Culture," *New Literary History* 10 (1979): 345–46.

3. Hasenohr, "Vie quotidienne," 21–23 (for the formulation of the model), 23–33 (for its use in pastoral literature).

4. "The episode came to symbolize the collapse of Muskie's Presidential campaign because of the perception that he was weak," Charlayne Hunter-Gault, "Remembering Ed Muskie," transcript of Online Newshour, March 26, 1996 (http://www.pbs.org/newshour/bb/remember/muskie_3-26.html).

5. "When [Pat Schroeder] withdrew from the 1988 Presidential race, she was hounded for her tears. Absolutely everyone, male, female, femininst, counterfeminist, had their say. See, we just knew women were wimps," Anne Taylor Fleming, "Crying If He Wants To," transcript, Online Newshour, July 10, 1996 (http://www.pbs.org/newshour/essays/fleming_7-10.html). Fleming argues that the injunction against politicians crying no longer holds for men but only, apparently, for women. One can only wonder if President Clinton, much beleaguered as we write, will deploy tears in his efforts to save his presidency.

6. Michel Foucault, "Why Study Power: The Question of the Subject," in *Beyond Structuralism and Hermeneutics: Michel Foucault*, ed. Herbert L. Dreyfus and Paul Rabinow, 2d ed. (Chicago: University of Chicago Press, 1983), 212.

7. Teresa de Lauretis, "Feminist Studies/Critical Studies: Issues, Terms, and Contexts," *Feminist Studies/Critical Studies,* ed. Teresa de Lauretis (Bloomington: Indiana University Press, 1986), 9.

8. Judith Butler, "Contingent Foundations: Feminism and the Question of 'Postmodernism,'" *Feminists Theorize the Political,* ed. Judith Butler and Joan W. Scott (New York: Routledge, 1992), 17.

9. Carroll Smith-Rosenberg, "Writing History: Language, Class, and Gender," in *Feminist Studies/Critical Studies,* 37.

10. Michel de Certeau, *The Practice of Everyday Life,* trans. Steven Rendell (Berkeley: University of California Press, 1984), 48.

11. Ibid., 45.

12. Ibid., xix.

13. Jean Gerson, "Sur l'excellence de la virginité," *Oeuvres complètes,* ed. Glorieux, 10 vols. (Paris: Desclée, 1966) 7: 416–21; briefly described in Hasenohr, "Vie quotidienne," 82–84.

14. Gerson, "Sur l'excellence de la virginité," 418.

15. All translations from the treatises and manuals are my own.

16. Paris, Bibliothèque Nationale, nouvelles acquisitions latines, 592. The manuscript is described in abbé Victor Leroquais, *Les livres d'Heures manuscrits de la Bibliothèque Nationale,* 2 vols. (Paris [Macon: Protat] 1927), 2: 260–66. One feature of the manuscript was clearly devised for the purpose of facilitating its use: on a number of pages a narrow strip appears in the outer margin beside certain prayers, each strip presenting a different pattern that is rendered more evident by use of blue and red inks for "coloring in." The first of these appears on fol. 32r next to the four verses of the cross attributed to Saint Anselm; the next one on fol. 33v next to a prayer of self-blessing. Thanks to this practical system, the lady could easily find her way about in her book.

17. An excellent introduction to Books of Hours is provided in Leroquais, vol. 1. See also Roger S. Wieck, *Time Sanctified: The Book of Hours in Medieval Art and Life* (New York: Braziller, 1988), 27–32.

18. A prayer of benediction and thanks to God; two prayers to the cross (the second consists of four verses of the cross attributed to Saint Anselm); a prayer consisting of the words "Jhesus nazarenus rex judeorum"; a prayer to Saint Cecilia; and a prayer of benediction attributed to Moses.

19. Two prayers to be said during the elevation of the Host (the second, a prayer to God by Saint Anselm); and a prayer to the Mother of God attributed to Saint Innocent.

20. Six verses of the Psalter; a prayer of thanks for the sacrifice of Christ on the cross; a prayer requesting God to bless the lady's resting place; the *Salve Regina;* prayers of intercession to the Virgin Mary and Saint John the Evangelist.

21. Some of these are translations of the long meditative prayers of Saint Anselm, for example, the prayer to Mary Magdalene quoted below.

22. Described in Hasenohr, "Vie quotidienne," 87–89. For another description of the text and citations of the early printed editions (the earliest of which dates from between 1512 and 1517), see Alice A. Hentsch, *De la littérature didactique du Moyen Age s'adressant spécialement aux femmes* (1903; Geneva: Slatkine, 1975), 223–26. Hentsch remarks

that this text is "un des nombreux traités mystico-ascétiques: il ne présente pas un très grand intérêt" (223).

23. As quoted in Hasenohr, "Vie quotidienne," 52.

24. Described in Hasenohr, "Vie quotidienne," 95–98.

25. Both passages here quoted from the *Decor puellarum* are given in French translation in Hasenohr, "Vie quotidienne," 96.

26. For example, the *Decor puellarum* and the *Regola del governo di cura familiare* of G. Dominici (Hasenohr, "Vie quotidienne," 67). According to Hasenohr, the tendency to transform the private chamber into an oratory and the use of images were more typical of Italian than French devotion.

27. [Se tenir] le plus reclusement que tu porras en ta chambre, car en sa chambre fu la glorieuse vierge saluee et ilecques concut ele le filz de Dieu (*La droite forme de vivre que doit mener l'ame qui se est donnee a Dieu en gardant sa virginité, sa veufveté, a tous jours ou monde,* as quoted in Hasenohr, "Vie quotidienne," 80).

28. *Comment on doit rigler sa vie,* included in the *Livret* attributed to Peter of Luxembourg (as quoted in Hasenohr, "Vie quotidienne," 83). The notion of the "inner chamber of the soul" was part of the Anselmian meditative tradition. See introduction, *The Prayers and Meditations of Saint Anselm,* trans. Benedicta Ward (New York: Penguin, 1973), 51–52. See also the appendix in the same volume, in which is quoted an early addition to Anselm's prayers, now attributed to Ralph of Battle, in which the latter writes: "My soul, my wretched, filthy soul, carefully gather within yourself all the senses of your body..." (279).

29. Georges Duby, "Avertissement," *De l'Europe féodale à la Renaissance: Histoire de la vie privée,* vol. 2 (Paris: Seuil, 1985), 13.

30. Liminality, from the Latin *limen,* or threshold, is a central concept in the work of the late British anthropologist Victor Turner. Turner described liminality as the state of being betwixt and between, the unstructured spaces that occur between an individual's or group's successive participations in clearly defined social structures. It is in these spaces that structures are negated or reversed by ritualistic actions and that rites of passage occur and bonds of *communitas* are reinforced. For a succinct but thorough presentation of Turner's theory of ritual, see Victor and Edith Turner, "Religious Celebrations," in *Celebration: Studies in Festivity and Ritual,* ed. Victor Turner (Washington, D.C.: Smithsonian Institution Press, 1982), 200–19.

31. It is particularly interesting that in an Italian manual the lady's children can play-pretend to perform the divine service at her private altar (Hasenohr, "Vie quotidienne," 67).

32. *Communitas* is rendered as "commonness of feeling" in Victor Turner and Edith Turner, *Image and Pilgrimage in Christian Culture: Anthropological Perspectives* (New York: Columbia University Press, 1978), 13. In the Turners' work, the term is applied to group ritual practices, but I seek to show that it is equally applicable to private rituals of the sort here described, in which the praying subject is perhaps less "identifying" than "communing" with Mary. I would like to thank Katherine Kong for suggesting this last distinction to me.

33. Described in Hasenohr, "Vie quotidienne," 84–86.

34. A note on the verso of the manuscript's final folio (141) states: "Iste liber est de conventu beate Marie fratorum Celestinorum Senonensis." The Celestine house of Sens was founded in 1366 (L. H. Cottineau, *Répertoire topo-bibliographique des abbayes et prieurés,* 3 vols. [Turnhout, France: Brepols, 1995], 2: 3006). From Sens the manuscript found its way to the Parisian house of the Celestines. Gerson had close ties with the Celestines, especially toward the end of his life. In 1419, when political turmoil prevented him from returning to Paris, he took refuge in Lyon in the Celestine house where his youngest brother, John the Celestine, was prior. Gerson spent his final years in Lyon, and John the Celestine would become his brother's literary executor.

35. Fol. 126v. Quoted with ellipsis in Hasenohr, "Vie quotidienne," 85.

36. Fol. 109v–10. Quoted in Hasenohr, "Vie quotidienne," 44–45.

37. De Certeau, *Practice of Everyday Life,* 37.

38. L'ame se gette toute entre les braz de son doulz amy et laisse raison et entendement dehors muser a la porte et amour la met dedans la chambre de retrait; la baise elle et acole son seigneur, non pas comme seigneur a craindre mais comme loial et amoureux espoux (fol. 89v).

39. Fol. 113v. According to the author, through excessive fasting and vigils would-be female mystics have brought on visions of the Antichrist and of crows as devils.

40. I would like to thank Katherine Kong for bringing to my attention this problem regarding agency.

8

Conducting Gender

Theories and Practices in Italian Confraternity Literature

Jennifer Fisk Rondeau

Why conduct literature? What is it in the first place, and why do we want to investigate it? Why do we care about what people wrote in the past about how they themselves or others ought to behave, to "conduct" themselves, to put it crudely? In addressing these very broad questions, I want to raise some theoretical issues that go well beyond the scope of this essay and this volume but to which both essay and volume speak. Briefly, I want to discuss the relationship between (post)modern theories of the subject on the one hand, and medieval studies on the other; I also want to problematize and theorize the category "conduct literature" using this discussion. In the second, longer part of the essay, I put my "theory" into "practice" in discussing the varieties of texts produced by and for the lay religious companies, or confraternities, of late medieval Italy.

It seems to me that our evident fascination with medieval conduct literature, however we choose to define it (and I will discuss this issue in more detail), rests at least in part on a fascination with issues of subjectivity and agency—with the complicated relationship between social structures of power, the production of the psychic and social self, and the possibilities for that self of action in the world. These are issues of evident contemporary concern, and efforts to historicize them have typically defined themselves in terms of the production of the modern self or subject. Medieval culture/s invite us to expand and complicate this project not only chronologically but also theoretically.

As Judith Butler has noted, theoretical considerations of the construction or production of the subject turn on the operations of power, understood both socially and psychically. Historicized theories of subjectivity, construed primarily as subjection but constituting also the subject's own power as agency, have tended to focus primarily on the social production of the subject in language, but Butler's formulations invite us to link the social and the psychic constitution of the subject. One of the problems historical investigations of subjectivity have continually faced is precisely the slipperiness of their central term—subjectivity—referring, as it so often is used, both to the process of hegemonic institutional subjection of individual subjects and to the creation in language (coming itself to constitute institutionalized hegemony in the early modern period) of a speaking subject. Although Butler's own project is not a historical one, she points precisely to the ambivalence of power inherent in the process of subjection/subordination. She writes, "Power considered as a condition of the subject is necessarily not the same as power considered as what the subject is said to wield. The power that initiates the subject fails to remain continuous with the power that is the subject's agency."[1]

It is precisely with the slippage between these forms of power, between these stances of the subject-in-formation, that I take the medievalist's project of discerning the multiple valences of conduct literature to be concerned. Butler is far more specific than any other theorist in her insistence that the "subject" is a linguistic one, not to be confused with—although always referring to—the individual. The historically informed approach I undertake in this essay also takes into account the social production of a discourse or discourses that are fundamentally intertwined with subject production. As Michel de Certeau writes, "History vacillates between two poles. On the one hand, it refers to a practice, hence to a reality; on the other, it is a closed discourse, a text that organizes and concludes a mode of intelligibility." To put it another way, history functions both as a mode of discourse (producing Butler's linguistic subject) and as the social processes whereby that discourse is itself produced. It is, furthermore, with the historical establishment of this distinction between what one might call history's stances that de Certeau is engaged. Writing, like myself, as a historian of religion, and echoing Foucault, he links the historical creation of the closed discourse of history—and of hegemonic "discourse" generally—to the claims to institutional power of the clergy. Clerics' claims to speak officially, in the name of religion—itself a historically defined category—both refer to and foreclose the possibility of examining transparently the "practice, hence . . . reality" of past cultures. Clerical claims to authority rest upon specific modes of linguistic control, framed in terms of the authority of the written word and Word—"discourse," in a word. In order to recoup a sense of the "réel," we must find ways of looking to "the formality of practices other than writing," in order to find "proof of popular practices that find a language for their expression in the margins of the religious tradition." Discourse, for de Certeau, is embedded in, perhaps is, "writing," and this discourse/writing is a quite specific form of ink on paper or parchment; it is a literate, highly constructed, elite written tradition. History is thus challenged to look somehow beyond itself—as produced in and by that discursive tradition—to the practice of the Other, and in particular to those oral traditions that are evidently encoded in language but which embody "practices" in ways that formal writing does not. The written, then, is discourse, the oral, practice—the one, a text, the other, a reality. History must function in both realms simultaneously—a difficult but necessary stance both practically and theoretically.[2]

History's ambivalent stance vis-à-vis discourse and practice, the written and the oral, can be fruitfully viewed as mirroring, producing, and being produced by the ambivalent stance of the power of the subject, itself the product of historical forces. It is, in fact, precisely the movement of these forces that de Certeau is concerned to trace. Such tracing, however, for him and for students of medieval conduct literature, involves also the recuperation of those aspects of the past that have been traced over, palimpsested by the seeming hegemony of the discursive tradition, of forces of subjecting power, by the project of Modernity, to put it another way.

Yet, as Butler reminds us, that hegemony is always already undone by the different and not-so-different power of the subject's agency. The ambivalence or slippage here—read theoretically or historically or both—and indeed the whole project of subject formation to begin with, is grounded in the foreclosure of particular erotic possibilities, which may in the modern world—as Butler argues—result in the melancholic production of a heterosexual subject, but that at crucial moments in the past have managed to exceed the possibilities for their containment.[3] This excess—especially available for examination in the Middle Ages—necessitates our consideration of subject formation as a profoundly gendered process. Desire is especially uncontainable in many confraternity laude, as we shall see, and the result is its expression in multiply gendered, complexly erotic languages that replicate precisely the ambivalence of their speaking subjects' social stances—and that also refuse the melancholic turn toward the necessity of the heterosexual.

If we take Butler's theories of subjection as a model for historical inquiry, we can describe our project as one that seeks not so much to discern the underlying traces of traditions—"popular," "oral," "mass"—as to describe the complex, ambivalent relations between discourse and practice, written and oral, power as subjection and power as agency. De Certeau's distinction between text/discourse on the one hand and the oral/practice on the other is, after all, "practically" a problematic one, since historians have little but texts to work with. Conduct literature provides us with a particularly useful body of materials for examining not so much the oscillations of a binary distinction as the vast ground between two extreme poles, neither of which can truly be said to manifest itself in the texts, materials, or sources of the past.

But what is "conduct literature" anyway? In this essay I work with two different but linked senses of the term. On the one hand, we can understand conduct fairly simply and straightforwardly as the ways in which people comport themselves, whether publicly or privately, although we generally tend to emphasize the former. According to this sense of the term, "conduct literature" is primarily a descriptive term, and texts that encode it tell us about how people behave or behaved. "Literature" is here thus broadly construed as that body of written materials that either wittingly or, more often, unwittingly tells us about what people did. One might call this the "historians'" sense of conduct literature, following de Certeau, with its emphasis on practice. I will argue in a moment that although this may seem like a naive definition, it is one that has been too often overlooked in the scholarship on medieval conduct literature.

That scholarship has tended to emphasize somewhat different meanings of our key terms. "Conduct" is seen rather as primarily prescriptive, as a set or sets of normative behaviors encoded in highly formalized texts, but "literature" is construed more narrowly as texts bounded by the requirements of genre or trope—in de Certeau's "writing" or "discourse." There is a highly, and very particularly, gendered component to this notion of conduct literature, since its texts are (almost) invariably addressed by men to women. Interestingly, even texts whose larger frame does not necessarily meet the requirements of the genre, and indeed may contest some of its assumptions, come to be read metonymically as conduct literature because a key part appears to fit the definition. One well-known example is that of Leonbattista Alberti's *Della Famiglia,* where Giannozzo's notorious advice to the young Lionardo on how to marry in book 3 has been made to stand both for the entirety of book 3 and for the work as a whole, which comprises four distinct dialogues between different Alberti family members on different subjects. One might, to pursue my previous comment, call this the "literary critics'" sense of "conduct literature."

There is, in the distinction of meanings I have drawn here, a distinction in definitions of source materials as well. A genre- or trope-bound reading of conduct literature has a sense of its materials embedded in its project at the outset. A more descriptively based reading also works with a sense of materials that define its project, but such materials come to be more arbitrarily bounded. Take, for example, my own work on Italian confraternity literature. I read statutes, chronicles, account books, and laude, or vernacular, hymns, all as potential descriptive (*and* prescriptive) conduct literature. I read them this way not because I began by defining "conduct literature" in a specific manner (although indeed I have ended by doing so), but because the category of conduct literature has proven useful to me as a tool for getting at the lives, and the discourses that structured and were structured by the lives, of pious laypeople in the late Middle Ages.

This discussion of "conduct literature" might well be taken to suggest an emphasis on Butler's production of a linguistic subject, and to a certain extent this essay does focus on linguistic production. The confraternity texts I examine, however—and many other examples of conduct literature as well—were also socially produced and performed, enacted within a public space where conduct, in all its ramifications, was always already a crucial indicator of an individual's social and personal "subjectivity." Here the formulations of the Marxian theorist Henri Lefebvre are useful. The subjectivities that conduct literature largely works to represent and establish are religious, social, economic, and political. In all of these guises they are thus bound up in the production and control of space, both interior domestic space and exterior public space. As Lefebvre writes,

> the problematic of space, which subsumes the problems of the urban sphere (the city and its extensions) and of everyday life (programmed consumption) has displaced the problematic of industrialization. It has not, however, destroyed that earlier set of problems: the social relationships that obtained previously still obtain; the new problem is, precisely, the problem of their *reproduction*.[4]

For both postmodern, postindustrial society and for medieval society, however, it is (problematically) within space that social relationships (and perhaps also the psychic subjection that Butler interrogates) are reproduced; the crucial difference lies in modes of reproduction. Lefebvre, not surprisingly, romanticizes the continuities between production and reproduction he sees as available in the experience of space in Italian communal urban life of the thirteenth and fourteenth centuries (the precise social and political setting of the confraternities I discuss here), where the citizen (confraternity member) experienced space

> in the traditional emotional and religious manner—that is to say, by means of the representation of an interplay of good and evil forces at war throughout the world, and especially in and around those places which were of special significance for each individual: his body, his house, his land, as also his church and the graveyard which received his dead.[5]

This is what Lefebvre calls "representational space," to be contrasted with a new, modern "representation of space," which emerges—again, where else?—in Italian Renaissance painting, with its "homogenous, clearly demarcated space complete with horizon and vanishing-point." The suggestion is of dissonance and distance; where the medieval citizen could enact himself within a representational space, the Renaissance/modern citizen must watch himself represented in space, removed by the process of representation from participation in it. Yet, as we shall see, representation in and of space could be profoundly problematic in thirteenth- and fourteenth-century urban Italy as well. Lefebvre's representational space turns out to be nearly as much a momentary escape from dissonance for the medieval citizen as its historical image might be for the (post)modern reader/viewer. For both, however, subjection, discourse, theory, practice—all are produced, enacted, reproduced in space, in and on the spaces of individual bodies and in the social space Lefebvre reminds us we must never forget. Let us explore some of these medieval spaces more particularly.

My readings of confraternity literature as conduct literature use the latter term in both the senses defined above, that is, as both descriptive and as prescriptive. In statutes and in laude, we can discern a body of practices and a larger concern with the practice of the body that have much in common with "conduct literature" more conventionally understood.

Most obviously perhaps, statutes regulate a plethora of conduct details for members. Unsurprisingly, much of this regulation concerns devotional practices: the saying of prayers, giving of alms, and providing for the ill and indigent, whether of the confraternity exclusively or of the larger community. The inclusion of rules forbidding certain social practices—frequenting taverns, playing at dice, associating with persons of evil reputation—may also seem unsurprising to us, given our familiarity with a (post-)Reformation morality. But I will argue that these proscriptions mark some of the most interesting and problematic aspects of confraternities' efforts to come to grips with the theory and practice of conduct.

Some more stringent practices were observed by only a few groups, most notably the ritual performance of flagellation, both publicly and privately. Such conduct is clearly expected in the interest of marking members both as devout Christians and, in the case of public processions, lauda singing, or flagellation, as devout members of the group as well. "Conduct" writ large thus concerns the bodies of individual confraternity members and the larger body of the confraternity as a whole—a vital relation of which the statutes are explicitly aware as well. Failure to observe the statutes, especially with regard to group participation, was punishable by a series of small money fines, private and public admonition or discipline (including flagellation on some occasions), and expulsion from the group.

There are two crucial aspects of this emphasis on conduct within confraternity life. First of all, conduct as external behavior in the statutes is coupled with the production of elaborate ceremonies—and especially the production of texts for use in those ceremonies—that are quite explicitly concerned with inculcation of particular attitudes, states of mind and heart, subjective conditions that are viewed as corresponding to but not completely delimited by objective behaviors. A number of commonly sung laude, for example, chastise the singer for his failure to feel as he ought toward, especially, Christ. "Alas, my cold and weary heart, why do you not sigh for love, so much that you should die from it?" or "Too much does he lose time who does not love you, sweet love, Jesus, over every other love!" Others call on their singers to sing joyously, or to praise lovingly the object of their devotion—simultaneously describing and prescribing the subjective state required of the devotee created by their singing, linking behavior and subjectivity through the act of singing itself and through the specific words sung. Singing laude is, in other words, itself a form of conduct, but one that must be performed precisely correctly in order to bring conduct and subjectivity, social and linguistic production, into line, as confraternity life seems designed to do.[6]

This assumption of a precise correspondence between inner and outer selves/lives—or, to put it another way, between discourse and practice—seems to me to lie at the heart of our contemporary fascination with conduct literature defined either narrowly or broadly. It offers a challenge to our (post)modern senses of the individuated self, of subjectivity writ however problematically as challenging, albeit challenged by, the institutional structures that would subject us rather than permit us to speak as subjects in our own right. Rather, the "medieval" construction of conduct appears to demand subjection to external and interiorized structures in place of subject-speaking—the antithesis of our subject-dreams.

At the same time, however, I suspect a kind of lurking pre-Raphaelite utopianism to inform some of our interest in medieval constructions of conduct and subjectivity. Subjection can look, after all, much easier than interrogation of the structures/institutions that constrain agency at the same time that they promise its fulfillment. Coupled with something like a post-Burckhardtian pity for the naive, undifferentiated, medieval world-soul we find sometimes a nostalgia for the "childlike" assumption that ritual can construct a self, that rules can create an actor, that exterior and interior states correspond, or can be made to correspond, so nearly perfectly.

Within the Christian tradition, of course, such a correspondence can be only approximate in this world; a perfect correspondence can be achieved only in the next world, only approximated imperfectly in this one. The gap between discourse and practice is always already there, and nowhere more insistently than in the language of conduct. We find in confraternity texts, in fact, both an explicit awareness of this troubling spiritual condition and an ongoing struggle to deal with it in sometimes perplexing terms (awareness and struggle perhaps not so unlike our own struggles with issues of subjection and autonomy as we might like to think). At the end of the thirteenth century, for example, the Florentine company of Sant'Egidio established a series of elaborate rituals for disciplining members who had disobeyed the confraternity's extensive conduct rules; one of their most striking components is their concern for the penitential attitude of the errant member. Indeed, failure of attitude, at least its outward expression, was in and of itself sufficient grounds for expulsion from the confraternity.[7]

Sant'Egidio's statutes' structure, moreover, suggests a remarkable awareness of the links not just between inner and outer states, but between conduct and grace. The text begins almost immediately with a fairly standard, but detailed, list of behaviors to be avoided, although some of the items included must give us some (baffled) pause. Members were specifically enjoined, for example, from going into places of cloistered women or having "any familiarity with them," or from going into any other church (than that of Sant'Egidio) for any pious purpose or staying there at night, without the express permission of the captains and the friar responsible for the company's spiritual guidance. There seem to be embedded in these unusual proscriptions concerns about the temptation of the company of women—even, or perhaps especially, religious women—and about overzealousness or possibly competition from other churches. Other confraternities, however, typically encouraged their members' private and public devotions, wherever they might be conducted.

More significant than the specific anxieties these details might point to, however, is the fact that such details appear at all—and that they form an integral part of what can only be described as the conduct of grace and conversion. It is immediately following the proscribed conduct list that the rituals for correction, together with admonitions about attitude, appear. Then, and only then, do we find rules for what members ought to do, rather than refrain from doing. For, as the statutes note:

> Here above are contained those things which it behooves us . . . to guard against doing. Here immediately below are contained those things which it concerns us to do. Since, according to Saint Augustine, it is not enough that a man refrain from evil, if afterward he do not take up the good.[8]

Conduct, in other words, serves as both outer and inner sign of conversion, marking both avoidance of evil and pursuit of good. It cannot coerce grace, but for the individual and the group it provides a crucial means and evidence for its pursuit. It is, moreover, both negative and positive: there are practices to be avoided, so that others may be pursued. Within this scheme of things, the Sant'Egidio statutes suggest, taverns, the company of (religious) women, or excessive devotional zeal are to be avoided precisely so that members may pursue such true signs of conversion as confession, daily prayers, lauda singing, and regular attendance at confraternity meetings—all practices demanded by the statutes.

That these assumptions of an at least theoretically seamless fit between personal conduct and the position of the confraternity itself vis-à-vis the world were hardly unproblematic is suggested by the fact that when the company came to revise its statutes several decades later, both the extensive concern for personal conduct and the preoccupation with inner attitude on the part of the penitent vanished. In their place we find a brief list of behaviors to be avoided and an even briefer admonishment to those who persisted in engaging in them. It is as though the confraternity had, officially at any rate, given up on conduct as signifier—in a volte-face all the more remarkable for the theoretical sophistication with which it had once articulated the importance of conduct for its members.

While explaining this change adequately lies well beyond both the scope of this essay and, I suspect, the capacity of historical inquiry, I would like to suggest that it represents precisely the vital importance of conduct as theoretical foundation for confraternity members and its highly problematic status as signifier. And it is here that we come to my second point regarding conduct and confraternity texts. A few examples will suffice to illustrate my argument. At the beginning of the fourteenth century, the confraternity of San Domenico in Prato, among other things, forbade its members to enter any tavern in or around the city for the express purpose of eating bread, meat, or cheese.[9] Around the same time, the company of Santa Croce in the same city prohibited its members from wearing gaudy, colorful clothing, "to set a good example and to extinguish all motive or appearance that could change into vice, or could give any help . . . to the members in pride and in all vain and curious honors." More remarkably, this same confraternity enjoined its members from buying or selling grain or other crops, linen, wine, or any other merchandise.[10]

Public consumption of food and clothing, public displays of wealth and power, public commercial transactions—all these were the precise hallmarks, the practices both theorized and undertaken, of the new urban layman of the late Middle Ages. It was in service to him that the new mendicant orders emerged. It was presumably by him that the confraternities were created. It was under his inspiration and in response to his concerns—and those of his sisters, mothers, daughters, and wives—that new forms of religious life and spiritual exploration proliferated. Yet here he is, presumably under the tutelage of an institution he helped to create, being admonished to abandon exactly those activities that had created him as a social actor in the first place. These statutes do not represent a call to formal religious profession; they are for the most part not very different from others of their genre. But in pushing the concern with a very urban set of practices, a very urban definition of conduct, as far as they do, they remind us both of the depths of the problematic spiritual and social issues with which confraternity members struggled and of our own need to read very carefully for "conduct."

To be blunt: just how far did these groups expect their members to be guided by their regulations? To what extent do these texts themselves represent not an effort to eliminate vice and its signifiers through regulation of practice, but rather a profound expression of the fundamental impossibility of their putative task? Conduct is as much a theory as a practice, as I have already argued. In the practical impossibility of injunctions against commerce, or in Sant'Egidio's abandonment of its early theories of member conduct, I would argue further that we find an acknowledgment that, for confraternities specifically, conduct had as much theoretical as practical importance. We might want to explore further, and in other contexts as well, the extent to which late medieval regulation of conduct both encodes and represents its problematic relations with the practices it purports to create and describe.[11]

It is most pressingly in the realm of the public that the relationship between theory and practice begins to unravel in confraternity texts explicitly regulating conduct—not surprisingly, since it was the creation of new public forms that typified the urban milieu within which confraternities proliferated and whose problems they attempted to address. Up to this point, I have explicitly assumed the masculine gender of both confraternity members and their institutional concerns, but it is now time to bring this issue more clearly into focus.

By the early fourteenth century, the public forum of Italian cities was a place explicitly and implicitly gendered masculine. To participate in public life in any of its myriad forms, as communal magistrate, as guildsman, as soldier, as confraternity member (although somewhat less insistently so), required that one be a man. A few confraternities seem to have included women from their inception, but the general assumption of a masculine culture is plainly demonstrated, for example, by the plaintive concession made by the Florentine confraternity of Santa Reparata in 1377. In that year, with the city under papal interdict and private and public spiritual life in crisis, the company reluctantly allowed women, whose prayers had been strident and insistent, admission as marginal members of their brotherhood. They were not allowed any of the public privileges of the confraternity, however, nor participation in any of their public rituals. Only the spiritual benefits of membership were to accrue to women, while the men continued their public lauda singing, financial assistance to one another, funeral rituals—and collection of substantial dues and alms, from women and men alike.[12]

Male confraternity members worked to further their groups' interests in other public forums, as well. Communal revenues were assigned to specific confraternities in a number of cities, and city-wide promotion of particular confraternity devotions was common. Guilds were sometimes associated with specific confraternities. And, I would suggest, it is a specifically masculine concern with conduct and reputation—with signification in the public sphere, to put it another way—that is reflected in the statutes I have discussed. It is tempting, given these parameters, to argue that in some of the statutes' more remarkable efforts to curtail public conduct we might read a generalized "feminization" of the masculine subject of confraternity texts. To the extent that masculinity in late medieval Italian cities was bound up with a particular set of public practices, and to the extent that the statutes challenge those practices, such an argument may indeed be an important one.[13]

But other confraternity rituals and texts themselves suggest a much richer, more particular, and more complex gendering of their subjects. It is particularly in the laude—in the texts themselves, and in the practices they simultaneously describe or create and are contained within—that theories and practices of gendered conduct work to create the subject, who is also agent or actor, of confraternity life. The troubled relationship between theory and practice I have argued characterizes confraternity statutes regulating conduct is at least partly resolved in the laude and in the act of lauda singing, precisely because they occupy a different, an alternative, public space to that otherwise occupied by confraternity members. That space is, moreover, one that can, if only momentarily, make room for a feminine speaking/singing subject among various Others. Indeed, it seems that a kind of spiritual cross-dressing becomes almost required by the texts of many laude. The most common forms of such cross-dressing, however, involve class and power as well as gender reversals. For example, the singer almost always relinquishes his power—specifically, his communal powers, *bailia* and *signoria*—to the objects of his lauda devotion. Indirectly, there is an association of powerlessness with femininity, especially in laude to Mary, but it is not often made explicitly. In some of the laude's more extreme explorations of what we might call a cross-dressed dynamic, however, gender transgression becomes a vital way in which to explore relations with the divine. It is precisely because lauda singing marks itself off as ritualized, liminal space that all these reversals and transgressions become possible and, indeed, within the spiritual dynamic they delimit, even necessary in their replication of the implications of extra-laude social relations.

The world of public conduct described by the discourse of confraternity statutes, and by contemporary guild regulations and communal statutes as well, was not only a masculine one, but one characterized by prudence and restraint.[14] The world of the laude themselves, if not of the rituals in which they were performed, was anything but. The interior state, the emotional condition most frequently conjured up in lauda texts is that of desire—insatiable longing, desperate passion, utterly unrestrained erotic abandon.[15] In this, as in much else, they reflect the themes and preoccupations of much contemporary spiritual writing. Read within the specific contexts of confraternity life and active engagement in urban life characteristic of their singers, however, their reiterations of desire, and the problematically gendered dynamics of that desire, take on particular significance.

Gender and desire construct the singer of the laude in two ways I want to discuss here. First, the act of singing itself is associated with desire, with the need to sing—to act, to engage in this particular practice—in order to inculcate a necessary desire, directed toward an Other object, within the singer. Second, insofar as this desire is frequently, although not always, eroticized, the singer becomes often ambiguously, always problematically, gendered.

Most lauda texts confine their invocations of desire and song to the kinds of examples I have already cited, to promises of spiritual union with the divine to those who sing the lauda with true desire, to admonitions to desire union, especially with Christ but sometimes with Mary, and to gain that desired desire through the "desire narrative" of the lauda itself. They assume tacitly their important but ultimately insufficient role in creating and manipulating a desiring singer. One remarkable text, however, pushes the implications of this common trope much further, and in so doing opens up for our inspection the laude's assumptions about the relationship between conduct (in this case, singing) and subjectivity (in this case, altogether subsumed/subjected by desire):

> It stupefies every mind
> that wishes to contemplate you;
> it is not to speak of nothing, to say
> that every human praise
> is almost a blasphemy;
> I so long to speak of you, though,
> that I am struck silent.
>
> I remain as silent
> in outward aspect
> as I cry aloud within
> what my lord is like,
> making a new song
> with desire in my heart
> crying aloud love, love,
> my pain is completed.

[Istupischa ogne mente / che te vuol contemplare / non e parli niente / chi ben ti vuol laudare / ch'ogne loda di gente / e quasi un bastemiare / percio si vo parlare / di te amutolischo. // Amutolischo al quanto / nel dimostrar di fuore / dentro grido alto tanto / che mod'e'l mie signore / facento un nuovo canto / col desider del cuore / gridando amor amore / la mie pena finischo.][16]

In other words, the singer's capacity to sing this text is utterly undone by the text itself. And yet, the act of singing makes it possible for the otherwise impossible to occur: the singer remains silent outwardly, while inwardly he cries aloud. And yet the practice of singing the text brings outer and inner desire and ability together. The utter incapacity of speech, of discourse, may demand a complete rupture between conduct and subjectivity (with which we postmoderns, in our preference for the ironic, may feel much more comfortable), but here song's very different power to articulate desire brings both language and desire back to the body, to the voice, and to the longing it embodies. In light of some of the other laude I discuss in this essay, one might call this move one that refuses, or historically has yet to be subjected to, the melancholic production of heteronormative desire. Desire in language struggles here with language itself, rather than with any particular erotic economy. Language, in a variation on Paul Zumthor's discussions of orality and vocality, offers a space within which to bridge that troubling gap between conduct and subjectivity, discourse and practice, desire and its object.[17]

This particular lauda appears only in a collection that belonged to a group of *disciplinati*—in other words, the evidence we have tells us it would have been used as part of private flagellant ceremonies, held in secret and in darkness, rather than in public, whether in open-air processions (as was most often the case) or as part of the Mass. As a practice, it offers its singers the redemption of desire and language only in an alternative space to the public, rather than in a transformed public space. Many other laude share its fundamental assumptions, however, and it is to them, and to their representations of gender, that we will now turn.

If desire is the subjective condition most frequently developed in lauda singing, can we say that it is, especially in its more highly eroticized representations, gendered? (Post)modern discussions of desire assume that it always already is gendered, but I wish to argue here that while gender may operate crucially in representing desire in the laude, it does so problematically and ambiguously. Indeed, it is gender's trouble that I wish to emphasize here, its disruptive union with desire to create a very different set of theories and practices of conduct from those articulated elsewhere in confraternity life. And yet, it is precisely its offering of an alternative to the impossible relationship between theory and practice of conduct in confraternity statutes that I want to argue makes that slippage bearable and that serves, however momentarily and liminally, even to remedy it.

The most gender-troubled rendering of desire in the laude appears in two different fourteenth-century collections. "Ben morro d'amore" rings a series of changes on its refrain—"I would die of love"—that powerfully evoke desire but that only indirectly, and perhaps troublingly, allow us to fix the gender/s of the desiring bodies depicted.

I would die of love
I would die of love
I would die of love
From the sighs alone
That he makes me cast forth
My great lord.

Sighs I send you.
Son of Mary;
I beg mercy of you,
Jesus, my life.
I die tormented
In my soul;
Yet still I cry
Laments of love.

Aching laments
I send out, languishing
For I am in such pain
That I am wholly broken,
And I am so beloved
More than I can take in,
So that I am wholly set alight
In a fire of love.

This fire surpasses
All other agony;
Everything transfixes me
In every vein.
All pain is erased
With a whisper.
My love has put me in bondage.

I am bound
In a prison
And locked inside;
I know not the cause,
Nor if I shall be helped
And I know
That this question
Is the end of love.

I would put an end to it,
That I might love no more;
I know that I would go mad
If it were to last too long.
And I would die soon
If he were to leave me,
If he carried me no longer
In the arms of love.

Carried in his arms, I swoon
from these great pains,
which I suffer, languishing in Christ;
then I am helped:
I rise to the heights;
and I give birth to a son of love.

[Ben morro d'amore/ ben morro d'amore/ ben morro d'amore/ pur delli sospiri/ che mi fa gittare/ lo mio grande singnore. // Sospiri ti mando / filgliuol di Maria / merce t'adimando /ihesu vita mia / morro tormentando / nell'anima mia / pero sempre cria / lamenti d'amore. // Lamenti dogliosi / io gitto languendo / che son si penosi / che tutto mi fendo / et son dilectosi / piu ch'io non comprendo / si che tutto incendo / d'un foco d'amore. //

> Questo foco passa / sopr'ongn'altra pena / tutto mi trapassa / in ciascuna vena / ongni dolgla cassa / che chiamat'a lena / in una catena / messo m'a l'amore. // Sono incatenato / in una pregione / et dentro serrato / non so la cagione / si saro aitato / et o la ragione / questa questione / termini l'amore. // Termine vorrei / ch'i piu amasse / so ch'impasserei / se troppo durasse / et tosto morrei / se non mi lassasse / piu non mi portasse / in braccio l'amore. // Im braccio mi tene / et io tramortisco / per le grandi pene / in Cristo rapisco / allor mi sovene / com'alto salisco / pero parturisco / un filgliuol d'amore.][18]

I quote at such length (although this is only a little over half of the entire text) in order to provide a sense of the relentless quality of desire depicted here, and I provide English and Italian texts in order to make my point about gender. If we read only my (admittedly crude but literal) English translation, we might be forgiven for assuming that the singer's gender is feminine. After all, not only is the singer plainly a fainting, desiring, utterly overcome subject, subjected to (her) desire for the beloved Christ, and suffering lamentably through and for that desire, but her longed-for union results in the birth of a child, a son of love. (Even when we recall that medieval discourses of love did not privilege languishing as a feminine condition or behavior, that moment of birth has to give us pause!)

If we look even cursorily at the Italian, however, we are forced to acknowledge that the singer is evidently masculine and consistently so throughout.[19] In spite of his grammatical gender, however, he gives birth—and we have to wonder about that graphically erotic union with Christ that produces his son of love. It seems rapturously and quite unproblematically homoerotic. Christ is not, it is true, specifically gendered in the first part of the lauda, quoted above—he is named only once, and appears more often as "love." In the second part of the lauda, however, he is called a husband (*sposo*). He also takes on the nonhuman figure of a "garland [*ghirlanda*—feminine] of love," which the masculine singer carries throughout the world, singing and dancing in joy for the spotless heart his beloved has brought him, but which also metamorphoses into a cloak (*amanto*—masculine and a pun on the word for male lover) that completely enfolds the singer.[20]

Furthermore, lest we be tempted to take the heteronormative way out and argue that this is a text primarily about desire, in which gender signifies rather a grammatical accident (a theoretically suspect move in any case), we have only to look at another lauda text that explicitly genders at least some of its singers feminine, with reference to precisely the same erotics as "Ben morro d'amore." This one undertakes creation of the same loving, desiring subject, using the same erotic tropes, and likewise linking human passion for Christ with Christ's Passion on the Cross. Following a stanza that addresses Christ in the second person as he hangs on the cross, the singer addresses it is not clear whom—his fellow singers? His audience?: "Weep with me, beloved brides, you who live chaste and converted: come, lovers and blessed virgins; let us rejoice in Christ! And may fire and flame remain in our hearts: refresh the rose with your love, and speak the Holy Spirit in us, and in your mercy confirm us in the Father." Again, we need the Italian: "Piangete meco, sponse inamorate, voi ke vivete cast'e adoctrinate: venite, amanti et virgine beate; di Cristo faciam gaudio et iubilanca! E fuoco et fianba stia nel nostro core: renfreskese la rose coll'amore, et lo Spiritu sancto parli 'n noi, e 'l Padre ne confirmi per pietanca." There is no doubt that the singer addresses women here, and given (his) use of the first person plural verb forms, that (he) is feminine as well.[21] My point is simple: when the laude use a given gender, it's no "accident," even if we wanted to argue the validity of "accidental" grammatical gender.

So we have an irretrievably masculine (and fertile!) singer of "Ben morro d'amore," addressing the object of his extravagant desire, Christ, for the most part quite clearly as a man. This gesture is remarkable for two reasons: first, and perhaps most obviously, because of the cultural taboo against sodomy, and the concomitant need to code same-sex desire far more subtly than this text does, in the urban world of which confraternities were a part; but second, and I think equally importantly, because it represents a radical departure from contemporary conventions about the gender of desire for Christ. I know of no other medieval representation of desire for Christ that so graphically depicts it as that of a man for a man. Of a woman for a man, to be sure (and most often from the pens of men); of a perhaps ambiguously gendered subject for a woman, yes; of a woman for a woman, yes; of a man for a man, no.

Gender is, in fact, an altogether remarkable signifier of place and of conduct in the laude generally. With the sole ambiguous example cited above, I have found no lauda texts that gender the singer directly as feminine. In other words, there are laude that represent the voices of explicitly female figures: occasionally the Magdalen, often Mary. But there are none that even hint at feminization of a singer who begins his song as a man. The Bernardine take on the Song of Songs appears nowhere, in spite of numerous laude devoted to the representation of desire. More common than "Ben morro d'amore" are texts that develop contemporary images of a feminized Christ, a Christ who bleeds and suffers and nourishes us with his body (although these images appear in conjunction with a masculine Christ who writes, judges, condemns)—a Christ, in other words, who is at least ambiguously enough gendered that a masculine singer can go relatively unremarked. Rarely, the specifically nuptial imagery of "Ben morro d'amore"—the garland, the cloak, even a possible reference to the dowry—appears elsewhere.[22] But there are no texts in which the singer imagines his desire as like that of a bride for her husband, let alone any that develop this trope in the astonishingly rich and varied ways characteristic of other forms of late medieval spiritual writing by both men and women.

Indeed, where there may be said to be spiritual cross-dressing (as opposed to the erotic transgression of laude to Christ) with respect to gender, it is of a sort that on first glance reads truly bizarrely. I refer to the Marian laments, those representations of the Passion through Mary's eyes and responses that always appear in the first person. Sometimes these laude begin with a third-person description of the Passion and Mary's grief; sometimes they offer no such frame, launching immediately into Mary's own frenzied expressions of distress and longing. As much as laude addressed to Christ or about the singer's response to Christ, their dominant subjective mode is one of desire. Mary does not simply mourn the loss of her son; she seeks to share his Passion in terms that go well beyond the popular notion of her "compassio," or imitation of her son's suffering. Her loss, she claims in a number of these texts, is that of a mother, but also of a wife, daughter, and sister. Her desire is to be reunited with her son, her beloved, in all these roles. Indeed, her desire is for union that obliterates all distinctions between self and other, (re)creating the two of them as One, as mother enclosing her son in pregnancy, as daughter enfleshed within her son/mother. In one particularly graphic extended expression of this desire, she imagines herself in turn as each instrument of the Passion, as the crown of thorns, the nails, the lance, the shroud or the tomb of Christ's burial, not simply so that she might share his torment, but so that she might become truly and completely one with his flesh. The shroud and the tomb would enable her to enclose him as she once did in her pregnancy; the nails and the lance would allow her to enter, to penetrate his flesh and in turn be fully enfleshed within him.[23]

These last astonishing, and powerfully erotic, images especially offer layers of cross-dressing and gender bending for our inspection. For these laude in Mary's voice were, of course, sung by men, men who, however momentarily, undertake the role of a woman graphically imagined as feminine desiring subject, yet who in her turn undertakes an aggressively masculine stance vis-à-vis the object of her desire, her beloved son/father/mother/husband. Singing is marked by the laude themselves as a special locus of union, of language and meaning, discourse and desire, theory and practice. It creates a place where conduct—singing—can signify unproblematically. But only here can it so signify. The "content"—the images—of the laude out of context would utterly undo the power of conduct to signify in theory or in practice in any other aspect of confraternity life. But singing as conduct can create an alternative space—one safe especially for the homoerotic potential of confraternity bonds to be explored and fruitfully exploited. Yet lauda singing's ability to resolve these tensions precisely marks them as elsewhere irresolvably conflicted, points inevitably to the impossibility of bridging the gap between theory and practice in the vital language of conduct.

My aim in this essay has not been to demolish altogether the category of "conduct literature" as an important component of medieval studies scholarship, although I hope to have offered some significant challenges to the way this category has been constructed up to now. I further hope that I have demonstrated some of the ways in which opening up and interrogating this category, with reference to both twentieth-century and fourteenth-century discourses and practices of conduct, can help us to understand both better. In particular, I hope to have convinced my readers that gender, however uneasily, provides one important avenue we must navigate in investigating the relations between contemporary and medieval discourses, languages, and practices.

NOTES

1. Judith Butler, *The Psychic Life of Power: Theories in Subjection* (Stanford, Calif.: Stanford University Press, 1997), 12 and passim.

2. Michel de Certeau, *The Writing of History*, trans. Tom Conley (New York: Columbia University Press, 1988), 21, 191, and passim. See also de Certeau, *The Mystic Fable*, vol. 1, *The Sixteenth and Seventeenth Centuries*, trans. Michael B. Smith (Chicago: University of Chicago Press, 1992).

3. Butler, *The Psychic Life of Power*, 132–50.

4. Henri Lefebvre, *The Production of Space*, trans. Donald Nicholson-Smith (Oxford, England: Blackwell, 1991), 89.

5. Ibid., 79.

6. The two specific texts I cite here appear in a number of fourteenth- and fifteenth-century lauda collections; they are probably most easily available in the volumes begun under the direction of Giorgio Varanini and appearing regularly since the early 1980s: for example, *Laude Cortonesi dal secolo XIII al XV*, vol. I, pt. 1, ed. Varanini, Luigi Banfi, and Anna Ceruti Burgio (Florence: Olschki, 1981), 217–34 (Troppo perde 'l tempo) and 240–45 (Oime lasso e freddo lo mio core). Any number of other examples could be cited, some more explicitly linked to lauda singing itself than these two: "Laudar vollio per amore," "Onne homo laudi con amore," "Allegramente e de buon core con fede," "Ciascun ke fede sente," and the list goes on.

7. The company's statutes are published in *Testi fiorentini del dugento e dei primi del trecento*, ed. Alfredo Schiaffini (Florence: Sansoni, 1926).

8. Ibid., 36–37.

9. Printed in Gilles Gerard Meersseman, *Ordo Fraternitatis: Confraternite e pieta dei laici nel medioevo*, 3 vols., with Gian Piero Pacini (Rome: Herder Editrice e Libreria, 1977), 1: 641.

10. *Testi pratesi della fine del dugento e dei primi del trecento*, ed. Luca Serianni (Florence: Presso l'Accademia della Crusca, 1977), 446–51.

11. A different, but if anything more pessimistic, articulation of this troubled relationship between theory and practice is to be found in a sermon preached in the convent of Santa Maria Novella in Florence (and probably commissioned by a confraternity that met in that church) by the Dominican Giordano da Pisa in 1306. In it, he excoriates the guildsmen of Florence—and of all Italian cities—for their deceitful trading practices. Rather than calling on them to give up commerce, however, he offers them instead a vision of an urban world in which it is precisely commerce that provides the means to salvation. We buy from and sell to one another, he argues, because we cannot provide for all our own wants and needs (*difatti*). Human society thus requires commerce. And if we buy and sell in a spirit of true charity and love, Giordano says, we would all be saints. Alas, however,

theory does not match practice, and deceit rules the world of commerce as it is rather than as it should be. See Carlo Del Corno, *La predicazione nell'eta comunale* (Florence: Sansoni, 1974), 98–104.

12. Archivio di Stato di Firenze, Compagnie Religiose Soppresse Z-1–2170, fasc. Z-1, f. 16v; printed in Luciano Orioli, *Le confraternite medievali e il problema della poverta: Lo statuto della compagnia di Santa Maria Vergine e di San Zenobio di Firenze nel secolo XIV* (Rome: Edizioni di storia e letteratura, 1984), 43.

13. Carol Lansing's work on mourning practices and their regulation offers another, related context within which to explore this view.

14. If we read guild and communal statutes as conduct literature (which my argument would suggest we indeed must), the gap between theory and practice (between discourse and practice?) becomes inescapable. In a time of virtually inescapable factionalism and public turmoil, textual regulation describes a world of order profoundly at odds with the political realities it attempts to control and restrain. Much contemporary discourse suggests awareness of this gap, in its location of peace, order, and tranquillity in a mythical, nostalgically invoked past.

15. While I do not have space to develop this aspect of my argument in detail, I would like to note here that the music of the laude could also have been "read" culturally as representing abandon and desire, if we read it within the context of contemporary discussions of music, especially liturgical music. By the fourteenth century, on those increasingly rare occasions when laypeople took communion, there was no formal liturgical music provided. Instead, communion was either received in silence, or, increasingly, vernacular music was sung, possibly including laude. (The statutes of one Florentine confraternity, Santa Reparata, suggest that the company sang laude during communion. ASF, CRS 2170 Z-1–2170, ff. 3v-4r; Orioli, *Le confraternite,* 22–23.)

16. Siena, Biblioteca Comunale degl'Intronati I.VI.9, f. 79v. Some of the laude in this manuscript are printed and discussed in Giuseppe Rondoni, "Laudi drammatiche dei disciplinati di Siena," *Giornale storico della letteratura italiana* II (1883), 273–301.

17. On the physicality of the vocal and the oral, see especially Paul Zumthor, "Ce que nous 'dit' le moyen age: Entretien avec Gerard le Vot," in his *Ecriture et nomadisme* (Montreal: L'Hexagone, 1990), 101–15. For a more conventional use of orality vs. writing, see, among many others, de Certeau, *The Writing of History,* 183–85.

18. Staaff, "Le laudario de Pise," 40–42; *Laude fiorentini,* 162–66.

19. He is, moreover, masculine also in the one collection belonging to a confraternity that admitted women as members and that not only allowed but encouraged them to sing laude.

20. We should also note here that the garland was traditionally carried by the bridegroom in late medieval and early modern marriage processions.

21. There is, admittedly, greater grammatical ambiguity in this text than in "Ben morro d'amore." But the feminine referent is sufficient to make the editors of the Italian text queasy. Their notes postulate an entirely hypothetical original written for a community of women, from which this version must have been copied. There is absolutely no evidence for such an original and no need for it, unless we must squirm uncontrollably in the face of what seems like pretty tame stuff however we read it, given the much more explicit gender bending of other lauda texts, let alone other contemporary spiritual writing in general.

22. Another context within which to read the homoerotic/homosocial aspects of these images is in contemporary betrothal practices, which were always undertaken exclusively between men—the groom or his father, and the bride's father. Cloaks were often exchanged between these men, and in one recorded instance even the betrothal kiss itself.

23. The text appears in four manuscripts; it is most accessible in the editions by Giorgio Varanini et al. For example, *Laude Cortonesi* I.2, 408–41.

9

Grace under Pressure

Conduct and Representation in the Norwich Heresy Trials

Ruth Nissé

One of the most intriguing tenets abjured by Robert Cavell, the renegade parish chaplain of Bungay, in the fifteenth-century Norwich Lollard trials is that "no honor should be given to images of the crucifix, Mary or any other saint, but that the trees growing in the woods have more vigor and power and should be worshiped rather than stone or dead wood carved in resemblance of a person."[1] As Margaret Aston points out, Cavell's idiosyncratic phrasing of the common Wycliffite criticism of images clearly derives from the teaching of his notorious associate, the guiding spirit of the Norwich group William White, who confessed to a similar statement in his 1428 trial.[2] I begin with this fascinating doctrinal formulation in order to consider the implications of its critique of the agency and authority involved in the cult of images and its polemical imagination of worship directed beyond the social order of "dead" or reified representations to the still living and growing *(crescentes)* trees. In this essay, I will explore how the Lollards translate their rejection of the *power* of images, as White and Cavell put it, into a new concept of devotional conduct. Like many of the writers in this volume, I am interested here in the relationship between conduct and other discursive practices in late medieval popular religious culture.

For the Norwich Lollards, devotional practice functions "heretically" as embodied polemic, as conduct that drains ritual acts of their historically established meanings by subjecting them to a radical inquiry into their scriptural authority. The Lollards' target, in their practices, is something like Bourdieu's concept of the habitus or "symbolic power," the organization of bodies "in accordance with schemes generated by history."[3] This particular kind of secular history, with all of its attendant narratives and practices, is, indeed, what Wyclif and his later followers derogatorily call "tradition."[4] All the orthodox practices that the Lollards define as mere traditions "ungrounded" in scripture hence become material for a kind of parodic theater in which they enact their ideas about spirituality and authority.[5]

By looking at the associative practices of Lollards in their homes and "schools"—groups that gathered to read vernacular texts—against the orthodox regulation of lay conduct exemplified by voluntary religious and craft guilds, I will show that the basis of Lollard social thought is a disruptive interpretation of the connections between dominion and representation. The Lollards reject both the affinities created by guilds and the authorizing language behind them, the traditional narratives that sustain the cults of saints and their visual manifestations. Lollard conduct, by delegitimizing and demystifying a system of devotional ritual centered on visual representation, creates in turn identities that function outside the social hierarchies, including the order of gendered bodies, that such images generate and maintain.

The views of White's followers survive in records made for Bishop William Alnwick between 1428–1431 of judicial proceedings against an enclave of sixty heretics from the Norwich diocese. The notary who produced these accounts, John of Exeter, seems to have been one of the officials put in charge by royal writ of rooting out heresy in Norfolk.[6] Remarkably, John chose to preserve many of the Lollards' confessions, which echo the vernacular idiom of earlier Wycliffite polemical tracts, in the original English.[7] The records reveal a heretical community that not only rehearses a version of Wyclif's reformist beliefs on the nature of the eucharist, secular disendowment of the church, and vernacular translation of the Bible, but that understands the academic theological debates of the 1370s and 1380s most profoundly in terms of polemical practice. It is, then, the glimpses the records afford us of what the Lollards claim to have *done,* rather than what they believe, that demonstrate the group's interpretation of reform as conduct.[8]

The beliefs that the Norwich Lollards adhere to, including the outright rejection of the sacraments and the defense of a priesthood of all good women and men, go much further than Wyclif's own ideas. So extreme are their anticlerical beliefs that they prove an embarrassment for John Foxe when he sets out to recount the Norwich persecution in the *Acts and Monuments*. Foxe only selectively incorporates the eccentric and outspoken views of the Lollards into his history of English Protestantism; he denies, for example, that the Lollards could ever have rejected the efficacy of infant baptism—which they clearly did—according this charge instead to the slander of the notaries.[9]

The trials, as Foxe cautions, are of course official records and therefore do reflect primarily the church's own principles of definition and historiography, no less than his rewritings of the narratives reveal his ideological stakes. Understood within the essentially theatrical account of power proposed by James Scott, however, the "hidden transcript" of Lollard vocabulary and conduct emerges with more or less its own voice from an ecclesiastical "public transcript" that can only "aspire" to hegemony.[10] Scott's interpretation of hegemonic relations as the simultaneous dramatic performances of dominant and subordinate groups theorizes what is evident from reading Alnwick's records: that the Lollards' ostensible renunciations of their practices nevertheless retain much of their subversive theatricality.

Not surprisingly, the Norwich heretics' beliefs, as recorded, mirror the strains of thought that the church found most dangerous in Wyclif's own writings. In 1415 the Council of Constance had condemned forty-five articles, wrenched out of context from Wyclif's works, that stressed the most dire consequences for both ecclesiastical and secular authorities of his attacks on church endowment, religious orders, and other nonscriptural "traditions." In addition to articles that deny the authority of canon law and the legitimacy of the papacy and the friars, others include assertions that "the common man can at his discretion correct deficient lords," that "oaths taken to confirm contracts between men and civil commerce are unlawful," and, perhaps most jarring, that saints "Augustine, Benedict, and Bernard are damned unless they repent of having had property and of having founded and joined religious orders."[11] William White and his followers apparently found in Wyclif's thought the same kinds of practical implications that the Council had feared. Their ecclesiopolitical beliefs are the basis for sweeping reinterpretations of social bonds and devotional conduct. White confessed to having preached that no one is allowed to plead for an inheritance or fight for a country (*patria*), a position echoed by several of his disciples.[12] The recantation of John Skylan of Bergh, recorded in English in 1430, includes the singular tenet that

> the foure doctors, Augustin, Ambrose, Gregory, and Jerom, which the Churche of Roome hath approved for seyntes, were heretikes and here doctrine, which Cristis puple calleth doctors draught, bey opin heresies. (148)

By rejecting the premises of all worldly or spiritual inheritance, fatherland and church fathers alike, the Lollards turn, as recent critics of these texts have argued, not just to a strict apostolic faith but to a concept of devotion based on direct experience instead of convention.[13] Discrediting the authority of all of the historical narratives that support the power of the institutional church, the Lollards reinvigorate the meanings of devotional practices as acts that must directly recall apostolic life. In their ideas of conduct, as they emerge in the records, bodies and practices must quote scripture directly, without commentary or mediating representations.

The Lollards' critical view of all forms of worldly alliance leads them to reinvent their terms of community outside the network of semicontractual relationships that characterize the orthodox devotional practices of guilds. Parish or village guilds drew their members—lay men and women, although only men held offices—from the same artisanal class that later produced the Lollards. Miri Rubin succinctly characterizes the guilds as "providers of essential personal, familial, religious, economic and political services" that typically included the offering of candles before an image of a saint or the eucharist, prayers for the guild's members, masses, charity of various kinds, burials, extralegal arbitration of quarrels, and processions and communal feasts on the patron saints' day or guild day.[14] Besides Corpus Christi fraternities, guilds dedicated to virgin martyrs such as Saint Katherine and Saint Margaret or to Thomas of Canterbury were especially popular. Pointing to the importance of payments in wax to guild organization, Barbara Hanawalt asserts that "in both the literal sense of providing candles and in the figurative sense of keeping alive the traditional religious ceremonies in spite of the decline of the church, the social-religious gilds may be called the keepers of the lights."[15] By the 1420s the more socially prestigious confraternities were also of central importance in oligarchic urban government; in Norwich, the Guild of St. George took the place of the Guild of the Annunciation as the most influential body in city politics.[16]

The Norfolk and Norwich guilds are amply documented by records of foundations, oaths, and ordinances from their returns to the inquiry of the Cambridge Parliament in 1388–89.[17] The royal writ ordering the guilds to account for their liberties and property reflects not only the crown's intent to confiscate their wealth but also the fear, in the wake of the 1381 Rising, that guild meetings could be occasions for planning rebellion.[18] The guilds responded directly to these concerns, often denying that they possessed any wealth and claiming rather too emphatically to uphold royal authority and civil and canon law. The Norwich Guild of Saint Christopher, for example, provides as an "ordinance" a long list of people whom its members pray for "at every time that the alderman and the brethren bene togedere," including the pope, "all Erchbissops and bisshops and specialy for our bisshope of Norwich," the king, dukes, earls, knights, burghers, and so on down the social ladder to "trewe tyliers and men of craft," and finally "for alle the men that ben in fals beleve, and wold be in gode beleve."[19] The Guild of St. Leonard in Lynn, besides explaining how it was founded to keep a candle burning on every festival day before an image of the saint, avows that "what man or woman of this gilde be rebel ageyne the lawe of holy chirche, he shal lese the fraternite of this gilde tille he come to amendment."[20] The Guild of St. Thomas of Canterbury in Wymondham denies having any oath of confederation beyond devotion to the saint, and the Guild of St. John the Baptist in Terrington claims that its members will "not hold congregations or private assemblies" *(congregationes neque conventicula)* other than those necessary for the running of the association itself.[21]

If the 1388 returns expose the perceived dangers of guilds as unpoliced lay gatherings, they demonstrate even more decisively an ideal of lay orthodoxy based on visual cues. Guilds ultimately derive their political legitimacy from the worship of images and, on a material level, from what Michael Camille has called "image investment," the lay endowment of church art "literally integrated into the ecclesiastical structure."[22] The saint whose representation is the manifest focus of the guild's devotional economy authorizes a system of corporate rule, ranging from regulations of manners, liveries, and sexual conduct to civic legislation.[23] Members are bound not only by the formal or informal contracts of oaths to the guild but by a sort of contractual relation to the exemplary and intercessory saint as well.[24] As Rubin argues of how guilds constructed subjects, "fraternities serviced identity in ways which combined the individual and the collective, binding them through elaborate presentations of their interdependence."[25]

The orthodox theoretical position on the worship of images defines the institutional limits of the guilds' lay devotion. The defenses of images sparked by the attacks of the early Wycliffites had reaffirmed—via Aquinas's *Summa Theologica*—the orthodoxy of the Second Council of Nicea's proclamations and John of Damascus's treatises. These English academic works lean heavily on the hierarchical idea of the worship of the prototype through the image as a defense against the Wycliffites' charges of idolatry in current practices.[26] For example, Walter Hilton's widely circulated contribution to the image question, *De adoracione ymaginum,* both defines the differences between pagan idolatry and correct worship (*latria, dulia* and *hyperdulia,* depending on the object of adoration) and emphasizes the importance of images for the devotion of the illiterate, the simple, and the spiritually weak.[27] The guilds, then, as upholders of orthodox ritual, are marked *as* lay associations by their focus on visual images, and thereby situated below the clergy on the ladder of spiritual understanding.

Wycliffite criticism of the religious guilds, beginning along with many of these organizations at the end of the fourteenth century, aims in part at debunking the discursive formations of devotional and political tradition that underwrite these associations—the historical cults of the saints that the guilds rework into their social ordinances as well as their own originary narratives.[28] The Wycliffite epistle sermon for the fifth Sunday after Trinity equates the fraternities with the divisive "new" fraternal orders: "And thus cristen men shulden be loveris of bretherhed, not of bretherhed of freris ne of bretherhed of gildis."[29] The Lollard tract "The Gret Sentence of Curs Expounded," moreover, fulminates that

> Alle newe fraternytes or gildis maad of men semen openly to renne in þis curse. For þei conspiren many false errours aȝenst þe common fraternyte of Crist . . . and aȝenst comyn charite and comyn profit of Crystene men. And þerto þei conspiren to

> bere up eche oþer, ȝe, in wrong, and oppresse oþere men in here riȝt bi here witt and power.... And þei bryngen in moche pride vanyte and wast, cost, and triste in mennus helpe more þan in Goddis; and þus þei bryngen in moche evyl, and no good, more þan God commaunded frist; but þei letten moche unyte pees and charite of Cristene peple, and meynteynen errour of wrong and gret discension, and moche symonye and letten pore mennus almes and liflode þat lyn bedrede blynd and feble.[30]

For the Wycliffite polemicist, the "new" guilds' pretensions to custom merely screen their coercive political and economic functions; they claim an essentially illegitimate communal identity upheld by their own agency (made by men, like the images) that by Christian doctrine is properly common to all. Significantly, the author—in a rhetorical move typical of Lollard attacks on images—imagines those "poor men" truly in need of charity as "blind," and therefore literally outside the guilds' light- and image-centered specular and spectacular economy.[31] The structures of both visual and economic representation that support the power of the guilds are for the Lollards illusory and "traditional."

The Norwich heresy trials reveal the Lollards' conceptual and practical responses to the guilds both in their subversions of corporate mechanisms of power and in their own associative style. The guilds' own potential, as lay religious organizations, for sedition and dissent is evident, as I have shown, from the returns to the 1388 inquiry. The channel for dissent inherent in lay control becomes apparent in the subversive and parodic form that the Lollard gatherings—the secret "scoles of heresie" *(scole privatae)*—take in relation to the guild structure.[32] Even the language used in the Norwich trials to describe the Lollard meetings recalls the earlier anxieties over the guilds: the defendants must swear to report all future "conventicula vel congregationes," private devotional gatherings.

The Lollards invent a type of guild set loose from its authorizing context by putting Wycliffite sacramental theology and political theory into practice. In particular, the Lollards observe Wyclif's theory of dominion and grace and the related unlawfulness of all oaths and contracts.[33] In *De Civili Dominio,* Wyclif had argued that only a person in a state of grace by predestination could hold dominion or lordship, a theory that, as the decree by the Council of Constance shows, was quickly recognized by the church as a challenge to all ideas of property, law, heredity, and ultimately political and social identity. In Lollardy, as in later forms of radical Protestant ideology, all aspects of devotional conduct, the entire ritual organization of time by Sabbaths, fasts, feasts and saints' days, collapse under the weight of the unknowability of salvation.[34] The Lollards' striking assertion, echoed through the trials, that "every good man and good woman is a priest" (147), breaks down the lay/clerical distinction and gender hierarchy at the basis of the guilds' civic devotion and therefore ultimately redefines the terms that govern representation.[35]

Lollard association in "autonomous textual communities," as Rita Copeland characterizes them, appropriates and domesticates the forms of corporate lay devotion to support the sole authority of vernacular doctrine.[36] The Norwich Lollards show an extraordinary attentiveness to the dynamics of such rituals if only to repudiate them all the more forcefully. On the evidence of the Norwich accounts, the "prive chambres" of Thomas and Hawisia Mone's house notably served as a center for instruction in scripture by the former priest White and his followers (140). The Mones' house was also the site of other transgressive observances like the Easter vigil feast reported by Mone's servant John Burrell:

> [He] said . . . that on Easter day, he saw in Thomas Mone's kitchen a quarter of a cold stuffed pig. And he supposed that this pig had been killed and cooked on the authority of Mone's wife and that the rest of this pig had been eaten by Thomas Burrell [his brother], the Mones, John Pert, the Mones' servant and by another man dressed in a russet robe whose name he didn't know, on the Easter vigil. And on the same Easter day, Thomas Mone's wife sent her daughter to Thomas Burell's house with the rest of the pig. (75–76)[37]

With practices like this lay celebration, a kind of parodic guild feast held at a forbidden time, the Lollards dramatize the lack of scriptural foundation for the Lenten fast. By inverting the "traditional" meal, they reveal its basis to be only tradition, human law rather than divine; the vigil becomes as good a time for a communal event as any, and Hawisia Mone's domestic authority *(consilium)* over the food supplants both ecclesiastical and political authority in determining its circumstances and location, right down to ostentatiously sending the leftovers to Thomas Burrell's house on Easter day. Similarly, Margery Baxter, another Lollard woman teacher, was said to have asserted that "it would be better for someone to eat the meat remaining from Thursday's leftovers on fast days than to go to the market and run up debts by buying fish" (46).[38] The Lollard approach to lay-controlled religious conduct is then, for the most part, to expose the radical discontinuity between the behavior regulated by the church and guilds and the behavior dictated directly by scripture and based on textual reception.

The trial of Margery Baxter, which uniquely includes lengthy depositions from her neighbor Joanna Clyfland and her two servants, Agnes Bethom and Joanna Grymle, is the most revealing record of actual Lollard instruction in devotional conduct. In the conversation by Baxter's fireplace that Clyfland reports, Baxter interrogates her on the beliefs expressed in public devotion, beginning with a curious warning recorded in English on oaths: "bewar of the bee, for every bee will styngge, and therefore look that ye swer nother by Godd ne by Our Ladi ne be non other seynt, and if ye do the contrarie the bee will styngg your tunge and veneme your sowle" (44). Most of the Norwich Lollards attest to the unlawfulness of swearing oaths and reject the legal identities, lineal and national, upheld by them. Baxter, however, deploys this view precisely to define the nature of her social position as a Lollard teacher to Clyfland and the other women; she parodically demonstrates her own authority by instead of demanding an oath, as in a guild induction, attacking the authorizing patriarchal power of ritualized language. As Copeland observes of Baxter's "feminine hermeneutic," "it is open and popular, vernacular and literal. All participants, women and men are discursively feminized, in sociolinguistic as well as metaphysical terms."[39] Baxter opposes her own "feminine" Lollard idiom to the tongue and soul poisoned by the institutional power of oaths over both body and language.

Having established her relation to Clyfland as distinctly outside such bonds, Baxter asks her to describe her daily worship and answers with an attack on images as well as the Eucharist that again underlines metaphorically the Lollard critique of the visual basis of these traditions. God will not, she says, "offer or grant you more merit for such genuflections, adorations or prayers made [before images] in such churches, any more than the burning light obscured by the cover of the baptismal font can offer light at nighttime to those in church" (44). Of images of the cross, Baxter tells Clyfland, no more honor should be shown to them than to the gallows her brother would be hanged on and that "lewed wrights of stokkes hewe and forme such crosses and ymages and after that lewed painters glorye thaym with colors" (44). Baxter then offers to show her the true cross of Christ, and stretching her arms out, tells her that she can and should see and worship this cross every day in her own home instead of "dead images" in church.

Following her teacher White's distinction between the respective powers of dead and living images, Baxter reappropriates the authority from the clergy to represent Christ with her own body by drawing a sharp distinction between the real force of representation in crafting the image and the ecclesiastical and political authority of investing it with the status of a devotional object. Just as Baxter's husband, himself a wright, could make a wooden image of a cross, it could only, like an actual gallows, represent the church's coercive power. This view, in its way like the guild movement, attaches new importance to the work of artisans in the devotional economy: several of the Norwich Lollards thus attest to the belief, similar to the argument of Tertullian's *De Idolatria,* that the makers of such images, complicitous in maintaining this false dominion, are themselves damned.[40] In contrast to the theological abstraction of the academic arguments in favor of images, the Lollards' objections had always been practical: they decry the waste of both wealth and labor on such "doumb simulacre."[41] Baxter, again echoing early patristic injunctions against pagan idols, voices the striking interpretation that the devils who fell with Lucifer remain lurking in images, an idea that vividly links the human agency behind such representations with illegitimate authority.[42] In Baxter's polemical conduct, the true cross can only be represented by the living body—the scriptural image of God—in an always available gesture of identification.

By addressing the material production of images, Baxter delegitimates the visual, devotional basis of guild as well as clerical authority. The redefinition of any *body,* regardless of gender or social position, as the visible true cross destabilizes the hierarchical ordering of vision inherent in the worship of images with lights and offerings. The guilds' devotion to images becomes, following the implications of this Lollard critique, a kind of misrecognition of exemplarity in patron saints.[43] With her unsparing iconoclasm, Baxter paves the way to a further attack on the conduct associated with the clerically ordained worship of saints. As William Hardy of Mundham phrases the Lollard position:

> All manner of prayer oweth to be maad only to God and to noon other seyntes, for alle seyntes be made be ordinances of popes and other prelates and prestes of the Churche, and therfor it is dowte whedir it be plesyng to God preyers to be maad to any seyntes or nay. (154)

For the Norwich Lollards, the saints are little more than a discursive "front" for the false social control of the church. William White had directed his vitriolic logic at Thomas Becket, one of the saints most associated with national identity:

> If the passion of Christ was profitable & valuable, then the death of St. Thomas, the martyred Archbishop of Canterbury, was worthless and should be scorned by the faithful because on account of his death the temporal dominion of the church was upheld. And if the death of this Thomas is commended, the passion of Christ is scorned.[44]

For White, the meaning of Thomas's "martyrdom" is the exact opposite of the implied *Imitatio Christi* narrative of his hagiographies, a sacrifice for clerical wealth instead of apostolic poverty. If, by the thirteenth century, the *Legenda aurea* emphasized Thomas' personal asceticism, his hairshirt, and his devotion to the poor as central to his *vita,* White is at pains to contrast the actual political meaning of the archbishop's death with the radical poverty decreed by Christ's life and crucifixion.

In Baxter's own account of Thomas Becket that she delivers to Clyfland:

> That Thomas of Canterbury whom the people call Saint Thomas Cantuar' was a false traitor and is damned in hell because he endowed churches with possessions to their injury and encouraged and supported many heresies in the church which seduce simple people, and therefore if God should be blessed then Thomas was and is cursed, and these false priests who say that

> Thomas patiently bore his own death before the altar are lying because he was killed in the door of the church while fleeing, just like a false and mad traitor. (45)[45]

"That cursed Thomma of Canterbury," she continues, is in fact the exemplar for the cursed worldly clergy who "cruelly killed" William White and other Lollard teachers and who deceive the people with "false mawmentries and lawes" (45). In a corollary to her scathing attack on Thomas Becket, Baxter presents White as a true saint *(magnus sanctus in celo et sanctissimus doctor ordinatus et missus a Deo)* and claims that she prays to him for intercession with God each day; she even provides a concise hagiographic narrative of his martyrdom at the stake:

> Margery herself was at the place of the said William White's death to see what would be done by this William White, and Margery herself saw that when the said W. White, at the place where he was burned, wished to preach the word of God, then a devil, a disciple of Bishop Caiaphas, struck this W. White upon the lips and stopped up the mouth of the said holy doctor with his own hand so that he could in no way proclaim the will of God. (47)[46]

White's sainthood is constituted by his preaching itself; Baxter's narrative only fills in for the Gospel that is silenced together with White's voice. As Steven Justice observes, Baxter contrasts Thomas of Canterbury's death in a church—his proper, corruptly rich place—with the simplicity of White's life and death.[47] Copeland, furthermore, convincingly argues that Baxter's treatment of White as a saint is consistent with the overall Lollard rejection of images and "symbolic mediation" in favor of literalism and direct experience.[48] However, I think a stronger polemical dimension of Baxter's claim is her clear recognition of the narrative fluidity of the traditions behind lay practices, the "images and laws" that make saints, and particularly the guilds' social uses of saints' cults. By refiguring Thomas's *vita* to undermine his popular status as a legitimating national figure, Baxter authorizes herself, a laywoman, to reassign Thomas's discursive role to White. Through her own capacity as a teacher to Clyfland, she defines him as a patron and intercessor for the Lollard community. Just as White himself, who in his confession had referred to Wyclif as "Beatus" in connection with his views on the freedom to preach the gospel, Baxter parodically invests White with the traditional sociopolitical functions of a saint yet preserves his position outside the dominant regulatory order.[49] Like White's own use of Wyclif's example to license the unlicensed to preach, Baxter's invocation of White serves to push the implications of lay exemplarity to extremes by eliminating clerical authority altogether. She thus reduces hagiography, as a political discourse, to its barest form. The saint, like the "true pope" is, for the Norwich Lollards, the person whose conduct, those acts that can be recorded as history, best approximates Christ's or St. Peter's. In the words of Hawisia Mone's abjuration, the head of the church could be "he only that is most holy and most perfit in lyving in erth" (141). In Baxter's polemical diatribe to Clyfland, White emerges not only as an exemplar but as a supplanter of the tenuous customs of lay devotion in the purity of his preaching.

In the same vein, Baxter goes on to single out another favorite Lollard target, pilgrimages to the shrine of Mary of Walsingham, called "Falsingham," which she juxtaposes with praise for Hawisia Mone as "the wisest woman in the doctrine of William White" (47).[50] Here she directly contrasts the worship of a "dead image" of Mary, a focus of regulated female exemplarity and piety, to Lollard devotion, that is, textual reception and interpretation that recasts women like herself and Mone as teachers. Lollard schools like the one Baxter invites Clyfland and her servant to attend reorder gender roles in the structure of a voluntary association, which, however, in contrast to the guilds' subjection of female members to the governance of both male guild officers and ultimately the clergy, allows for laywomen to attain the authority of "true priests" by teaching doctrine. Together with this radical revaluation of women's authority, the Lollard rejection of the sacraments as well as images involves a recuperation of the female body as a potential site of grace. Baxter's cryptic and much-discussed remark that she would not be burned if convicted of Lollardy because she has "a charter of salvation in her womb" [una carta salvacionis in utero suo] (49) echoes the Lollards' denunciations of what one defendant, John Kynget, calls the "shakelment" of baptism (81) and the corresponding belief that, as Robert Cavell asserts, a child is baptized in the womb when its soul is joined to its body (94–95). Baxter's striking declaration extends Cavell's replacement of the visible church with the female body as a possible locus of salvation to a metaphorical displacement of the institutional or customary authority suggested by a written "charter" by her "unshackled" womb itself. The body as a living image of Christ generates its authority—its "charter"—from within and, therefore, is not truly subject to the orders of church or state authority. Baxter's bodily "charter" is, in a sense, a conceptually ingenious if ultimately ineffectual answer to the texts of the sealed indentures of their abjurations given to the Norwich heretics to remind them, in part, of the fatal punishment for relapse.[51]

Evident in Margery Baxter's decidedly strong opinions, the Lollards' ideas of conduct and community depend on their interpretation of the authority of representations and on the social and political consequences of iconoclasm. Lollard criticism of the practices associated with image worship, offerings, and pilgrimages, denouncing their expense as well as idolatry, strikes at the core of guild piety, the rhetoric of mutual charity. By claiming that pilgrimages should be made only to the poor or, as the defendant John Pyry puts it, that "the poor are the true images of Christ" (71), the Norwich Lollards, like the earlier Wycliffite critic, divorce the charity generated by the image-centered guilds from the idea of true charity or "common profit" based on the body as a living image. The Lollards' own conduct, then, emerges from their rejection of the guilds' prescriptive tenets in favor of a reenactment of scripture. The social bonds maintained by devotional images become, in the Lollards' accounts, as illegible as the materials used to make them. William Colyn, therefore, acknowledges telling a parish churchwarden that he would rather pay for an image to be burned than painted (91). In his testimony, John Burell affirms that a Lollard clerk of Loddon had burned images and admits to attacking a crucifix himself with a "fagothook," declaring that: "No matter how strongly or sharply I strike this cross, even with a sharper instrument, this cross will never bleed" (76).

Burrell's violence against the cross perfectly captures the dynamics of the Norwich Lollards' reimagination of conduct. In his narrative, the image itself, made, invested with illusory power, and unmade, is the focus of a polemic performed and meant to be repeated. In order to return the focus of devotion not only back to scripture but to a radically "untraditional" lay idea of community supported by the Wycliffite denial of true dominion to anyone in a state of sin, the Lollards direct their attacks at the corporate bodies of guilds—bodies that would likewise never bleed—through the images that embody their ideology. The Lollards destroy the representations that produce and are produced by the guilds' false authority, dramatically revealing them as the dead wood that they become in the absence of shaping power.

Notes

1. *Heresy Trials in the Diocese of Norwich, 1428–31*, ed. Norman Tanner (London Historical Society, 1977), 95: "quod nullus honor est exhibendus ymaginibus crucifixi, Beate Marie nec alicuis sancti, eo quod arbores crescentes in silvis sunt maioris viriditatis et virtutis et eo cicuis adorande quam lapis vel lignum mortuum sculptum ad similitudinem hominis." Unless otherwise noted, translations are my own.

2. Margaret Aston, "William White's Lollard Followers," *Lollards and Reformers* (London: Hambledon, 1984) 89–90. White's statement is: "Nam arbores, crescentes in silva sunt majores virtutis, et vigoris, et expressiorem gerunt similitudinem Dei et imaginem quam lapis vel lignum mortuum ad similitudinem himinis scultptum; et ideo huiusmodi arbores crescentes magis sunt adorandae orationibus, genuflectionibus, oblationibus, peregrinationibus et luminibus, quam aliquod idolum in ecclesia mortuum" (*Fasciculi Zizaniorum* [RS 5, 1858], 430). For more on the Lollards' iconoclasm, see Aston, "Lollards and Images," in *Lollards and Reformers* and Anne Hudson, *The Premature Reformation* (New York: Oxford University Press, 1988), 301–9.

3. Pierre Bourdieu, *The Logic of Practice*, trans. Richard Nice (Stanford, Calif.: Stanford University Press, 1990), 54. Bourdieu goes on to define the habitus as "embodied history, internalized as a second nature and so forgotten as history" (56). Bourdieu's concept of *hexis* offers much the same analysis of conduct: "bodily *hexis* is political mythology realized, em-bodied, turned into a permanent disposition, a durable way of standing, speaking, walking, and thereby of thinking and feeling" (70).

4. John Wyclif's own polemical writings are marked by constant attacks on human "tradition," especially with reference to the "four new sects" of friars and other religious orders; see, for example, "De Nova Praevaricantia Mandatorum" in *Polemical Works in Latin*, vol. 1, ed. Rudolf Buddensieg (London, 1883), 116–50. For later Lollard invective against "tradition," see "The Great Sentence of Curs Expounded" in *Select English Works of John Wyclif*, vol. 3, ed. Thomas Arnold (Oxford, 1871), 267–337; and "Of Dominion" in *The English Works of John Wyclif*, ed. F. D. Matthew (London: EETS, 1880; 2d ed., 1902), 282–93.

5. On the uses of parodic ritual in the German Reformation, see R. W. Scribner's brilliant "Ritual and Reformation," in *Popular Culture and Popular Movements in Reformation Germany* (London: Hambledon, 1987), 103–22.

6. Henry VI's letters to John of Exeter and Jacolet Germain, keeper of the tower of Colchester, ordering the arrest of White and other Lollards are preserved in Foxe's *Acts and Monuments* (John Foxe, *Acts and Monuments*, vol. 3, ed. George Townsend [New York: AMS Press, 1965], 586–87). Steven Justice considers John of Exeter's career in "Inquisition, Speech, and Writing: A Case from Late-Medieval Norwich," *Representations* 48 (1994): 1–29.

7. For an argument about John of Exeter's motives for recording the Lollards' confessions in English, see Justice, 5–8.

8. The Norwich Lollards' inevitable translation of Wycliffite theory into practice informs Aston's controversial conclusion that the "limited intelligence of glovers & skinners" and "the domestic talk of enthusiastic women" had "weakened" the Magister's theology (99).

9. Foxe, 589.

10. James Scott, *Domination and the Arts of Resistance: Hidden Transcripts* (New Haven, Mass.: Yale University Press, 1990) 18. For Scott the "hidden transcript" is "the privileged site for nonhegemonic, contrapuntal, dissident, subversive discourse" (25). Scott's theory of power, indebted to theatrical metaphors, is a direct critique of Bourdieu's version of the "false consciousness" paradigm, which he characterizes as the "thin" account of ideological hegemony (73–76).

11. Hermann Van der Hardt, ed., *Magnum Oecumenicum Constantiense Concilium,* vol. 4 (Berlin, 1700), 149–55; translations from C. M. D. Crowder, ed., *Unity, Heresy, and Reform, 1378–1460* (New York: St. Martin's, 1977), 85–87. See also Edith Tatnall, "The Condemnation of John Wyclif at the Council of Constance," in *Councils and Assemblies,* ed. G. J. Cumin and Derek Baker (Cambridge University Press, 1971), 209–18.

12. As John Skilly of Flixton abjures this point: "Also that Y held, taght, and afermed that it is not leful ony mon to fighte or do bataile for a reawme or a cuntre, or to plete in law for any right or wrong" (58).

13. Rita Copeland, "Why Women Can't Read: Medieval Hermeneutics, Statutory Law, and the Lollard Heresy Trials," in *Representing Women: Law, Literature, and Feminism,* ed. Susan Heinzelman and Zipporah Wiseman (Durham, N.C.: Duke University Press, 1994). See also Justice, 21–25.

14. Rubin, *Corpus Christi* (New York: Cambridge University Press, 1991), 233. See also Eamon Duffy, *The Stripping of the Altars* (New Haven, Mass.: Yale University Press, 1992), 131–54; H. F. Westlake, *The Parish Gilds of Medieval England* (New York: Macmillan, 1919); Gervase Rosser, "Communities of Parish and Guild in the Late Middle Ages," *Parish, Church, and People: Local Studies in Lay Religion 1350–1750,* ed. S. J. Wright (London: Hutchinson, 1988), 29–55.

15. Barbara Hanawalt, "Keepers of the Lights: Late Medieval Parish Gilds," *Journal of Medieval and Renaissance Studies* 14, no. 1 (1984): 21.

16. Norman Tanner, *The Church in Late Medieval Norwich 1370–1532* (Toronto: PIMS, 1984), 67–82; and, especially, Ben McRee, "Religious Gilds and Civic Order: The Case of Norwich in the Late Middle Ages," *Speculum* 67 (1992): 69–97. For the history of the Guild of St. George, see Mary Grace, ed., *Records of Gild of St. George in Norwich, 1389–1547: A Transcript with an Introduction* (Norfolk Record Society, 1937).

17. For an overview, see Catherine Firth, "Village Gilds of Norfolk in the Fifteenth Century," *Norfolk Archaeology* 18 (1914): 161–203.

18. The writ of Richard II to the sheriffs ordering returns from the guilds specifies that the guilds account for "the manner and form and authority of the foundation and beginning and continuance and governance of the gilds and brotherhoods aforesaid: And as to the manner and form of the oaths, gatherings (*congregationes*), feasts, and general meetings (*assemblias*) of the brethren and sistren" (*English Gilds,* ed. Toulmin Smith and Lucy Toulmin Smith [EETS, 1870], 128). The petition of the Commons at the 1388 Cambridge Parliament, which prompted the inquiry into the guilds, is preserved in *The Westminster*

Chronicle: 1381–1394, ed. L. C. Hector and B. Harvey (New York: Oxford University Press, 1982) 356–57.

19. *English Gilds*, 22–23.

20. *English Gilds*, 49–50.

21. Walter Rye, ed. "Some Norfolk Gild Certificates," *Norfolk Archaeology* 11 (1892): 134–36; 128–131.

22. Michael Camille, *The Gothic Idol* (New York: Cambridge University Press,1989), 215.

23. See Ben McRee, "Religious Gilds and the Regulation of Behavior in late Medieval Towns," *People, Politics, and Community in the Later Middle Ages*, ed. Joel Rosenthal and Colin Richmond (Gloucester: Sutton, 1987), 108–22.

24. Duffy, *Stripping of the Altars* 183–86.

25. Miri Rubin, "Small Groups: Identity and Solidarity in the Late Middle Ages," *Enterprise and Individuals in Fifteenth-Century England*, ed. Jennifer Kermode (Gloucester: Sutton, 1991) 37.

26. See, for example, the lengthy tract by the Dominican Thomas Palmer, British Library MS. Harley 31, ff. 182r–194v. Aquinas's definitive discussion of the kinds of worship is the *Summa Theologica*, Part 3, Question 25. For a discussion of the image debate in the universities, see Hudson, *The Premature Reformation*, 92–94. On the theology of images propounded by the Second Council of Nicea, see Hans Belting, *Likeness and Presence: A History of the Image before the Era of Art*, trans. E. Jephcott (Chicago: University of Chicago Press, 1994), 144–63. See also Camille, 206–7.

27. *Hilton's Latin Writings*, vol. 1, ed. John P. H. Clark and Cheryl Taylor (Salzburg: *Analecta Cartusiana*, 1987), 175–214. See also Joy M. Russell-Smith, "Walter Hilton and a Tract on the Defence of the Veneration of Images," *Dominican Studies* 7 (1954): 180–214.

28. See Rubin, "Small Groups" for an analysis of the guilds' "historically constructed identities" (135).

29. *English Wycliffite Sermons*, vol. 1, ed. Anne Hudson (New York: Oxford University Press, 1983), 627.

30. "The Great Sentence of Curs Expounded," in Arnold, vol. 3, 333.

31. See, for example, the Lollard text on images and pilgrimages from the "Tenison Tracts" in BL. Ms. Additional 24202, in *Selections from English Wycliffite Writings*, ed. Anne Hudson (New York: Cambridge University Presss, 1978), 83–88. My understanding of the Lollard attack on visual representation is indebted to Martin Jay's *Downcast Eyes: The Denigration of Vision in Twentieth-Century French Thought* (Berkeley: University of California Press, 1993), especially chapters 6–7, which focus on recent theories of vision and social control: "Lacan, Althusser, and the Specular Subject of Ideology" and "From the Empire of the Gaze to the Society of the Spectacle: Foucault and Debord."

32. For more on Lollard "schools" and "conventicles," see Hudson, *The Premature Reformation*, 180–200, and Shannon McSheffrey's new survey, *Gender and Heresy: Women and Men in Lollard Communities 1420–1530* (Philadelphia: University of Pennsylvania Press, 1995), 49–66.

33. On Wycliffe's theory of dominion and grace see M. Wilks, "Predestination, Property and Power: Wycliffe's Theory of Dominion and Grace," *SCH* 2 (1965): 220–36.

34. Euan Cameron, *The European Reformation* (New York: Oxford University Press,

1991), 111–35; Steven Ozment, *The Age of Reform, 1250–1550* (New Haven: Yale University Press, 1980), 340–51.

35. McSheffrey concludes that Lollardy was unappealing to women precisely because it rejected traditional "female piety" such as "the practices associated with the cult of saints" (148); see especially 137–49.

36. Copeland, 26–27.

37. Johannes Burrell dixit . . . quod die Pasche . . . vidit in le botery retro altum scannum aule mansionis Thome Mone de Lodne unum quarterium porcelli coctum facitum frigidum. Et iste Johannes suspicatur quod dictus porcellus fuit occisus et paratus ac coctus de consilio uxoris Thome Mone; et eciam quod residuum eiusdem porcelli fuit comestum per Thomam Burrell fratrem istius Johannis Burrell, ac uxorem Thome Mone, et per Johannem Pert, famulum dicti Thome Mone, ac per alium hominem toga de russeto indutum, cuius nomen iste Johannes dixit nescire, in vigilia Pasche predicta. Et dicto Pasche uxor Thome Mone misit per filiam suam dictum residuum porcelli ad domum Thome Burrell.

38. [Q]uod melius esset cuilibet carnes remanentes die Jovis de fragmentis in diebus ieiunalibus quam ire in mercatum et indebitare se emendo pisces.

39. Copeland, 26.

40. Tertullian, *De Idolatria,* trans. and ed. J. H. Wazink and J. C. M. Van Winden (Leiden: Brill, 1987).

41. *An Apology for Lollard Doctrines,* ed. J. H. Todd (London, 1842), 85. This text contains the most trenchant Lollard critique of images.

42. For patristic sources that present arguments against images, see Tertullian, *De Idolatria;* Minucius Felix, *Octavius,* trans. and ed. G. Rendall (Cambridge, Mass.: Harvard University Press, 1931); Origen, *Contra Celsum,* trans. and ed. H. Chadwick (Cambridge, Mass.: Cambridge University Press, 1953). See also Camille, 27–49.

43. See Bourdieu's account of ritual and "misrecognition" in "Authorized Language: The Social Conditions for the Effectiveness of Ritual Discourse," in *Language and Symbolic Power,* ed. John B. Thompson, trans. G. Raymond and M. Adamson (Cambridge, Mass.: Harvard University Press, 1991), 107–16. For the Lacanian antivisual sense of "méconnaissance," see Jay, 347–50.

44. Si passio Christi fuit utilis et pretiosa, mors S, Thomae martyris Cantuariensis archepiscopi fuit vilis, et a fidelibus vituperanda, quia propter dominium ecclesiae temporalis mortis sustinet passionem: et si ipsius Thomae mors fuerit commendanda, passio Christi fuit reprobanda (*Fasciculi Zizaniorum,* 430).

45. [I]lle Thomas Cantuariensis quem populus vocat Sanctum Thomam Cantuar' fuit falsus proditor et est dampnatus in infrno eo quod dotavit ecclesias iniuriose possessionibus et suscitavit ac supportavit plures hereses in Ecclesia que seducunt simplicem populum, et ideo si Deus fuerit benedictus idem Thomas fuit et est maledictus, et si Thomas fuerit et sit benedictus Deus fuit et est maledictus, et isti falsi presbiteri qui dicunt quod idem Thomas pacienter sustinuit mortem suam coram altari menciuntur quia tanquam falsus vecors proditor, fugiendo, occisus fuit in ostio ecclesie.

46. [I]psa Margeria fuit ad locum mortis dicti W. White ut videret quid fieret per ipsum Willlelmum White, et ipsa Margeria videbat quod quando dictus W. White, in loco ubi fuit combustus, voluit predicasse populo verbum Dei, tunc ibi diabolus, discipulus

Cayphe episcopi, percuciebat ipsum W. White super labia et obturabat manu sua os dicto sancti doctoris sic quod nullo modo potuit proponere voluntatem Dei.

47. Justice, 24.

48. Copeland, 31.

49. For White's invocation of Wycliffe, see *Fasciculi Zizaniorum,* 429. For a perceptive discussion of Lollard redefinitions of sainthood, see Christina Von Nolcken, "Another Kind of Saint: A Lollard Perception of John Wyclif," in *From Ockham to Wyclif,* ed. Anne Hudson and Michael Wilks (Oxford: SCH, 1987), 429–43.

50. [U]xor Thome Mone est secretissima et sapientissima mulier in doctrina W. White.

51. Aston, 97.

Contributors

Mark Addison Amos is assistant professor of English at Southern Illinois University at Carbondale. His scholarship focuses on reading practices, early book production, and other relationships between late medieval cultures and their literatures.

Kathleen Ashley is professor of English at the University of Southern Maine. Her books include *Writing Faith: Text, Sign, and History in the Miracles of Sainte Foy* (with Pamela Sheingorn) and two edited volumes, *Interpreting Cultural Symbols: Saint Anne in Late Medieval Society* (also with Pamela Sheingorn) and *Victor Turner and the Construction of Cultural Criticism.* She is completing a translation of *Miroir des bonnes femmes* that will accompany a study of the manuscript's owners during the fifteenth and sixteenth centuries.

Robert L. A. Clark is associate professor of French at Kansas State University. He has published on medieval dramatic, romance, and devotional texts and the opera *Carmen,* and has translated the *Chanson de Sainte Foy* into English. Current projects include an edition of the *Mistere de la sainte Hostie* and a collaborative volume in honor of C. Clifford Flanigan. He is founder and owner of MEDGAY-L, the electronic forum on gay and lesbian issues in medieval studies.

Anna Dronzek is assistant professor of history at the University of Minnesota at Morris. Her research focuses on gender and culture in fifteenth-century England.

Roberta L. Krueger is professor of French at Hamilton College. She is author of *Women Readers and the Ideology of Gender in Old French Verse Romance* and has edited the *Cambridge Companion to Medieval Romance.* Her chapter on the *Livre du Chevalier de la Tour Landry,* the *Ménagier de Paris,* and Christine de Pizan's *Livre des Trois Vertus* is part of a book project on late medieval French didactic literature.

Ruth Nissé teaches English and cultural studies at the University of Nebraska, Lincoln. She is currently completing a book on medieval theater, *Defining Acts: Drama and the Politics of Interpretation in Premodern England.*

Ann Marie Rasmussen is associate professor of German at Duke University. She is author of *Mothers and Daughters in Medieval German Literature* and has written articles on courtly love poetry, *Tristan and Isolde,* medieval German romance, and gender studies. Her current research explores the construction of gender in fifteenth-century German compilation manuscripts.

Jennifer Fisk Rondeau teaches history at the University of Oregon. Her teaching and research interests include the histories of gender, religion, and society, particularly in late medieval and Renaissance Italy. She has published articles on Italian confraternities and continues to write about the connections between late medieval and contemporary theoretical and spiritual concerns.

Claire Sponsler writes about late medieval culture, especially drama. She teaches English at the University of Iowa and is author of *Drama and Resistance: Bodies, Goods, and Theatricality in Late Medieval England* (Minnesota, 1997) and editor of *East of West: Crosscultural Performance and the Staging of Difference.*

Medieval Cultures

Volume 26
Paul Strohm
Theory and the Premodern Text

Volume 25
David Rollo
Glamorous Sorcery: Magic and Literacy in the High Middle Ages

Volume 24
Steve Ellis
Chaucer at Large: The Poet in the Modern Imagination

Volume 23
Edited by Barbara A. Hanawalt and Michal Kobialka
Medieval Practices of Space

Volume 22
Michelle R. Warren
History on the Edge: Excalibur and the Borders of Britain, 1100–1300

Volume 21
Olivia Holmes
Assembling the Lyric Self: Authorship from Troubadour Song to Italian Poetry Book

Volume 20
Karen Sullivan
The Interrogation of Joan of Arc

Volume 19
Clare A. Lees
Tradition and Belief: Religious Writing in Late Anglo-Saxon England

Volume 18
David Matthews
The Making of Middle English, 1765–1910

Volume 17
Jeffrey Jerome Cohen
Of Giants: Sex, Monsters, and the Middle Ages

Volume 16
Edited by Barbara A. Hanawalt and David Wallace
Medieval Crime and Social Control

Volume 15
Kathryn Kerby-Fulton and Denise L. Despres
Iconography and the Professional Reader: The Politics of Book Production in the Douce "Piers Plowman"

Volume 14
Edited by Marilynn Desmond
Christine de Pizan and the Categories of Difference

Volume 13
Alfred Thomas
Anne's Bohemia: Czech Literature and Society, 1310–1420

Volume 12
Edited by F. R. P. Akehurst and Stephanie Cain Van D'Elden
The Stranger in Medieval Society

Volume 11
Edited by Karma Lochrie, Peggy McCracken, and James A. Schultz
Constructing Medieval Sexuality

Volume 10
Claire Sponsler
Drama and Resistance: Bodies, Goods, and Theatricality in Late Medieval England

Volume 9
Edited by Barbara A. Hanawalt and David Wallace
Bodies and Disciplines: Intersections of Literature and History in Fifteenth-Century England

Volume 8
Marilynn Desmond
Reading Dido: Gender, Textuality, and the Medieval "Aeneid"

Volume 7
Edited by Clare A. Lees
Medieval Masculinities: Regarding Men in the Middle Ages

Volume 6
Edited by Barbara A. Hanawalt and Kathryn L. Reyerson
City and Spectacle in Medieval Europe

Volume 5
Edited by Calvin B. Kendall and Peter S. Wells
Voyage to the Other World: The Legacy of Sutton Hoo

Volume 4
Edited by Barbara A. Hanawalt
Chaucer's England: Literature in Historical Context

Volume 3
Edited by Marilyn J. Chiat and Kathryn L. Reyerson
The Medieval Mediterranean: Cross-Cultural Contacts

Volume 2
Edited by Andrew MacLeish
The Medieval Monastery

Volume 1
Edited by Kathryn L. Reyerson and Faye Powe
The Medieval Castle

Index

Created by Eileen Quam